ANNUAL EDITIONS

Business Ethics 08/09

Twentieth Edition

G000056795

Editor

John E. Richardson
Pepperdine University

Dr. John E. Richardson is professor of marketing in the George L. Graziadio School of Business and Management at Pepperdine University. He is president of his own consulting firm and has consulted with organizations such as Bell and Howell, Dayton-Hudson, Epson, and the U.S. Navy, as well as with various service, nonprofit, and franchise organizations. Dr. Richardson is a member of the American Management Association, the American Marketing Association, the Society for Business Ethics, and Beta Gamma Sigma honorary business fraternity.

McGraw Hill **Higher Education**

Boston   Burr Ridge, IL   Dubuque, IA   New York   San Francisco   St. Louis
Bangkok   Bogotá   Caracas   Kuala Lumpur   Lisbon   London   Madrid   Mexico City
Milan   Montreal   New Delhi   Santiago   Seoul   Singapore   Sydney   Taipei   Toronto

Higher Education

ANNUAL EDITIONS: BUSINESS ETHICS, TWENTIETH EDITION

Published by McGraw-Hill, a business unit of The McGraw-Hill Companies, Inc., 1221 Avenue of the Americas, New York, NY 10020.
Copyright © 2008 by The McGraw-Hill Companies, Inc. All rights reserved. Previous edition(s) 1987–2007. No part of this publication
may be reproduced or distributed in any form or by any means, or stored in a database or retrieval system, without the prior written consent
of The McGraw-Hill Companies, Inc., including, but not limited to, in any network or other electronic storage or transmission, or broadcast
for distance learning.

Some ancillaries, including electronic and print components, may not be available to customers outside the United States.

Annual Editions® is a registered trademark of The McGraw-Hill Companies, Inc.
Annual Editions is published by the **Contemporary Learning Series** group within the McGraw-Hill Higher Education division.

 This book is printed on recycled, acid-free paper containing 10% postconsumer waste.

1 2 3 4 5 6 7 8 9 0 QPD/QPD 0 9 8

ISBN 978–0–07–352849–6
MHID 0–07–352849–8
ISSN 1055–5455

Managing Editor: *Larry Loeppke*
Senior Managing Editor: *Faye Schilling*
Developmental Editor: *Dave Welsh*
Editorial Assistant: *Nancy Meissner*
Production Service Assistant: *Rita Hingtgen*
Permissions Coordinator: *Shirley Lanners*
Senior Marketing Manager: *Julie Keck*
Marketing Communications Specialist: *Mary Klein*
Marketing Coordinator: *Alice Link*
Project Manager: *Sandy Wille*
Design Specialist: *Tara McDermott*
Senior Administrative Assistant: *DeAnna Dausener*
Senior Production Supervisor: *Laura Fuller*
Cover Graphics: *Kristine Jubeck*

Compositor: Laserwords Private Limited
Cover Images: Tom Grill/CORBIS and Brand X Pictures

Library in Congress Cataloging-in-Publication Data
Main entry under title: Annual Editions: Business Ethics 2008/2009.
  1. Business Ethics—Periodicals by John E. Richardson, *comp.* II. Title: Business Ethics.
658'.05

www.mhhe.com

Editors/Advisory Board

Members of the Advisory Board are instrumental in the final selection of articles for each edition of ANNUAL EDITIONS. Their review of articles for content, level, currentness, and appropriateness provides critical direction to the editor and staff. We think that you will find their careful consideration well reflected in this volume.

Correlation Guide

The *Annual Editions* series provides students with convenient, inexpensive access to current, carefully selected articles from the public press. **Annual Editions: Business Ethics 08/09** is an easy-to-use reader that presents articles on important topics such as *workplace misconduct, social and environmental issues, global ethics, ethics in the marketplace,* and many more. For more information on *Annual Editions* and other *McGraw-Hill Contemporary Learning Series* titles visit www.mhcls.com.

This convenient guide matches the units in **Annual Editions: Business Ethics 08/09** with the corresponding chapters in our McGraw-Hill *Business Ethics* text by *Ghillyer* (ISBN: 0073403040).

Annual Editions: Business Ethics 08/09	**Business Ethics: The Challenges of Ethical Organizational Performance, Ghillyer**
Unit 1: Ethics, Values, and Social Responsibility in Business	**Chapter 1:** Understanding Ethics
	Chapter 2: Defining Business Ethics
	Chapter 4: Corporate Social Responsibility
Unit 2: Ethical Issues and Dilemmas in the Workplace	**Chapter 2:** Defining Business Ethics
	Chapter 3: Organizational Ethics
	Chapter 7: Blowing the Whistle
Unit 3: Business and Society: Contemporary Ethical, Social, and Environmental Issues	**Chapter 2:** Defining Business Ethics
	Chapter 9: Ethics and Globalization
Unit 4: Ethics and Social Responsibility in the Marketplace	**Chapter 3:** Organizational Ethics
	Chapter 8: Ethics & Technology
	Chapter 10: Making it Stick: Doing What's Right in a Competitive Market
Unit 5: Developing the Future Ethos and Social Responsibility of Business	**Chapter 10:** Making it Stick: Doing What's Right in a Competitive Market

Preface

In publishing ANNUAL EDITIONS we recognize the enormous role played by the magazines, newspapers, and journals of the public press in providing current, first-rate educational information in a broad spectrum of interest areas. Many of these articles are appropriate for students, researchers, and professionals seeking accurate, current material to help bridge the gap between principles and theories and the real world. These articles, however, become more useful for study when those of lasting value are carefully collected, organized, indexed, and reproduced in a low-cost format, which provides easy and permanent access when the material is needed. That is the role played by ANNUAL EDITIONS.

Recent events have brought ethics to the forefront as a topic of discussion throughout our nation. And, undoubtedly, the area of society that is getting the closest scrutiny regarding its ethical practices is the business sector. Both the print and broadcast media have offered a constant stream of facts and opinions concerning recent unethical goings-on in the business world. Insider trading scandals on Wall Street, the marketing of unsafe products, money laundering, and questionable contracting practices are just a few examples of events that have recently tarnished the image of business.

As corporate America struggles to find its ethical identity in a business environment that grows increasingly complex, managers are confronted with some poignant questions that have definite ethical ramifications. Does a company have any obligation to help solve social problems such a poverty, pollution, and urban decay? What ethical responsibilities should a multinational corporation assume in foreign countries? What obligation does a manufacturer have to the consumer with respect to product defects and safety?

These are just a few of the issues that make the study of business ethics important and challenging. A significant goal of *Annual Editions: Business Ethics 08/09* is to present some different perspectives on understanding basic concepts and concerns of business ethics and to provide ideas on how to incorporate these concepts into the policies and decision-making processes of businesses. The articles reprinted in this publication have been carefully chosen from a variety of public press sources to furnish current information on business ethics.

This volume contains a number of features designed to make it useful for students, researchers, and professionals. These include the *table of contents* with summaries of each article and key concepts in italics, and a *topic guide* for locating articles on specific subjects related to business ethics.

Also, included in this edition are selected *Internet References* sites that can be used to further explore article topics.

The articles are organized into five units. Selections that focus on similar issues are concentrated into subsections within the broader units. Each unit is preceded by an overview that provides background for informed reading of the articles, emphasizes critical issues, and presents key points to consider that focus on major themes running through the selections.

Your comments, opinions, and recommendations about *Annual Editions: Business Ethics 08/09* will be greatly appreciated and will help shape future editions. Please take a moment to complete and return the postage-paid *article rating form* at the back of this book. Any book can be improved, and with your help this one will continue to be.

John E. Richardson
Editor

The concepts in bold italics are developed in the article. For further expansion, please refer to the Topic Guide.

80

UNIT 3
Business and Society: Contemporary Ethical, Social, and Environmental Issues

Unit Overview

84

Part A. Changing Perspectives in Business and Society

UNIT 4
Ethics and Social Responsibility in the Marketplace

The concepts in bold italics are developed in the article. For further expansion, please refer to the Topic Guide.

UNIT 5
Developing the Future Ethos and Social Responsibility of Business

The concepts in bold italics are developed in the article. For further expansion, please refer to the Topic Guide.

Topic Guide

This topic guide suggests how the selections in this book relate to the subjects covered in your course. You may want to use the topics listed on these pages to search the Web more easily.

On the following pages a number of Web sites have been gathered specifically for this book. They are arranged to reflect the units of this *Annual Edition*. You can link to these sites by going to the student online support site at *http://www.mhcls.com/online/*.

ALL THE ARTICLES THAT RELATE TO EACH TOPIC ARE LISTED BELOW THE BOLD-FACED TERM.

Internet References

The following Internet sites have been carefully researched and selected to support the articles found in this reader. The easiest way to access these selected sites is to go to our student online support site at *http://www.mhcls.com/online/*.

Annual Editions: Business Ethics 08/09

The following sites were available at the time of publication. Visit our Web site—we update our student online support site regularly to reflect any changes.

General Sources

Center for the Study of Ethics in the Professions
http://ethics.iit.edu

Sponsored by the Illinois Institute of Technology, this site links to a number of world business ethics centers.

GreenMoney Journal
http://www.greenmoneyjournal.com

The editorial vision of this publication proposes that consumer spending and investment dollars can bring about positive social and environmental change. On this Web site, they'll tell you how.

Markkula Center
http://www.scu.edu/SCU/Centers/Ethics/

Santa Clara University's Markkula Center strives to heighten ethical awareness and to improve ethical decision making on campus and within the community. A list of published resources, links to ethical issues sites, and other data are provided.

U.S. Department of Labor
http://www.dol.gov

Browsing through this site will lead to a vast array of labor-related data and discussions of issues affecting employees and managers, such as the minimum wage.

U.S. Equal Employment Opportunity Commission (EEOC)
http://www.eeoc.gov

The EEOC's mission "is to ensure equality of opportunity by vigorously enforcing federal legislation prohibiting discrimination in employment." Consult this site for facts about employment discrimination, enforcement, and litigation.

Wharton Ethics Program
http://ethics.wharton.upenn.edu/

The Wharton School of the University of Pennsylvania provides an independently managed site that offers links to research, cases, and other business ethics centers.

UNIT 1: Ethics, Values, and Social Responsibility in Business

Association for Moral Education (AME)
http://www.amenetwork.org/

AME is dedicated to fostering communication, cooperation, training, and research that links moral theory with educational practices. From here it is possible to connect to several sites of relevance in the study of business ethics.

Business for Social Responsibility (BSR)
http://www.bsr.org

Core topic areas covered by BSR are listed on this page. They include Corporate Social Responsibility; Business Ethics; Community Investment; the Environment; Governance and

Accountability; Human Rights; Marketplace; Mission, Vision, Values; and finally Workplace. New information is added on a regular basis. For each topic or subtopic there is an introduction, examples of large and small company leadership practices, sample company policies, links to helping resources, and other information.

Enron Online
http://www.enron.com/corp/

Explore the Enron Web site to find information about Enron's history, products, and services. Go to the "Press Room" section for Enron's spin on the current investigation.

Ethics Updates/Lawrence Hinman
http://ethics.sandiego.edu/index.html

This site provides both simple concept definitions and complex analysis of ethics, original treatises, and sophisticated search engine capability. Subject matter covers the gamut, from ethical theory to applied ethical venues.

Institute for Business and Professional Ethics
http://commerce.depaul.edu/ethics/

Sponsored by DePaul College of Commerce, this site is interested in research in the field of business and professional ethics. It is still under construction, so check in from time to time.

National Center for Policy Analysis
http://www.ncpa.org

This organization's archive links lead you to interesting materials on a variety of topics that affect managers, from immigration issues, to affirmative action, to regulatory policy.

Open Directory Project
http://dmoz.org/Business/Management/Ethics

As part of the Open Directory Project, this page provides a database of Web sites that address numerous topics on ethics in business.

Working Definitions
http://www.workingdefinitions.co.uk/index.html

This is a British, magazine-style site devoted to discussion and comment on organizations in the wider social context and to supporting and developing people's management skills.

UNIT 2: Ethical Issues and Dilemmas in the Workplace

American Psychological Association
http://www.apa.org/homepage.html

Search this site to find references and discussion of important ethics issues for the workplace of the 1990s, including the impact of restructuring and revitalization of businesses.

International Labour Organization (ILO)
http://www.ilo.org

ILO's home page leads you to links that describe the goals of the organization and summarizes international labor standards and human rights. Its official UN Web site locator can point you to many other useful resources.

www.mhcls.com/online/

UNIT 3: Business and Society: Contemporary Ethical, Social, and Environmental Issues

National Immigrant Forum
http://www.immigrationforum.org

The pro-immigrant organization offers this page to examine the effects of immigration on the U.S. economy and society. Click on the links to underground and immigrant economies.

Workopolis.com
http://sympatico.workopolis.com

This Canadian site provides an electronic network with a GripeVine for complaining about work and finding solutions to everyday work problems.

United Nations Environment Programme (UNEP)
http://www.unep.ch

Consult this UNEP site for links to topics such as the impact of trade on the environment. It will direct you to useful databases and global resource information.

United States Trade Representative (USTR)
http://www.ustr.gov

This home page of the U.S. Trade Representative provides links to many U.S. government resources for those interested in ethics in international business.

UNIT 4: Ethics and Social Responsibility in the Marketplace

Business for Social Responsibility (BSR)
http://www.bsr.org/

BSR is a global organization that seeks to help companies "achieve success in ways that respect ethical values, people, communities, and the environment." Links to Services, Resources, and Forum are available.

Total Quality Management Sites
http://www.nku.edu/~lindsay/qualhttp.html

This site points to a variety of interesting Internet sources to aid in the study and application of Total Quality Management principles.

U.S. Navy
http://www.navy.mil

Start at this U.S. Navy page for access to a plethora of interesting stories and analyses related to Total Quality Leadership. It addresses such concerns as how TQL can improve customer service and affect utilization of information technology.

UNIT 5: Developing the Future Ethos and Social Responsibility of Business

International Business Ethics Institute (IBEI)
http://www.business-ethics.org/index.asp

The goal of this educational organization is to promote business ethics and corporate responsibility in response to the growing need for transnationalism in the field of business ethics.

UNU/IAS Project on Global Ethos
http://www.ias.unu.edu/research/globalethos.cfm

The United Nations University Institute of Advanced Studies (UNU/IAS) has issued this project abstract, which concerns governance and multilateralism. The main aim of the project is to initiate a process by which to generate jointly, with the involvement of factors from both state- and nonstate institutions in developed and developing countries, a global ethos that could provide or support a set of guiding principles for the emerging global community.

We highly recommend that you review our Web site for expanded information and our other product lines. We are continually updating and adding links to our Web site in order to offer you the most usable and useful information that will support and expand the value of your Annual Editions. You can reach us at: *http://www.mhcls.com/annualeditions/*.

UNIT 1

Ethics, Values, and Social Responsibility in Business

Unit Selections

Key Points to Consider

- Do you believe that corporations are more socially responsible today than they were 10 years ago? Why or why not?

- In what specific ways do you see companies practicing social responsibility? Do you think most companies are overt or covert in their social responsibility activities? Explain your answer.

- What are the economic and social implications of "management accountability" as part of the decision-making process? Does a company have any obligation to help remedy social problems, such as poverty, urban decay, and pollution? Defend your response.

- Using recent examples of stock, financial, and accounting debacles, discuss the flaws in America's financial system that allows companies to disregard ethics, values, and social responsibility in business.

Student Web Site

www.mhcls.com/online

Internet References

Further information regarding these Web sites may be found in this book's preface or online.

Association for Moral Education (AME)
   http://www.amenetwork.org/
Business for Social Responsibility (BSR)
   http://www.bsr.org
Enron Online
   http://www.enron.com/corp/
Ethics Updates/Lawrence Hinman
   http://ethics.sandiego.edu/index.html
Institute for Business and Professional Ethics
   http://commerce.depaul.edu/ethics/
National Center for Policy Analysis
   http://www.ncpa.org
Open Directory Project
   http://dmoz.org/Business/Management/Ethics
Working Definitions
   http://www.workingdefinitions.co.uk/index.html

Ethical decision making in an organization does not occur in a vacuum. As individuals and as managers, we formulate our ethics (that is, the standards of "right" and "wrong" behavior that we set for ourselves) based upon family, peer, and religious influences, our past experiences, and our own unique value systems. When we make ethical decisions within the organizational context, many times there are situational factors and potential conflicts of interest that further complicate the process.

Decisions do not only have personal ramifications—they also have social consequences. Social responsibility is really ethics at the organizational level, since it refers to the obligation that an organization has to make choices and to take actions that will contribute to the good of society as well as the good of the organization. Authentic social responsibility is not initiated because of forced compliance to specific laws and regulations. In contrast to legal responsibility, social responsibility involves a voluntary response from an organization that is above and beyond what is specified by the law.

The nine selections in this unit provide an overview of the interrelationships of ethics, values, and social responsibility in business. These essays offer practical and insightful principles and suggestions to managers, enabling them to approach the subject of business ethics with more confidence. They also point out the complexity and the significance of making ethical decisions.

Thinking Ethically

A Framework for Moral Decision Making

MANUEL VELASQUEZ ET AL.

Moral issues greet us each morning in the newspaper, confront us in the memos on our desks, nag us from our children's soccer fields, and bid us good night on the evening news. We are bombarded daily with questions about the justice of our foreign policy, the morality of medical technologies that can prolong our lives, the rights of the homeless, the fairness of our children's teachers to the diverse students in their classrooms.

Dealing with these moral issues is often perplexing. How, exactly, should we think through an ethical issue? What questions should we ask? What factors should we consider?

The first step in analyzing moral issues is obvious but not always easy: Get the facts.

The first step in analyzing moral issues is obvious but not always easy: Get the facts. Some moral issues create controversies simply because we do not bother to check the facts. This first step, although obvious, is also among the most important and the most frequently overlooked.

But having the facts is not enough. Facts by themselves only tell us what *is*; they do not tell us what *ought* to be. In addition to getting the facts, resolving an ethical issue also requires an appeal to values. Philosophers have developed five different approaches to values to deal with moral issues.

The Utilitarian Approach

Utilitarianism was conceived in the 19th century by Jeremy Bentham and John Stuart Mill to help legislators determine which laws were morally best. Both Bentham and Mill suggested that ethical actions are those that provide the greatest balance of good over evil.

To analyze an issue using the utilitarian approach, we first identify the various courses of action available to us. Second, we ask who will be affected by each action and what benefits or harms will be derived from each. And third, we choose the action that will produce the greatest benefits and the least harm. The ethical action is the one that provides the greatest good for the greatest number.

The Rights Approach

The second important approach to ethics has its roots in the philosophy of the 18th-century thinker Immanuel Kant and others like him, who focused on the individual's right to choose for herself or himself. According to these philosophers, what makes human beings different from mere things is that people have dignity based on their ability to choose freely what they will do with their lives, and they have a fundamental moral right to have these choices respected. People are not objects to be manipulated; it is a violation of human dignity to use people in ways they do not freely choose.

Of course, many different, but related, rights exist besides this basic one. These other rights (an incomplete list below) can be thought of as different aspects of the basic right to be treated as we choose.

- *The right to the truth*: We have a right to be told the truth and to be informed about matters that significantly affect our choices.
- *The right of privacy*: We have the right to do, believe, and say whatever we choose in our personal lives so long as we do not violate the rights of others.
- *The right not to be injured*: We have the right not to be harmed or injured unless we freely and knowingly do something to deserve punishment or we freely and knowingly choose to risk such injuries.
- *The right to what is agreed*: We have a right to what has been promised by those with whom we have freely entered into a contract or agreement.

In deciding whether an action is moral or immoral using this second approach, then, we must ask, Does the action respect the moral rights of everyone? Actions are wrong to the extent

The Case of Maria Elena

Maria Elena has cleaned your house each week for more than a year. You agree with your friend who recommended her that she does an excellent job and is well worth the $30 cash you pay her for three hours' work. You've also come to like her, and you think she likes you, especially as her English has become better and you've been able to have some pleasant conversations.

Over the past three weeks, however, you've noticed Maria Elena becoming more and more distracted. One day, you ask her if something is wrong, and she tells you she really needs to make additional money. She hastens to say she is not asking you for a raise, becomes upset, and begins to cry. When she calms down a little, she tells you her story:

She came to the United States six years ago from Mexico with her child, Miguel, who is now 7 years old. They entered the country on a visitor's visa that has expired, and Maria Elena now uses a Social Security number she made up.

Her common-law husband, Luis, came to the United States first. He entered the country illegally, after paying smugglers $500 to hide him under piles of grass cuttings for a six-hour truck ride across the border. When he had made enough money from low-paying day jobs, he sent for Maria Elena. Using a false green card, Luis now works as a busboy for a restaurant, which withholds part of his salary for taxes. When Maria Elena comes to work at your house, she takes the bus and Luis baby-sits.

In Mexico, Maria Elena and Luis lived in a small village where it was impossible to earn more than $3 a day. Both had sixth-grade educations, common in their village. Life was difficult, but they did not decide to leave until they realized the future would be bleak for their child and for the other children they wanted to have. Luis had a cousin in San Jose who visited and told Luis and Maria Elena how well his life was going. After his visit, Luis and Maria Elena decided to come to the United States.

Luis quickly discovered, as did Maria Elena, that life in San Jose was not the way they had heard. The cousin did not tell them they would be able to afford to live only in a run-down three-room apartment with two other couples and their children. He did not tell them they would always live in fear of INS raids.

After they entered the United States, Maria Elena and Luis had a second child, Jose, who is 5 years old. The birth was difficult because she didn't use the health-care system or welfare for fear of being discovered as undocumented. But, she tells you, she is willing to put up with anything so that her children can have a better life. "All the money we make is for Miguel and Jose," she tells you. "We work hard for their education and their future."

Now, however, her mother in Mexico is dying, and Maria Elena must return home, leaving Luis and the children. She does not want to leave them because she might not be able to get back into the United States, but she is pretty sure she can find a way to return if she has enough money. That is her problem: She doesn't have enough money to make certain she can get back.

After she tells you her story, she becomes too distraught to continue talking. You now know she is an undocumented immigrant, working in your home. What is the ethical thing for you to do?

This case was developed by Tom Shanks, S.J., director of the Markkula Center for Applied Ethics. Maria Elena is a composite drawn from several real people, and her story represents some of the ethical dilemmas behind the immigration issue.

This case can be accessed through the Ethics Center home page on the World Wide Web: http://www.scu.edu/Ethics/. You can also contact us by e-mail, ethics@scu.edu, or regular mail: Markkula Center for Applied Ethics, Santa Clara University, Santa Clara, CA 95053. Our voice mail number is (408) 554-7898. We have also posted on our homepage a new case involving managed health care.

that they violate the rights of individuals; the more serious the violation, the more wrongful the action.

The Fairness or Justice Approach

The fairness or justice approach to ethics has its roots in the teachings of the ancient Greek philosopher Aristotle, who said that "equals should be treated equally and unequals unequally." The basic moral question in this approach is: How fair is an action? Does it treat everyone in the same way, or does it show favoritism and discrimination?

Favoritism gives benefits to some people without a justifiable reason for singling them out; discrimination imposes burdens on people who are no different from those on whom burdens are not imposed. Both favoritism and discrimination are unjust and wrong.

The Common-Good Approach

This approach to ethics presents a vision of society as a community whose members are joined in the shared pursuit of values and goals they hold in common. This community comprises individuals whose own good is inextricably bound to the good of the whole.

The common good is a notion that originated more than 2,000 years ago in the writings of Plato, Aristotle, and Cicero. More recently, contemporary ethicist John Rawls defined the common good as "certain general conditions that are . . . equally to everyone's advantage."

In this approach, we focus on ensuring that the social policies, social systems, institutions, and environments on which we depend are beneficial to all. Examples of goods common to all include affordable health care, effective public safety, peace among nations, a just legal system, and an unpolluted environment.

Appeals to the common good urge us to view ourselves as members of the same community, reflecting on broad questions concerning the kind of society we want to become and how we are to achieve that society. While respecting and valuing the freedom of individuals to pursue their own goals, the common-good approach challenges us also to recognize and further those goals we share in common.

The Virtue Approach

The virtue approach to ethics assumes that there are certain ideals toward which we should strive, which provide for the full development of our humanity. These ideals are discovered through thoughtful reflection on what kind of people we have the potential to become.

Virtues are attitudes or character traits that enable us to be and to act in ways that develop our highest potential. They enable us to pursue the ideals we have adopted.

Honesty, courage, compassion, generosity, fidelity, integrity, fairness, self-control, and prudence are all examples of virtues.

Virtues are like habits; that is, once acquired, they become characteristic of a person. Moreover, a person who has developed virtues will be naturally disposed to act in ways consistent with moral principles. The virtuous person is the ethical person.

In dealing with an ethical problem using the virtue approach, we might ask, What kind of person should I be? What will promote the development of character within myself and my community?

Ethical Problem Solving

These five approaches suggest that once we have ascertained the facts, we should ask ourselves five questions when trying to resolve a moral issue:

- What benefits and what harms will each course of action produce, and which alternative will lead to the best overall consequences?
- What moral rights do the affected parties have, and which course of action best respects those rights?
- Which course of action treats everyone the same, except where there is a morally justifiable reason not to, and does not show favoritism or discrimination?
- Which course of action advances the common good?
- Which course of action develops moral virtues?

This method, of course, does not provide an automatic solution to moral problems. It is not meant to. The method is merely meant to help identify most of the important ethical considerations. In the end, we must deliberate on moral issues for ourselves, keeping a careful eye on both the facts and on the ethical considerations involved.

This article updates several previous pieces from *Issues in Ethics* by **MANUEL VELASQUEZ**—Dirksen Professor of Business Ethics at SCU and former Center director—and **CLAIRE ANDRE,** associate Center director. "Thinking Ethically" is based on a framework developed by the authors in collaboration with Center Director **THOMAS SHANKS, S.J.,** Presidential Professor of Ethics and the Common Good **MICHAEL J. MEYER,** and others. The framework is used as the basis for many Center programs and presentations.

Ethical Leadership

Maintain an Ethical Culture

RONALD E. BERENBEIM

In the United States, the consensus regarding the need for ethical business practice has been codified in *The Revised Sentencing Guidelines,* which is widely accepted as an authoritative business conduct guidance document in the United States and elsewhere—a template for sound business practice.

Compliance with the *Guidelines* requires that a high-level person be responsible for the company's ethics program and foster an ethical culture within the company. Such an environment affords assurance that people are free to ask questions and raise concerns. Meeting the demands of the *Guidelines* demands ethical leadership. For example, in Australia, a company can be criminally liable if it fails to maintain a culture that requires compliance with the law—if the culture directs, tolerates, or leads to noncompliance with the criminal provisions proscribing the bribery of foreign public officials. This standard helps companies avoid these problems with descriptions of the necessary structural, operational, and maintenance elements for effective compliance.

Three Lessons from Nehru

As an example of ethical leadership of the highest order, consider the case of Jawaharlal Nehru. In 1937, Nehru had just been elected to a second, consecutive term as President of the Indian National Parliament. Rabindrath Tagore, the Indian poet, philosopher, writer, and Nobel laureate hailed him as "representing the season of youth and triumphant joy." Even a British official wrote of him at the time, "there is no doubt that his manliness, frankness, and reputation for sacrifice attracts a large public."

Though widely held, this favorable view was not unanimous. One anonymous writer vigorously dissented. In a severe attack published in the *Modern Review,* the critic said: "He has all the makings of a dictator in him—vast popularity, a strong will directed to a well-defined purpose, energy, pride, organizational capacity, ability, hardness, and with his love of the crowd, an intolerance of others and a certain contempt for the weak and inefficient. His conceit is formidable. He must be checked. We want no Caesars."

The author of this vitriolic article was none other than Nehru himself. Recalling this episode is not to make a judgment about Nehru but to demonstrate how his behavior in this situation shows an intuitive grasp of the essence of ethical leadership. Nehru understood that a leader is most ethical and effective when his or her power is limited—by institutional arrangements and the criticism that results from harsh public scrutiny. If the Congress Party and the Indian press lacked these resources, he believed that it was necessary for him to supply the discipline that these countervailing forces ordinarily would have imposed.

From this great example of ethical leadership, I draw three lessons:

1. *Ethical leaders don't hide from debate.* An ethical leader understands that open and contentious debate is essential to making the best possible decisions. And openly debated decisions result in better outcomes. Some years ago, a research study focused on the behavior of members of investment clubs, small and somewhat informal gatherings of private individual investors, in the United States. Those groups in which the members enjoyed one another's company, reached consensus quickly, and were polite and civil, had a much poorer performance record than the clubs whose investment choices were the result of contentious debate.

An ethical leader understands that open and contentious debate is essential to making the best possible decisions. Although encouraging debate is essential, ethical leadership must balance the need for robust discussion with the requirement of commitment to a common purpose. Where such a consensus is lacking there is a danger of polarization, which will cause people to avoid the risk of winding up on the wrong side and in so doing limit their comments to information that everyone already has.

These findings tell us something that most of us already know—and often forget—or at least choose to believe is good advice for other organizations (perhaps even our competitors), but not our own. Leaders who ignore this wisdom put their enterprises at great risk. For confirmation of this view, one need look no further than the U.S. Presidential Commission report released March 30, 2005, on the intelligence failures in Iraq. The report recommended moving "away from the intelligence community's tradition of searching for consensus, in favor of opening up internal debate and including a more diverse spectrum of views."

2. *Ethical leaders are active participants.* Leaders need to be active participants in the debate over alternatives. In some circles, it has become a fashionable corporate model for the CEO to say to the senior executives, "You people thrash it out, reach a consensus, and send me your recommendation." Such a decision-making process has serious flaws. The most robust internal processes are of no avail if the leader is exempt from them. Good leaders don't just subject themselves to the need to test their ideas—they welcome the opportunity and have a zest for intellectual combat. They realize that there is more to leadership than giving orders. Ethical leaders understand that their views and decisions are in large measure determined by their contact with the people they lead.

Among other advantages, these discussions provide a necessary dose of reality. Nehru's self-criticism attacked his own "conceit" and what he believed to be his "intolerance of others and [a certain] contempt for the weak and the inefficient." He seemed to understand that however decisive and effective a leader's decision-making powers may be, the implementation of a decision requires great patience and tolerance. Or to put it another way, as the 19th-century Prussian general Helmuth von Moltke once said, "No plan survives contact with the enemy." And one can only add that untested ideas are likely to be a plan's first casualty.

Another consequence of the arrogance resulting from a leader's isolation and immunity from full disclosure and accountability is a loss of the public esteem that is essential for maintaining power. In the end, Enron was destroyed by the incompetence of its leadership. Had that not been the case, it is still entirely possible that the company would have met a similar fate anyway if and when the public learned of senior management's greed and wanton extravagance.

3. *Institutional sustainability comes first.* This principle entails an understanding of limits—not those that are imposed by institutional arrangements, the need for public approval, or even self discipline—but rather the limits of human mortality. The final task of ethical leadership is to put in place the requirements for institutional sustainability that survives the loss of any one person. Perhaps the best test of leadership is the state of the enterprise 20 years after the leader has left. Are decisions made in an orderly way? Is the leadership accountable? Is the transfer of power completed without serious disruption? Has the founding vision survived but also accommodated itself to changing economic, social, and political realities? The final task of ethical leadership is to put in place the requirements for institutional sustainability that survives the loss of any one person.

Judged by those standards, Nehru gets high marks. He understood that leaders function best when they are subject to limits, understand those constraints, and strive in a human way to function within these boundaries. And as Nehru concluded somberly, the ultimate limit is mortality. At the head of the epilogue to his autobiography, he placed this epigraph from the Talmud: "We are enjoined to labor; but it is not granted to us to complete our labors."

RONALD E. BERENBEIM is a principal researcher and director of The Conference Board's Working Group on Global Business Ethics Principles. This article is based on his presentation at The Conference Board 2005 Global Leadership Development Conference in Mumbai, India, and used with permission.

Business Ethics

Back to Basics

With business news dominated in recent years by some spectacular examples of ethical malfeasance, confidence in the business world has been shaken. Never mind that the Enrons of the world are actually few and far between. No business or organization can afford even a suspicion of unethical behavior and must take proactive steps to ensure that no suspicions arise. Ethical behavior begins at the top with actions and statements that are beyond reproach and ambiguity. Managements may want to follow an eight-point action list presented here for establishing a strong ethical culture and also a decision checklist when ethical dilemmas loom. Sterling reputations are valuable business assets: they are earned over time but can be lost almost overnight.

WILLIAM I. SAUSER, JR.

Introduction

Enron, Arthur Andersen, Tyco, ImClone, Martha Stewart, WorldCom, Global Crossing, Merrill Lynch, Rite-Aid, Qwest, Adelphia, Kmart, HealthSouth—the list of formerly respected businesses (and business leaders) being charged with breaches of ethical conduct seems to be growing by the day. This is having adverse effects on our economic well-being, on investor confidence, and on the perceived desirability of pursuing business as a respectable calling.

Commenting on the ethical crisis in business leadership, Eileen Kelly (2002) observed, "Recently a new business scandal seems to surface each day. The current volatility of the market reflects the apprehension, the sense of betrayal, and the lack of confidence that investors have in many large corporations and their managements" (p. 4). Marcy Gordon (2002), reporting on a speech by United States Securities and Exchange Commissioner Paul Atkins, noted, "The string of accounting failures at big companies in the last year has cost U.S. households nearly $60,000 on average as some $5 trillion in market value was lost."

Accounting failures are not the only ethical concerns facing modern business organizations. The Southern Institute for Business and Professional Ethics (2002) lists on its Web site an array of issues that put pressures on business enterprises. These include the globalization of business, work force diversification, employment practices and policies, civil litigation and government regulation, and concerns about environmental stewardship. The institute (on the same Web site) concluded, "Despite such powerful trends, few managers have been adequately equipped by traditional education to recognize, evaluate, and act upon the ethical dimension of their work."

Columnist Malcolm Cutchins (2002), an emeritus professor of engineering at Auburn University, summed up the problem concisely: "We have seen the effect of not teaching good ethics in business schools. If we continue to neglect the teaching of good principles on a broad scale, we all reap the bad consequences."

Business Ethics

Ethics has to do with behavior—specifically, an individual's moral behavior with respect to society. The extent to which behavior measures up to societal standards is typically used as a gauge of ethicality. Since there are a variety of standards for societal behavior, ethical behavior is often characterized with respect to certain contexts. The Ethics Resource Center says, "*Business Ethics* refers to clear standards and norms that help employees to distinguish right from wrong behavior at work" (Joseph, 2003, p. 2). In the business context, ethics has to do with the extent to which a person's behavior measures up to such standards as the law, organizational policies, professional and trade association codes, popular expectations regarding fairness and rightness, plus an individual's internalized moral standards.

Business ethics, then, is not distinct from ethics in general, but rather a subfield (Desjardins, 2003, p. 8). The subfield refers to the examination and application of moral standards within the context of finance; commerce; production, distribution, and sale of goods and services; and other business activities.

It can be argued that an ethical person behaves appropriately in all societal contexts. This may be so, in which case one might prefer the term "ethics in business" to "business ethics." The distinction is subtle, but serves as a reminder that morality may be generalized from context to context. Adam Smith, for example, saw no need for ethical relativism when it comes to business. "It is impossible to determine just how business became separated from ethics in history. If we go back to Adam Smith, we find no such separation. In addition to his famous book on business and capitalism, *The Wealth of Nations*, Adam Smith also wrote *The Theory of Moral Sentiments*, a book about our ethical obligations to one another. It is clear that Smith believed that business and commerce worked well only if people took seriously their obligations and, in particular, their sense of justice" (Bruner, Eaker, Freeman, Spekman, and Teisberg, 1998, p. 46).

May (1995) echoed this important point: "The marketplace breaks down unless it can presuppose the virtue of industry, without which goods will not be produced; and the virtues of honesty and integrity, without which their free and fair exchange cannot take place."

Standards of Behavior

The law (including statutory, administrative, and case law) is an important and legitimate source of ethical guidance. Federal, state, and local laws establish the parameters (Fieser, 1996), and violation of the law is almost always considered unethical (with the possible exception of civil disobedience as a mechanism for putting the law itself on trial). Pursuing business outside the law is regarded as an obstructionist approach to business ethics (Schermerhorn, 2005, p. 75). Such an individual would almost certainly be labeled unethical.

A second important source of authority is organizational policies, which are standards for behavior established by the employing organization. Typically they are aligned with the law (which takes precedence over them) and spell out in detail how things are done. All employees are expected to adhere to organizational policies. It is very important that managers at the highest level set the example for others by always working within the law and the policies of the organization.

Another important source of ethical guidance is the code of behavior adopted by professional and trade associations. These codes are often aspirational in nature and frequently establish higher standards for behavior than the law requires. Members of a profession or trade association typically aspire to meet these higher standards in order to establish and uphold the reputation of a profession or trade.

A fourth type of standard—often unwritten and commonly the community's concept of morality. These social mores, based on commonly held beliefs about what is right and wrong and fair and unfair, can be powerful determinants of a person's reputation. Behavior that—in the strictest sense—meets legal requirements, organizational policies, and even professional standards may still be viewed by the general public as unfair and wrong (Krech, Crutchfield, and Ballachey, 1962).

A fifth set of standards reflects the individual conscience. Coleman, Butcher and Carson (1980, p. Glossary IV) define "the conscience" as "the functioning of an individual's moral values in the approval or disapproval of his or her own thoughts

and actions," and equate it roughly with the Freudian concept of the superego. Highly ethical business leaders typically have moral standards that exceed all four of the lesser standards just listed. These values, learned early in life and reinforced by life's experiences, are internalized standards often based on personal, religious or philosophical understandings of morality (Baelz, 1977, pp. 41–55)

Ethical Dilemmas

An ethical dilemma is a situation where a potential course of action offers potential benefit or gain but is unethical, in that it violates one or more of the standards just described. Behaviors violating laws are, by definition, illegal as well as unethical. The key question for the business leader when presented with an ethical dilemma is: "What to do?" Behavior determines a person's ethical reputation, after all. Ethical leadership is exhibited when ethical dilemmas are resolved in an appropriate manner.

Here is a sampling of some ethical dilemmas that frequently rise in the business setting. Many of these behaviors are illegal as well as unethical.

- Providing a product or service you know is harmful or unsafe
- Misleading someone through false statements or omissions
- Using insider information for personal gain
- Playing favorites
- Manipulating and using people
- Benefiting personally from a position of trust
- Violating confidentiality
- Misusing company property or equipment
- Falsifying documents
- Padding expenses
- Taking bribes or kickbacks
- Participating in a cover-up
- Theft or sabotage
- Committing an act of violence
- Substance abuse
- Negligence or inappropriate behavior in the workplace.

Poor Ethical Choices

Why do people sometimes make poor choices when faced with ethical dilemmas? One set of reasons has to do with flaws of *character*. Such character defects include malice (intentional evil); sociopathy (lack of conscience); personal greed; envy, jealousy, resentment; the will to win or achieve at any cost; and fear of failure. There are also flaws in *corporate culture* that lead even good people to make poor ethical judgments. Weaknesses in corporate culture include indifference, a lack of knowledge or understanding of standards on the part of employees; poor or inappropriate incentive systems; and poor leadership, including the use of mixed signals such as:

- I don't care how you do it, just get it done.
- Don't ever bring me bad news.

- Don't bother me with the details, you know what to do.
- Remember, we always meet our financial goals somehow.
- No one gets injured on this worksite . . . period. Understand?
- Ask me no questions, I'll tell you no lies.

Such statements by managers to their subordinates too often imply that unethical behaviors that obtain the intended results are acceptable to the organization. While it may be difficult—other than through termination or other sanctions—to rid the organization of employees with character flaws, correcting a poor organizational culture is clearly a matter of leadership.

Establishing a Strong Ethical Culture

Business leaders who wish to take proactive measures to establish and maintain a corporate culture that emphasizes strong moral leadership are advised to take the following steps:

1. **Adopt a code of ethics.** The code need not be long and elaborate with flowery words and phrases. In fact, the best ethical codes use language anyone can understand. A good way to produce such a code is to ask all employees of the firm (or a representative group) to participate in its creation (Kuchar, 2003). Identify the commonly-held moral beliefs and values of the members of the firm and codify them into a written document all can understand and support. Post the code of ethics in prominent places around the worksite. Make certain that all employees subscribe to it by asking them to sign it.

2. **Provide ethics training.** From time to time a leader should conduct ethics training sessions. These may be led by experts in business ethics, or they may be informal in nature and led by the manager or employees themselves. A highly effective way to conduct an ethics training session is to provide "what if" cases for discussion and resolution. The leader would present a "real world" scenario in which an ethical dilemma is encountered. Using the organization's code of ethics as a guide, participants would explore options and seek a consensus ethical solution. This kind of training sharpens the written ethical code and brings it to life.

3. **Hire and promote ethical people.** This, in concert with step four, is probably the best defense against putting the business at risk through ethical lapses by employees. When making human resources decisions it is critical to reward ethical behavior and punish unethical behavior. Investigate the character of the people you hire, and do your best to hire people who have exhibited high moral standards in the past. Remember that past behavior is the best predictor of future behavior, so check references carefully. Formal background investigations may be warranted for positions of fiduciary responsibility or significant risk exposure. Base promotional decisions on matters of character in addition to technical competence. Demon-

strate to your employees that high ethical standards are a requirement for advancement.

4. **Correct unethical behavior.** This complements step three. When the organization's ethical code is breached, those responsible must be punished. Many businesses use progressive discipline, with an oral warning (intended to advise the employee of what is and is not acceptable behavior) as the first step, followed by a written reprimand, suspension without pay, and termination if unethical behavior persists. Of course, some ethical lapses are so egregious that they require suspension—or even termination—following the first offense. Through consistent and firm application of sanctions to correct unethical behavior, the manager will signal to all employees that substandard moral behavior will not be tolerated.

5. **Be proactive.** Businesses wishing to establish a reputation for ethicality and good corporate citizenship in the community will often organize and support programs intended to give something back to the community. Programs that promote continuing education, wholesome recreation, good health and hygiene, environmental quality, adequate housing, and other community benefits may demonstrate the extent to which the business promotes concern for human welfare. Seeking and adopting best practices from other businesses in the community is also a proactive strategy.

6. **Conduct a social audit.** Most businesses are familiar with financial audits. This concept can be employed in the context of ethics and corporate responsibility as well. From time to time the leader of the business might invite responsible parties to examine the organization's product design, purchasing, production, marketing, distribution, customer relations, and human resources functions with an eye toward identifying and correcting any areas of policy or practice that raise ethical concerns. Similarly, programs of corporate responsibility (such as those mentioned in step five) should be reviewed for effectiveness and improved as needed.

7. **Protect whistleblowers.** A whistleblower is a person within the firm who points out ethically questionable actions taken by other employees—or even by managers—within the organization. Too often corporate whistle blowers are ignored—or even punished—by those who receive the unfortunate news of wrongdoing within the business. All this does is discourage revelation of ethical problems. Instead the whistle blower should be protected and even honored. When unethical actions are uncovered within a firm by one of the employees, managers should step forward and take corrective action (as described in step four). Employees learn from one another. If the owners and managers of a business turn a blind eye toward wrongdoing, a signal is sent to everyone within the firm that ethicality is not characteristic of that organization's culture. A downward spiral of moral behavior is likely to follow.

8. **Empower the guardians of integrity.** The business leader's chief task is to lead by example and to empower every member of the organization to demonstrate the firm's commitment to ethics in its relationships with suppliers, customers, employees, and shareholders. Turn each employee of the firm, no matter what that individual's position, into a guardian of the firm's integrity. When maliciousness and indifference are replaced with a culture of integrity, honesty, and ethicality, the business will reap long-term benefits from all quarters.

A Checklist for Making Good Ethical Decisions

A business leader who takes seriously the challenge of creating a strong ethical culture for the firm must, of course, make good decisions when faced personally with ethical dilemmas. Here is a checklist a manager might wish to follow:

1. Recognize the ethical dilemma.
2. Get the facts.
3. Identify your options.
4. Test each option: Is it legal, right, beneficial? Note: Get some counsel.
5. Decide which option to follow.
6. Double-check your decision.
7. Take action.
8. Follow up and monitor decision implementation.

Number six is key: Double-check your decision. When in doubt consider how each of the following might guide you. Take the action that would allow you to maintain your reputation with those on this list you believe adhere to the highest ethical standards: Your attorney, accountant, boss, co-workers, stakeholders, family, newspaper, television news, religious leader, and Deity.

How would you feel if you had to explain your decision—and your actions—to each of these? If you would not feel good about this, then it is quite likely that you are about to make a poor decision. Double check your decision in this manner before you take any action you may later regret.

Conclusion

A firm's reputation may take years—even decades—to establish, but can be destroyed in an instant through unethical behavior. That is why it is so important for business leaders to be very careful about the things they say and do. Taking the time and effort to establish and maintain a corporate culture of morality, integrity, honesty, and ethicality will pay important dividends throughout the life of the firm. While taking ethical shortcuts may appear to lead to gains in the short term, this type of corporate strategy almost always proves tragic in the longer term.

Every business leader will be faced at one time or another with an ethical dilemma. Many face even daily temptations. How the leader manifests moral integrity when faced with ethi-

cal dilemmas sets the tone for everyone else in the organization. This is why it is so important to "walk the talk" by making good ethical decisions every day. Understanding and applying the concepts presented in this article will enable you, as a business leader, to create and maintain an ethical corporate culture in your business. As Carl Skoogland, the former vice president and ethics director for Texas Instruments, recently advised, if you want to create an ethical business, you must *know what's right, value what's right, and do what's right* (Skoogland, 2003).

References

Baelz, P. (1977). *Ethics and belief*. New York: The Seabury Press.

Bruner, R. F., Eaker, M. R., Freeman, E., Spekman, R.E., and Teisberg, E. O. (1998). *The portable MBA, 3rd ed*. New York: Wiley.

Coleman, J. C., Butcher, J. N., and Carson, R. (1980). *Abnormal psychology and modern life, 6th ed,* Glenview, IL: Scott Foresman.

Cutchins, M. (2002, November 20). Business ethics must be taught or we all pay. *Opelika-Auburn News*, p. A4.

Desjardins, J. (2003). *An introduction to business ethics*. Boston: McGraw-Hill.

Fieser, J. (1996). Do businesses have moral obligations beyond what the law requires? *Journal of Business Ethics, 15*, 457–468.

Gordon, M. (2002, November 18). Accounting failures cost $60,000 on average, SEC commissioner says. *Opelika-Auburn News*, p. C4.

Joseph, J. (2003). *National business ethics survey 2003: How employees view ethics in their organizations*. Washington, DC: Ethics Resource Center.

Kelly, E. P. (2002). Business ethics—An oxymoron? *Phi Kappa Phi Forum, 82*(4), 4–5.

Krech, D., Crutchfield, R. S., and Ballachey, E. L. (1962). Culture. Chapter 10 in *Individual in society* (pp. 339–380). New York: McGraw-Hill.

Kuchar, C. (2003). Tips on developing ethics codes for private companies. *GoodBusiness*, 2(3), pages unnumbered.

May, W. F. (1995). The virtues of the business leader. In M. L. Stackhouse, D. P. McCann, S. J, Roels, and P. N. Williams (Eds.), *On moral business* (pp. 692–700). Grand Rapids, MI: Eerdmans.

Schermerhorn, J. R., Jr. (2005). *Management, 8th ed*. New York: Wiley.

Skoogland, C. (2003, October 16). *Establishing an ethical organization*. Plenary address at the Conference on Ethics and Social Responsibility in Engineering and Technology, New Orleans, LA.

The Southern Institute for Business and Professional Ethics. (2002). *The certificate in managerial ethics*. Retrieved August, 14, 2002, from http://www.southerninstitute.org.

DR. SAUSER is Associate Dean for Business and Engineering Outreach and Professor of Management at Auburn University. His interests include organization development, strategic planning, human relations in the workplace, business ethics, and continuing professional education. He is a Fellow of the American Council on Education and the Society for Advancement of Management (SAM). In 2003, he was awarded the Frederick W. Taylor Key by SAM for his career achievements.

From *SAM Advanced Management Journal*, 2005, No. 2, pp. 1–4. Copyright © 2005 Society for Advancement of Management. Reprinted by permission.

The Value of an Ethical Corporate Culture

CURTIS C. VERSCHOOR

An independent U.S. research study conducted by LRN, a provider of governance, ethics, and compliance management, shows additional evidence that a company's ability to maintain an ethical corporate culture is key to the attraction, retention, and productivity of employees. In other words, money invested in ethics education, help lines, assessment of ethics programs, and risk evaluation is money well spent. *The LRN Ethics Study* involved 834 full-time employees from various industries across the United States. Respondents included both men and women, all 18 or older.

According to the LRN study, 94% of employees said it is either critical or important that the company they work for is ethical. This compares to 76% who said so in a similar survey six months earlier. Eighty-two percent said they would rather be paid less but work at a company that had ethical business practices than receive higher pay at a company with questionable ethics. More than a third (36%) had left a job because they disagreed with the actions of either fellow employees or managers. This is true across all ages, genders, and socioeconomic factors.

Other findings of the survey include 80% of respondents reporting that a disagreement with the ethics of a supervisor, fellow employee, or management was the most important reason for leaving a job and 21% citing pressure to engage in illegal activity.

Working for an ethical company is slightly more critical to women (63%) than to men (53%). Full-time employees in the western and southern U.S. consider the factor more important than those in the north central and northeast. Two-thirds of those in managerial and professional occupations find ethics important, compared to 45% of blue collar workers.

The LRN study found that a majority (56%) of Americans working full-time say their current employer embraces ethics and corporate values in everything they do. Despite this, about 25% have witnessed unethical or even illegal behavior at their job in the past six months. Among those, only 11% say they weren't affected by it. About 30% of respondents say their company merely toes the line by following the letter of the law and company policy. Nine percent say they work at a company where they either do what they are told and aren't encouraged

to ask questions about what is right or wrong or they often see management and peers acting in questionable ways.

Among those who witness unethical behavior, about one in four say they do so at least once a week, including 12% who say it is a daily occurrence. Unethical behavior affects a company's costs and ability to recruit, train, and retain employees; increases the legal, regulatory, and compliance risks a company faces; and has an impact on productivity. Half of all respondents indicated that unethical behavior was a distraction on the job. While most merely spent time discussing ethical issues with colleagues, nearly one third (32%) made a formal complaint or went to speak with management about a specific issue.

Dov Seidman, chairman and CEO of LRN, believes, "An ethical culture where employees and management use values and not rules to self-govern can only take root when executives, managers, supervisors, and employees understand and embrace the company's principles and values and incorporate them into their daily conduct."

George S. May International Company, a consulting firm that specializes in helping small and midsize businesses, has developed the three "Rs" of business ethics: respect, responsibility, and results.

Respect includes behavior such as:

- Treating everyone (customers, coworkers, vendors, etc.) with dignity and courtesy.
- Using company supplies, equipment, time, and money appropriately, efficiently, and for business purposes only.
- Protecting and improving your work environment and abiding by laws, rules, and regulations that exist to protect our world and our way of life.

Responsibility applies to customers, coworkers, the organization, and yourself. Included are behaviors such as:

- Providing timely, high-quality goods and services.
- Working collaboratively and carrying your share of the load.
- Meeting all performance expectations and adding value.

Essential for attaining results is an understanding that the way they are attained—the "means"—are every bit as and maybe more important than the ultimate goal—the "ends." The phrase "the ends justify the means" is an excuse that is used too often to explain an emotional response or action that wasn't well planned or considered carefully.

The May firm suggests that considering the three "Rs" before taking action will help you avoid the following common rationalizations:

- Everyone else does it.
- They'll never miss it.
- Nobody will care.
- The boss does it.
- No one will know.
- I don't have time to do it right.
- That's close enough.
- Some rules were meant to be broken.
- It's not my job.

Professionals Desire Independence

In spite of the fact that independent professionals don't receive many of the fringe and other benefits that regular employees generally do, a study by the Hudson Highland Group, a global staffing, executive search, and consulting firm, shows them to be consistently happier and better compensated than their counterparts in full-time positions. The survey covered 2,168 participants, with about half located in the U.S.

Titled *The Lure of Autonomy: A Global Study of Professional Workers,* the survey finds that these workers hold similar views on the importance of competence and knowledge, balance between work and life, compensation, and interesting work. Independent professionals are likely to be slightly older and more experienced, and they are considerably more likely to value both autonomy in their work situation and a flexible work schedule than do full-time employees. Independents also want to develop their professionalism, broaden their skill sets, and get the type of experiences that will advance their careers while keeping their work interesting.

According to John Chalt, chair and CEO of Hudson Highland, "The study is a wake-up call for employers . . . to fundamentally rethink the way they manage their workforce." He adds, "Smart employers are not only focusing on their full-time employees but developing strategies to relate to and manage highly skilled and productive professionals who are not under their direct control."

Full-timers in the U.S. give the highest weight to paid vacation and the lowest to having to deal with office politics. They also report very low satisfaction with their employment security, which they rate as one of the most important objectives. Independent professionals generally cite greater satisfaction than their full-time counterparts with the type of work they do, the people with whom they work, the industry, and their employer. They report less satisfaction with the lack of paid vacations and the need to provide their own retirement benefits.

Robert Morgan, chief operating officer of Hudson Talent Management in North America, states, "This segment of nontraditional employees is fast approaching 10% of the total workforce and is expected to show continued strong growth in future years."

Perhaps one way to better motivate full-time employees is to provide them with some of the benefits of independence, such as more flexible work hours, additional varied temporary work assignments, and more developmental activities.

CURTIS C. VERSCHOOR is the Ledger & Quill Research Professor, School of Accountancy and MIS, DePaul University, Chicago, and Research Scholar in the *Center for Business Ethics* at Bentley College, Waltham, Mass. You can reach him at cverscho@tdepaul.edu.

From *Strategic Finance,* November 2006, pp. 21–22. Copyright © 2006 by Institute of Management Accountants (IMA). Reprinted by permission via Copyright Clearance Center.

Building an Ethical Framework

10 questions to consider in encouraging an ethical corporate culture.

THOMAS R. KRAUSE AND PAUL J. VOSS

Although we are now several years into the new and land-mark regulatory environment that mandates an organizational culture of ethical conduct, there remains little guidance on how to get there. Many companies are engaged in a scramble to create a paper and electronic trail to ward off prosecution, rather than in a well-designed effort to promote or govern the culture of their organizations. While procedure is essential, the lesson we have learned from organizational change efforts is that leadership, rather than rules, finally determines behaviors and their outcomes.

This article suggests 10 primary questions every executive should ask—and expect to have answered thoroughly and well—in order to initiate a culture that encourages and sustains ethical conduct. These questions are meant to be asked and answered among leaders themselves, as well as with employees throughout the organization.

1. What is the relationship between ethics and other performance metrics in the company?

The relative cost of preventing a protracted ethical dilemma or full-fledged scandal is exponentially lower than the costs associated with fixing ethical problems. For example, see "The Cost to Firms of Cooking the Books," by J. Karpoff, D. Lee and G. Martin, forthcoming in *The Journal of Financial and Quantitative Analysis,* for a study of the substantial costs in fines and lost market value to almost 600 firms subject to SEC enforcement before the enactment of the Sarbanes-Oxley Act. Current research demonstrates that ethical companies are more competitive, profitable and sustaining than unethical companies. The challenge for the ethical leader is to find that connection and reveal it to the organization.

2. Have we, as required by the 2004 federal sentencing guidelines, offered ethics training for all of our employees? Does the training provide more than rote introduction of the company's code of conduct?

Ethics training comes in all shapes and sizes, with the most successful moving from theory to practice and from the conceptual to the real. Companies must first settle on an ethical vocabulary, define terms and establish core values. Live case studies can then help leadership and management "solve" relevant ethical dilemmas, both real and hypothetical.

3. What is the relationship between exercising sound ethics and retaining great talent?

Fortune magazine's annual list of the top 100 companies to work for contains a wide variety of companies with no obvious common denominator. Salary, benefits, career opportunities, location and profession all vary. What they do have in common is trust between employee and employer. Ethical behavior with and among employees, then, can lay the groundwork for attracting and retaining the best talent.

4. Have we conducted a "risk assessment" to determine our exposure to major ethical damage? What is our potential Enron?

While each company may have its unique "ethical nightmare," most companies face similar ethical exposures (e.g., to theft and accounting irregularities). Companies must examine the potential hazards of perverse incentives (e.g., compensation based 100 percent on financial goals) and the various "unintended consequences" of policy, procedures and protocols. Companies can reduce or eliminate adverse incentives by never rewarding, intentionally or unintentionally, improper behavior.

Research literature identifies several characteristics predictive of ethical outcomes: management credibility, upward communication, perceived organizational support, procedural justice and teamwork.

5. How can we be proactive in the area of ethics, culture and corporate citizenship?

Leaders need to own and shape the culture as much as they manage, for example, quality initiatives. Research literature identifies several characteristics predictive of ethical outcomes: management credibility, upward communication, perceived organizational support, procedural justice and teamwork. Well-tested diagnostic tools allow leaders to measure these characteristics and specific behaviors that foster the culture desired.

6. What tone should executive leadership set regarding ethics, integrity and transparency?

Setting an example is just one part of the executive leadership's responsibility. What leaders say, think and feel affects the tone as much as their actions. Mistrust, cynicism or indifference from topmost leaders can erode others' loyalty to the organization, to its mission, to employees and to shareholders. Left unchecked, this tone from the top can also potentially push ethical leaders out the door.

7. What does management need from the board of directors and senior leadership to enhance and buttress corporate ethics?

Employees who see the governing board and executive leadership as unconcerned will discount any directives about ethics that come from them. Consistency and authenticity from the board and executive leadership play a signal role in establishing an ethics initiative. At a minimum this means providing a reasonable budget of time, talent and money.

8. Who is driving ethics and compliance in the company?

The recent American Management Association report *The Ethical Enterprise* (2006) shows that ethical companies do not happen by accident. Companies need to designate internal drivers who move along the discussions, training and initiatives, producing ethical outcomes.

9. Do we have consistency of message between and among the board, the CEO, the senior executive team and the associates in terms of ethics and culture?

We all need to be on the same page, but finding the proper tone and guidance can be tricky. Establishing a common vocabulary can help with this process. For example, what does it mean to act unethically? What is an ethical dilemma? Who were Aristotle, Plato and Machiavelli, and how can they help provide a vocabulary for our company? What ethical model do we want to follow? What can we do to make it stick?

10. What roadblocks now discourage ethical conversations and the implementation of ethical practices, procedures and protocols?

Most people want to act with ethics and integrity, "to do the right thing." Yet our current approach to ethical conversation often does not advance our thinking or practice past our own perspectives. The object of dialogue, as advocated by physicist David Bohm, is "not to analyze things, or to win an argument, or to exchange opinions. Rather, it is to suspend your opinions and . . . to listen to everybody's opinions, to suspend them, and to see what all that means. . . . And if we can see them all, we may then move more creatively in a different direction." (For more information, see "On Dialogue," Ojai, Calif.: David Bohm Seminars, 1990.)

> **Most people want . . . "to do the right thing." Yet our current approach to ethical conversation often does not advance our thinking past our own perspectives.**

Starting the Conversation

Asking these 10 questions at board meetings, in leadership team meetings, and in the course of day-to-day interactions with employees engenders a climate that leads, over time, to zero tolerance for ethical lapses and impropriety. They also help executives assure their own diligence and oversight of ethical risks and threats, and deliver on their promise to employees, shareholders, customers and the community at large.

THOMAS R. KRAUSE, PhD is author of several books and Chairman and Co-founder of Behavioral Science Technology, Inc. (BST), an international performance solutions consulting company. He focuses on executive leadership development and coaching for clients including NASA, BHP Billiton and the FAA. PAUL J. VOSS, PhD is Ethics Practice Leader with BST. An author, scholar and lecturer, Dr. Voss' clients include Home Depot, the FBI lab, General Electric and Russell Athletics.

Moral Leadership

Inspire Ethical Behavior

Deborah L. Rhode

Given the centrality of ethics to the practice of leadership, it is striking how little research has focused on key questions: How do leaders form, sustain, and transmit moral commitments? Under what conditions are those processes most effective? What is the impact of ethics officers, codes, training programs, and similar initiatives? How do practices vary across context and culture? What can we do to foster moral leadership?

One difficulty plaguing analysis of moral leadership is the lack of consensus on what exactly it means. Leadership requires a relationship, not simply a title; leaders must inspire, not simply compel or direct their followers.

Leadership is inescapably value-laden. All leadership has moral dimensions. The essence of effective leadership is ethical leadership, which requires morality in means, as well as ends. Whether such leadership is cost-effective in the short term, is uncertain. "Ethics pays" is the mantra of most leadership literature. But when and how much depends on various factors.

Ethical Culture and Financial Value

Most studies that attempt to assess the value of values find positive relationships between ethical behaviors and financial results. For example, companies with stated commitments to ethical behavior have a higher mean financial performance. Employees who view their organization as supporting fair and ethical conduct and its leadership as caring about ethical issues observe less unethical behavior and perform better; they are more willing to share information and knowledge and to go the extra mile in meeting job requirements.

Employees also show more concern for the customer when employers show more concern for them. Workers who feel justly treated respond in kind; they are less likely to engage in petty dishonesty such as pilfering, fudging on hours and expenses, or misusing business opportunities. The financial payoffs are obvious: employee satisfaction improves customer satisfaction and retention; enhances workplace trust, cooperation, and innovation; and saves substantial costs resulting from misconduct and surveillance designed to prevent it.

People perform better when they believe that their workplace is treating them with dignity and respect and ensuring basic rights and equitable reward structures. Workers also respond to cues from peers and leaders. Virtue begets virtue, and observing moral behavior by others promotes similar conduct. Employers reap the rewards in higher morale, recruitment, and retention. Employee loyalty and morale are higher in businesses that are involved in their communities, and corporate giving correlates with public image and financial performance.

A reputation for ethical conduct by leaders and organizations also has financial value. Such a reputation can attract customers, employees, and investors, and build relationships with government regulators. Most individuals believe that companies should set high ethical standards and contribute to social goals.

Foundations of Ethical Leadership

Moral leadership involves ethical conduct on the part of leaders, as well as the capacity to inspire such conduct in followers and create ethical cultures.

Most organizations have ethical codes and compliance programs. In principle, their rationale is clear. Codes of conduct can clarify rules and expectations, establish standards, and project a responsible public image. If widely accepted and enforced, codified rules can also reinforce ethical commitments, deter ethical misconduct, promote trust, reduce the risks of liability, and prevent free riders (those who benefit from others' adherence to moral norms without observing them personally).

In practice, however, the value of codes is subject to debate. Skeptics often fault current documents as either too vague or too specific. Also, isolated ethical codes and compliance structures are viewed as window dressing—public relations gestures or formalities to satisfy federal guidelines.

Efforts to institutionalize ethics can succeed only if they are integral to the culture and taken seriously by leaders. A commitment to moral leadership requires the integration of ethical concerns into all activities. That means factoring moral considerations into day-to-day functions, including planning, resource allocations, hiring, promotion, compensation, performance evaluations, auditing, communications, public relations, and philanthropy. Responsibilities to stakeholders need to figure in strategic decision-making, and assessments of performance need to reflect values in addition to profits.

Ethical Commitment

The leader's own ethical commitment is critical in several respects. First, leaders set a moral tone and a moral example by their own behavior. Employees take cues about appropriate behavior from their leaders. Whether workers believe that leaders care about principles as much as profits influences their conduct.

Consistency between words and actions is important in conveying a moral message. Decisions that mesh poorly with professed values send a powerful signal. No mission statement can counter the impact of seeing leaders withhold crucial information, play favorites with promotion, stifle dissent, implement corrosive reward structures, or pursue their own self-interest.

One overlooked opportunity for moral leadership is for those in top positions to keep their own compensation within reasonable bounds. Another is to create more safe spaces for reports of misconduct and moral disagreements. Doing so prevents the far greater costs of external whistle-blowing.

Not only do we need more rewards for leadership that is ethically and socially responsible, but we also need fewer rewards for leadership that is not. We need to alter compensation structures that unduly favor short-term profit maximization, and define success to include ethical and social responsibility as well as financial profitability.

DEBORAH L. RHODE is the Ernest W. McFarland Professor of Law and director of the Stanford Center on Ethics. This article is adapted from her book *Moral Leadership (Jossey-Bass)* and used with permission. Email rhode@stanford.edu.

From *Leadership Excellence*, by Deborah L. Rhode, January 2007, pp. 10. Copyright © 2007 by Leadership Excellence. Reprinted by permission. www.LeaderExcel.com

A Measure of Success?

Ethics after Enron

CHERYL ROSEN

The guilty verdicts were not the end of the story. Only six weeks after his conviction for conspiracy and fraud, Enron founder and former chief executive Kenneth Lay was dead, the victim of a heart attack. Jeffrey Skilling, Lay's successor at the now defunct energy giant, continues to maintain his innocence and has vowed to appeal; nonetheless, he's likely to receive a hefty prison term when sentenced. As the drama plays to its final conclusion, corporate America watches with bemusement and searches for lessons. Is the Enron case a "Verdict on an Era" gone by—as *The New York Times* suggests? Or do the "Guilty Verdicts Provide 'Red Meat' to Prosecutors Chasing Companies?"—as *The Wall Street Journal* speculates?

There's probable truth in both scenarios. In interviews we've conducted with executives of companies large and small, it's clear that the Enron case will influence discussions and decisions in corporate boardrooms for years to come. Here's a look at some of the lessons already learned—and how many executives are gearing up to meet the challenges of increased scrutiny and expense, organizational change and a mandate for measurement to help ensure ethics programs are far more than just corporate window-dressing.

New Players in the C-Suite

Perhaps the most noticeable change is in the new roles and titles to which Enron has given life. One of the newest is chief accounting officer.

"Enron has made us all just nervous," says Joyce Bastoli, vice president and regional director of Ajilon Finance Solutions. "CFOs don't want to be blamed for weaknesses in accounting functions, so companies are bringing in this extra layer of management, hiring chief accounting officers to handle reporting and compliance and work with outside auditors. And they have found that their stocks usually rise when they do."

Ajilon, headquartered in Saddle Brook, N.J., provides companies with senior level finance and operations professionals on a project or interim basis. But like many of its clients, Ajilon is cleaning its own house, "enforcing the rules a lot more and not letting it slide when there's no process in place," Bastoli says. In fact, the company recently dismissed one employee for misreporting his key-performance indicators. "We're really holding managers accountable for ensuring their numbers are accurate, and doing more due diligence to make sure the people we hire are credible and ethical."

Steve Skalak, partner in the corporate investigations practice of PricewaterhouseCoopers in New York, agrees that "the whole area of forensic accounting is being pretty aggressively installed in major companies, though the jury is out on whether the measures are worth the cost." In early returns, the data suggest that one area where the return on investment is palpable is the lessening risk of legal actions. There were 168 securities-related, class-action cases last year, down from more than 200 for the first time in 10 years, he notes. According to PwC's Global Economic Crime survey, a company's two most effective investments are in whistleblower access and internal audit.

The big-picture lesson, Skalak says, is that whatever the specifics of a corporate system of internal controls, ethics office and hotline, it's important to constantly reinforce the concept of "We trust our employees but we verify what they do." He suggests a supervisory review by management, scheduled on an appropriate cycle, at all levels of the organization. In corporate governance, for example, that means questioning what management is doing deep in the clerical operations. And it translates into making sure payments for routine goods and services are being properly reviewed at all levels.

Skalak says companies also shouldn't forget one of the most important—and most counter-intuitive—lessons learned from Enron and other business-ethics scandals. The old saw that communicating stories of bad behavior only inspires others to try it themselves has proven untrue. "One key best practice in corporate investigations is communicating that you have detected and mitigated a problem," he says. "That has a substantial deterrent effect and is definitely preferable to keeping everything confidential."

For ethics and compliance officers, the most obvious post-Enron trend is the evolution of their job responsibilities into a field in itself, separate from law, human resources and audit. The Ethics and Compliance Officer Association, Waltham, Mass., reports that in the five years since Enron collapsed, the association has grown more than 70%, to 1,260 members.

One ongoing challenge for most compliance and ethics professionals is that they "still don't really have the power to say no to a CEO or CFO," says Joseph E. Murphy, partner in the Compliance Systems Legal Group, Warwick, R.I. Murphy suggests that compliance officers be accountable to corporate boards, not to senior management, with employment agreements that need the approval of a company's full audit committee.

Adding It All Up

Measurement. That's what companies are increasingly looking for with regard to their ethics and compliance programs, partly to determine whether the programs are working but also to tweak and fine-tune business systems and processes in the hopes of recouping some return on the vast sums being spent on post-Enron compliance.

"The new wave is business-process improvement through accurate, real-time reporting," Ajilon's Bastoli says, "looking at how finance can leverage technology to capture efficiencies, savings and activity-based costing, to trace profits and be sure you're running a lean operation."

At Boeing Co., the huge Chicago-based aerospace company, the goal is to "be in a position to see ahead, predict what's happening and get ahead of it," rather than responding after the fact to negative behaviors or publicity, says Martha Ries, vice president of ethics and business conduct. Ries told a packed room at a recent Conference Board conference on ethics and compliance, "We're starting to take our survey data, our H.R. data, data from a number of companies we benchmark within the defense industry and focus-group data, and look at it altogether."

In January, each business head at Boeing identified three key business risks to focus on for 2006. They each get a daily summary report that tracks current cases, backlog, cycle time and customer satisfaction. An internal Ethics Report, posted on the corporate intranet, communicates the disposition of any cases that arise for all employees to see, with only the names of the perpetrators deleted.

Dow Chemical Co., Midland, Mich., is also looking at the numbers and the data, trying to measure how employees perceive it's ethics program. It's also working to develop a standard process and database to identify and track issues, apply consistent discipline or remedial action and eliminate the possibility of double standards based on management levels, says director of global ethics and compliance Tom McCormick.

At PBS&J, a Florida-based, employee-owned engineering firm with 3,800 employees, chief ethics and compliance officer C. Lee Essrig identifies best practices as focusing on risk assessment, measuring program effectiveness and putting a real emphasis on culture and leadership. "The key is to encourage and reward right behaviors instead of punishing after the fact," she says. They're also "relentless about communicating with employees. The point is to breathe life into the program by following through on what you promise."

"Does your company have mandatory ethics training?" she asks. "Is it truly mandatory? What happens to people who don't go?"

The question of over-promising also concerns Lisa Ruca, director of corporate compliance at law firm Holland Knight

A Little Light in Portland

Enron may be gone, but its legacy continues in a most unlikely place.

In April, on the same day former Enron CEO Jeffrey Skilling took the stand in his own defense, Enron subsidiary Portland General Electric spun off from its bankrupt parent and made its debut on the New York Stock Exchange. Enron creditors received 27 million newly-issued shares of the utility, or about 43% of its outstanding stock, for a payout worth $568 million. The remaining shares are being held by a disputed claims reserve for future distribution to Enron's creditors—including the 401(k) accounts of Portland General's retirees.

Portland General, Oregon's oldest utility, delivers electricity to about 780,000 customers. When it was bought by Enron for $3.1 billion in 1997, its pension plan largely remained unchanged—but its 401(k) plan shifted to Enron securities, which today are virtually without value.

"It's a relief to have the Enron chapter behind us and we're excited to be an independent company again," CEO Peggy Fowler told Business Ethics. Now, the remaining issue is personal, as employees "are still dealing with their 401(k) losses in varying ways and are watching closely how the 401(k) settlements will work out, including if there will be any noticeable recovery of those lost investments."

Some folks have delayed their retirement plans and stayed on longer than they had planned. Others are hoping for a successful outcome to Portland General's efforts to convince Congress to pass catch-up retirement legislation for employees of companies like Enron. Portland General, meanwhile, is offering retirement planning advice and job training for workers who want to move into other areas of the company.

"Most of us have moved on," says Fowler, and certainly her focus is on the future rather than the past. In the works at the newly public utility are an infrastructure investment plan that will add the 400 megawatt (MW) natural gas-fired Port Westward Generating Plant [by 2007], and a wind project that will produce 450 MW more, as well as new metering technologies and information platforms to better monitor customers' daily needs.

But the lessons of Enron are not forgotten—especially not by Fowler. "Would Enron have been different with different people? Probably," she says. "It's important to have the right people in the right jobs, especially when they are key leadership positions. And it's extremely important to protect your company's reputation. It's far too easy to damage or lose your reputation these days—and far harder to earn it back."

LLP. "Enron is the perfect example of a window-shelf compliance program," she notes, with a state-of-the-art ethics program and a CEO who talked the talk. The lesson? It's not what you put in your code; it's about how your executives embrace and own the program. "The important thing is to integrate compliance and ethics into the business. Companies don't know how to do that yet, but they have learned that paper programs just aren't going to work. There's more of an emphasis on measurement than ever, even though it's very difficult," Ruca says.

Looking to the Future

In the autumn of 2001, Enron was beginning its final slide into corporate oblivion, taking with it the Arthur Andersen accounting firm and the jobs of thousands of employees. Few could have imagined then what has unfolded since. Certainly no one could have predicted that the financial and business ramifications of the Enron debacle would continue on into the second half of the decade.

Yet that's what is happening. In Washington, the debate continues regarding Sarbanes-Oxley and required levels of compliance, especially for smaller publicly-held businesses. Ajilon's Bastoli predicts a wave of small companies privatizing as their executives simply give up trying to meet the compliance standards. "We'll see a lot of activity in investment banking and M&A in 2007," she says.

But larger companies also will continue to search for efficiencies. "There's no question that investors are better served today than before Enron, and that the system has delivered better processes," says PricewaterhouseCoopers partner Ray Beier. "But the question is, at what cost? I do see where the system has acknowledged that maybe there's too much regulation. What's the balance between regulation and getting things done in the marketplace? That's the debate that will go on. That's going to be one key question for 2007."

Meanwhile, getting the accounting right is particularly important, Beier says. The IRS likely will be looking carefully at how companies account for liabilities in terms of reserves and complex hedging transactions, and whether they account for revenue properly. Executive compensation will draw attention in 2007—and so will the role of the board.

And the age-old question will remain: "How do you make sure your people do the right thing? Are your incentives directing behaviors the way you want them directed?"

Former federal prosecutors Chuck La Bella and Thomas McNamara, now white-collar, criminal-defense lawyers at their own San Diego firm, predict that enforcement activities by the Securities and Exchange Commission will continue at the current level, "though federal prosecutions may have reached a peak." Regulators and law enforcement agents have been so aggressive that companies are starting to fight back a little. Still, they note, "the SEC is pooling hundreds of millions of dollars in resources (into) an enforcement apparatus it didn't have five years ago. They have to do something."

At Boeing, an internal Ethics Report, posted on the corporate intranet, communicates the disposition of any cases that arise for all employees to see, with only the names of the perpetrators deleted.

Another "subtle aftermath of Enron" is the increased role of the institutional investor. "They're flexing their muscles, and we're going to see more and more of that," LaBella and McNamara predict. Insurance companies and pensions funds are going to demand good corporate governance—and their involvement "is a much more effective solution than an Enron trial, because they are interested in the survival—the growth and prosperity—of companies, and in creating real value."

Smart companies will fine-tune their use of good governance not just to satisfy market analysts but as a public relations vehicle, the former prosecutors predict. "Good corporate governance," they note, "can be as effective a marketing tool as a good quarter."

CHERYL ROSEN (crosen2@optonline.net) is a New York-based freelance business journalist.

Why Good Leaders Do Bad Things
Mental Gymnastics behind Unethical Behavior

In making ethical decisions, let virtuous values guide your judgments and beware of the mental games that can undermine ethical decision making.

CHARLES D. KERNS, PHD

As the General Manager for an industrial distributor, you have recently learned that your consistently top performing purchasing manager has violated company policy by accepting an expensive gift from a supplier. Since you believe that this was likely a one-time lapse in judgment, what would you say or do? Your response could range from "looking the other way" to firing the manager.

In this situation, as in all ethical choices or dilemmas, the leader's thought pattern (cognitive process) will significantly influence what action he or she takes. People's patterns of thinking will be influenced by their values, what they say to themselves (self-talk), and what they imagine will happen in response to their actions. At its most basic level, ethical managerial leadership involves discerning right from wrong and acting in alignment with such judgment.

Leaders with strong virtuous values are more likely to act ethically than are leaders who are operating with a weak or non-existent value system. One set of values that seems to be universally accepted includes wisdom, self-control, justice, transcendence, kindness, and courage.[1] When faced with challenging decisions, leaders who have not internalized a value system that includes these values will probably respond with more variability than will one who has such a system. It is primarily in the situation in which the leader does not have an internalized value system that mental gymnastics or mind games may cause an otherwise good person to make unethical decisions.

In this article we will review mind games that leaders may play when they face difficult decisions and lack both a strong value system and a professional and ethical approach to management. These leaders tend to react to circumstances on a situational basis. Some suggestions on how managerial leaders can deal with challenging decisions are offered throughout the following discussion.

Mind Games

Decision making can often result in managerial missteps, even those decisions that involve ethical considerations. Many common themes emerge as we look at these problematic decisions. Most significantly, various cognitive processes that leaders often unwittingly employ and which may be called "mental gymnastics" or mind games may serve to support and sustain unethical behavior.

Mind Game #1: Quickly Simplify— "Satisficing"

When we are confronted with a complicated problem, most of us react by reducing the problem to understandable terms. We simplify. Notwithstanding the considerable power of our human intellect, we are often unable to cognitively process all of the information needed to reach an optimal decision. Instead, we tend to make quick decisions based on understandable and readily available elements related to the decision. We search for a solution that is both satisfactory and sufficient. Full rationality gives way to bounded rationality, which finds leaders considering the essential elements of a problem without taking into account all of its complexities. Unfortunately, this process, called "satisficing," can lead to solutions that are less than optimal or even ethically deficient.[2]

"Satisficing" leads the managerial leader to alternatives that tend to be easy to formulate, familiar, and close to the status quo. When one grapples with complex ethical considerations, this approach to decision making may not produce the best solutions. Ethical dilemmas can often benefit from creative thinking that explores ideas beyond the usual responses. If a decision maker uses satisficing when crafting a solution to an ethical problem, the best alternative may be overlooked. David Messick and Max Bazerman, researchers in decision making, tell us that when executives "satisfice," they often simplify, thereby overlooking low probability events, neglecting to consider some stakeholders, and failing to identify possible long-term consequences.[3]

One of the best ways to guard against oversimplifying and reaching less than optimal solutions to ethical challenges is to discuss the situation with other trusted colleagues. Have them play devil's advocate. Ask them to challenge your decision. The resulting dialogue can improve the quality of your ethical decision making.

Scholar and ethics consultant Laura Nash suggests twelve questions that can help leaders avoid the mind game of over simplifying.[4] The following questions may raise ethical issues not otherwise considered, or help generate a variety of "out of the box" alternatives. Before settling on a solution, ask yourself the following questions:

- Have I specified the problem accurately?
- How would I describe the problem if I were on the opposite side of the fence?
- How did this situation begin?
- To whom and to what do I give my loyalties as a person or group and as a member of the organization?
- What is my intention in making this decision?
- How does this intention compare with the likely results?
- Whom could my decision or action harm?
- Can I engage those involved in a discussion of the problem prior to making a decision?
- Am I confident that my position will be valid over the long term?
- Could I disclose without reservation my decision or action to my boss, our CEO, the Board of Directors, my family, or society as a whole?
- What is the symbolic impact of my action if it is understood?
- Under what conditions would I allow exceptions to my position?

These questions initiate a thought process that underscores the importance of problem identification and information gathering. Such a process can help leaders guard against over simplifying an otherwise complicated ethical decision.

Mind Game #2: The Need to Be Liked

Most people want to be liked. However, when this desire to be liked overpowers business objectivity, ethical lapses can occur. For instance, when managers witness ethical transgressions, the need to be liked may cause them to overlook these transgressions. Such a situation is particularly acute for those recently promoted into management from within the same organization. Because they want to be liked by their former peers, they may have a difficult time saying, "No." Dr. Albert Ellis, author of *A New Guide to Rational Living*,[5] notes that one of eleven irrational beliefs that some people hold is the belief that one can or should always be liked. He states that people who are affected by this need carry around in their heads statements such as, "I believe I must be approved by virtually everyone with whom I come in contact."

Such an overriding desire to be liked can ultimately adversely affect the ethics of people in an organization and thus can decrease the firm's bottom line. For instance, a retail store manager who wants her employees to like her may readily give them additional hours when they request them to enable employees to earn more money. However, in so doing, the manager contributes to the accumulation of too many hours of labor relative to sales volume. Over time, excessive labor costs can then begin to eat into profit margins.

After recognizing that she is playing this mind game, one way that the manager might stem this problem is to distance herself from her subordinates (e.g., reduce unnecessary socializing) until she can establish some objective boundaries. Another successful approach would be to respond warmly and assertively toward employees while still going forward with appropriate but possibly less popular decisions. (If necessary, the manager could even take assertiveness training.) Finally, in such situations, the newly appointed manager might want to read Alberti and Emmons' book, *Your Perfect Right*.[6] This book provides excellent advice on how to say "no" while preserving a quality relationship.

Mind Game #3: Dilute and Disguise

In trying to strike a diplomatic chord, leaders can disguise the offensiveness of unethical acts by using euphemisms or softened characterizations. Words or phrases such as "helped him make a career choice" are used to describe firing someone, or "inappropriate allocation of resources" is used to describe what everyone knows is stealing. Regardless of whether people want to be seen as kinder and gentler, or just politically correct, this process merely helps wrongdoers and those associated with them to get away with unethical behavior.

Such softened characterizations serve to reduce the anxiety of the leader, but these euphemisms are dishonest. They serve to dilute and disguise unethical behavior. This form of mental gymnastics defuses discomfort that may otherwise develop among those involved in unethical "mischief," but such an approach dilutes the necessary intensity of ethical constraints that should be brought to bear in the situation. The antidote is for leaders to talk straight and to avoid euphemistic labeling or recharacterizing unethical behavior.

Mind Game #4: "Making Positive"

The mental gymnastic of comparing one's own unethical behavior to more heinous behavior committed by others serves only to avoid self-degradation. For example, the salesperson who occasionally cheats when reporting his expenses may say to himself, "I do this only a few times a year, while Tom, Dick, and Harry do it all the time." Or, "If you think I disregard my colleagues' feelings, you ought to see Andy in action. He is a bona fide bully!" Unethical behavior appears more ethical by comparing it to worse behavior.

Such justifications for unethical behavior are not valid. The tendency to diminish misdeeds by making dishonest comparisons also contributes to sustaining unethical conduct. To avoid this mind game, ask three questions about the comparison:

- Am I comparing apples to oranges?
- How self-serving is this comparison?
- What would three objective observers say about me and my objectivity regarding this comparison?

While behavior may often legitimately be compared to that of others, when ethical transgressions are involved, relativity does not excuse ethical lapses.

Mind Game #5: Overconfidence

Overconfident managers tend to perceive their abilities to be greater than they actually are. Self-perception often does not match objective reality. By indulging in the mental gymnastics of overconfidence, such leaders can discount others' perceptions and thus easily overlook the insights and talents of other people. Without benefit of input from those around them, overconfident managerial leaders may be blind to the most appropriate ethical choices in given circumstances and may consider only their own ideas regarding the best course of action. Overconfident managers act as though they are "above it all," relegating their people, useful information, and learning opportunities to the sidelines while pursuing their own courses of action.

Overconfident decision makers deny themselves fresh perspectives and thus perhaps better solutions to ethical problems. The overconfident manager is typically perceived as arrogant. Research tells us that the manager labeled thusly is headed for career derailment.[7] Arrogant managerial leaders who have performance problems, which may include ignoring, overlooking, or causing ethical concern, are likely to receive less understanding and support from others in their time of trouble. Their air of overconfidence not only interferes with the practice of quality ethical decision making, but it can also virtually wreck their careers.

One tool to counterbalance this unproductive and potentially deadly tendency is for the overconfident managerial leader to catch himself or herself when preparing to make declarative, "This is the way it is" statements, and replace them with more open ended, "What do you think?" types of inquiries. If practiced conscientiously, this simple communication tool can help the overly confident manager begin to consider others' perspectives. Accepting input from other people will improve the manager's decision making ability generally, including those issues that involve ethical consideration. Applied broadly, this practice will positively impact the ethical problem solving climate within the entire organization.

These five mind games can influence an otherwise good leader to act unethically. Each of the mental maneuvers provides an easy way around difficult decisions, with the likely outcome that some of those decisions will result in unethical behavior. However, the intrinsic benefit of pursuing an ethical course will be a source of motivation for leaders to get on track ethically and stay there. By staying the course and behaving in a way that is consistent with his or her virtuous values and attitudes, the ethical managerial leader will have less need to play these types of mind games.

A Call to Action

Examine your thoughts when confronted with ethical choice points. In making ethical decisions, let virtuous values guide your judgments, and avoid playing mental games that undermine ethical behavior. If unchecked, indulging in these games can lead you to do bad things while feeling justified by your wrongdoing, at least temporarily. You are encouraged to heed the following suggestions that can help defend against participating in these mind games.

As you approach an ethical decision, to what extent do you do the following?

- Deliberate the obvious and not so obvious circumstances surrounding the issue.
- Decide objectively without regard to being liked.
- Talk about transgressions and ethical breaches using straightforward words.
- Make valid comparisons when discussing specific ethical behavior.
- Act with an appropriate level of confidence.

If you responded favorably to these questions, then perhaps these five mind games are not stumbling blocks for you. Less favorable or more uncertain responses may impel you to consider how your patterns of thinking may be adversely affecting your approach to ethical decision making.

Notes

1. Martin Seligman, *Authentic Happiness* (New York: Free Press, 2002). For definitions of these "virtuous values," and a discussion about their role in the business environment see Charles D. Kerns, "Creating and Sustaining an Ethical Workplace Culture," Graziadio Business Report, 6, Issue 3.
2. Stephen P. Robbins, *Essentials of Organizational Behavior*, 7th ed., New Jersey: Prentice-Hall (2003).

3. David M. Messick and M. H. Bazerman, "Ethical Leadership and the Psychology of Decision Making," *Sloan Management Review* 37 (Winter, 1996), p. 9.

4. Laura L. Nash, "Ethics Without the Sermon," in K. R. Andrews (ed.) *Ethics in Practice: Managing the Moral Corporation,* Boston: Harvard Business School Press, (1989), p. 243–257.

5. Albert Ellis and R. A. Harper, *A New Guide To Rational Living*, 3rd ed., 1997, (North Hollywood, CA: Wilshire).

6. Robert Alberti and M. L. Emmons, *Your Perfect Right: A Guide to Assertive Living,* 7th ed. (San Luis Obispo, CA: Impact, 1995).

7. Morgan W. McCall, *High Flyers: Developing the Next Generation of Leaders*, (Boston: Harvard Business School Press, 1998).

Best Resources for Corporate Social Responsibility

Karen McNichol

What most of us lack these days isn't data but time. The World Wide Web is a marvelous research tool, but the sheer amount of information available can be overwhelming. How do you weed through it to find the very best sites, where someone has already synthesized masses of material for you? Well, consider the offerings below a garden without the weeds: a selection of the best of the best sites in corporate social responsibility (CSR).

1. Best Practices and Company Profiles

www.bsr.org—This may well be the best CSR site of all. Run by the business membership organization Business for Social

Responsibility, its focus is on giving business hands-on guidance in setting up social programs, but data is useful to researchers as well, particularly because of "best practice" examples. Topics include social auditing, community involvement, business ethics, governance, the environment, employee relations, and corporate citizenship. New topics are being researched all the time. One recent report, for example, looked at companies linking executive pay to social performance, while others have looked at how to implement flexible scheduling, or become an "employer of choice." Visitors can create their own printer-friendly custom report on each topic, selecting from sections like Business Importance, Recent Developments, Implementation Steps, Best Practices, and Links to Helping Resources. To receive notices about updates, plus other CSR news, subscribe

Figure 1 www.worldcsr.com offers one-stop access to the leading business-led organizations on corporate social responsibility in Europe and the U.S.

to BSR Resource Center Newsletter by sending a message to centerupdates@bsr.org with "subscribe" in the subject line.

www.ebnsc.org—You might call this the BSR site from Europe. It is sponsored by Corporate Social Responsibility Europe, whose mission is to help put CSR into the mainstream of business. This site includes a databank of best practices from all over Europe on topics like human rights, cause-related marketing, ethical principles, and community involvement. To give just one example of the site's capability, a search on the topic "reporting on CSR" came up with a dozen news articles available in full, plus a case study, and a list of 20 books and reports on the topic. One unique feature is the "CSR Matrix," which allows visitors to call up a complete social report on companies like IBM, Levi Strauss, or Procter & Gamble. The "matrix" is a grid, where the visitor clicks on one box to view the company's code of conduct, another box to see how the company interacts with public stakeholders, a third box to access the company's sustainability report, and so forth.

www.worldcsr.com is a World CSR portal offering one-stop access to the leading business-led organizations on corporate social responsibility in Europe and the U.S., including the two sites mentioned above. Another site on the portal—www.businessimpact.org—offers a useful databank of links to related organizations, such as the Global Reporting Initiative, Institute for Global Ethics, and World Business Council for Sustainable Development. Readers can also subscribe to the Business Impact News e-mail newsletter.

www.responsibleshopper.org—For individuals wishing to shop with or research responsible companies, Responsible Shopper from Co-op America offers in-depth social profiles on countless companies. A report on IBM, for example, looks at everything from Superfund sites, toxic emissions, and worker benefits to laudatory activities. Different brand names for each company are listed, and social performance is summarized in letter ratings—as with IBM, which got an "A" in Disclosure, and a "B" in the Environment.

2. Social Investing

www.socialfunds.com—Run by SRI World Group, Social Funds is the best social investing site on the web. A staff of reporters researchers breaking news and posts it without charge. For socially responsible mutual funds, the site offers performance statistics plus fund descriptions. There's an investing center where you can build your own basket of social companies, plus a community banking center with information on savings accounts and money market funds with responsible banking organizations. A shareholder activism section offers a status report on social resolutions and is searchable by topic (equality, tobacco, militarism, etc.). Also available is a free weekly e-mail newsletter, SRI News Alert—which goes beyond social investing. One recent issue, for example, looked at new labeling programs for clean-air office construction, an Arctic Wildlife Refuge resolution against BP Amoco, and why greener multinationals have higher market value. A new service from SRI World Group, offered jointly with Innovest Strategic Advisors, offers subscribers ($100 annually) ratings of companies

in various industries, based on environmental and financial performance.

www.socialinvest.org—This is the site of the nonprofit professional membership association, the Social Investment Forum, and is a useful pair to the above site. One unique feature is the collection of Moskowitz Prize-winning papers on research in social investing. The 2000 winner, for example, was "Pure Profit: The Financial Implications of Environmental Performance." Also available is a directory to help visitors find a financial adviser anywhere in the country; a mutual funds chart; a guide to community investing (showing resources by state and by type); and materials on SIF's campaign to end predatory lending. You can also access the Shareholder Action Network-which shows how to submit shareholder resolutions, and offers information on both current campaigns and past successes.

www.goodmoney.com.—Offering some unique investing features of its own is the Good Money site, which showcases the Good Money Industrial Average: a screened index which outperformed the Dow in 2000. Also available are social profiles and performance data for a variety of public companies—including the 400 companies in the Domini Social Index, companies with the best diversity record, the Council on Economic Priorities "honor roll" list, and signers of the CERES Principles (a voluntary environmental code of conduct). Another section on Eco Travel has dozens of links and articles.

3. Corporate Watchdogs

www.corpwatch.org—For activists, this may be the best site of all. Calling itself "The Watchdog on the Web," CorpWatch offers news you may not find elsewhere on human rights abuses abroad, public policy; and environmental news—plus on-site reporting of protests. Its director Josh Karliner was nominated by Alternet.org (an alternative news service) as a Media Hero 2000, for using the web to fight the excesses of corporate globalization. CorpWatch puts out the bimonthly Greenwash Awards, and runs a Climate Justice Initiative, as well as the Alliance for a Corporate-Free UN. An Issue Library covers topics like the WTO and sweatshops, while the Hands-on Guide to On-line Corporate Research is useful for research ideas. A free twice-monthly e-mail newsletter updates readers on recent CorpWatch headlines. One recent issue of "What's New on CorpWatch" looked at topics like the World Bank's record, the protests at the World Economic Forum, California's deregulation troubles, plus the regular "Take Action" feature urging readers to send e-mails or faxes on a specific issue. To subscribe to the e-letter, send blank message to corp-watchers-subscribe@igc.topica.com.

www.corporatepredators.org—Featuring Russell Mokhiber, editor of the weekly newsletter *Corporate Crime Reporter*, this site offers a compilation of weekly e-mail columns called "Focus on the Corporation," written by Mokhiber and Robert Weissman. They offer a valuable, quirky voice in corporate responsibility. Taking on topics not covered elsewhere, the columns have looked at how the chemical industry responded to Bill Moyers TV program on industry coverup, how little academic research focuses on corporate crime, and why it's inappropriate to legally view corporations as "persons." At this site (which also features

Figure 2   For activists, www.corpwatch.org may be the best site of all.

the book *Corporate Predators* by Mokhiber and Weissman), readers can access weekly columns back through 1998. Subscribe free to the column by sending an e-mail message to corp-focus-request@lists.essential.org with the text "subscribe."

4. Labor and Human Rights

http://oracle02.ilo.org/vpi/welcome—Sponsored by the International Labor Organization, this web site offers a new Business and Social Initiatives Database, compiling Internet sources on employment and labor issues. It covers topics like child labor, living wage, dismissal, investment screens, monitoring, international labor standards, glass ceilings, safe work, and so forth. It features information on corporate policies and reports, codes of conduct, certification criteria, labeling and other programs. A search feature allows visitors to retrieve information on specific companies, regions, and business sectors. This is one of the most comprehensive labor sites out there.

www.summersault.com/~agj/clr/—Sponsored by the Campaign for Labor Rights, this site keeps activists up to date on anti-sweatshop struggles and other pro-labor activities around the world. Particularly useful is the free e-mail newsletter Labor Alerts, which updates readers on recent news about trade trea-

ties, plant shutdowns, labor organizing, job postings, upcoming protests, recent books, and so forth. One recent issue contained a "webliography" of sites about the pending creation of the Free Trade Area of the Americas (FTAA). To subscribe contact clr-main@afgj.org.

5. Progressive Economics

www.epn.org—For the best thinking in progressive economic policy, this site managed by *The American Prospect* magazine is a one-stop source. It's the Electronic Policy Network, an on-line consortium of over 100 progressive policy centers nationwide, like the Center for Public Integrity, the Brookings Institution, the Financial Markets Center, and many more. (The focus of member groups is heavily though not exclusively economic.) A feature called Idea Central offers on-line bibliographies on topics like globalization, poverty, and livable cities. Certain topics get "Issues in Depth" treatment: One, for example, looks at campaign finance reform—including history, alternatives, and legal background, with numerous links to sites like a database of soft-money contribution, research from the Center for Responsive Politics, ACLU factsheets, and more. Another feature, "What's New," looks at recent reports and research papers by member

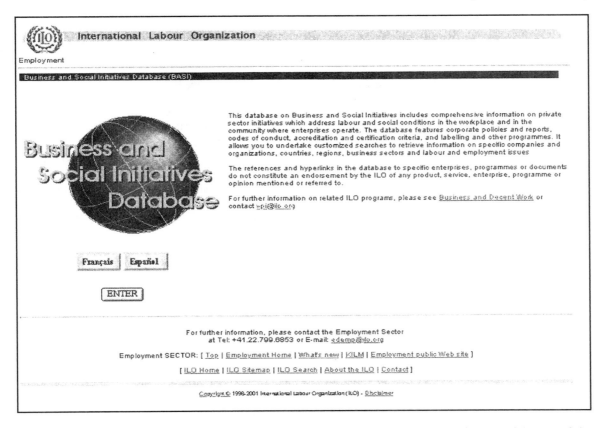

Figure 3 The Business and Social Initiatives Database (http://oracle02.ilo.org/vpi/welcome) is one of the most comprehensive labor compilations out there.

policy centers—like a recent report from the Economic Policy Institute on privatization, or a report on state initiatives for children from the National Center for Children in Poverty. Readers can receive summaries of new research reports by subscribing to the e-mail EPN News; send an e-mail to majordomo@epn.org with "subscribe epnnews" in the message body.

www.neweconomics.org—This valuable site is run by The New Economics Foundation (NEF), a UK nonprofit think tank created in 1986 to focus on "constructing a new economy centered on people and the environment." Different areas on the site focus on powerful tools for economic change, like alternative currencies, social investment, indicators for sustainability, and social accounting. A monthly web-based newsletter reports on topics like Jubilee 2000 (the movement to cancel the debt of developing nations), May Day plans, an "indicator of the month," and more. A new bimonthly e-briefing is called "mergerwatch," which looks at the hidden costs behind mergers, and who pays the price. Its first issue in April 2001 reported, for example, that a 1999 KPMG study showed 53 percent of mergers destroy shareholder value, and a further 30 percent bring no measurable benefit.

6. *Employee Ownership*

http://cog.kent.edu—For researchers in employee ownership, the Capital Ownership Group site is indispensable. COG is a virtual think tank of individuals—including academics, employee

ownership specialists, and business leaders worldwide—who aim to promote broadened ownership of productive capital. The site's library allows visitors to browse ongoing discussions, on topics like promoting employee ownership globally, getting economists more involved in issues of capital ownership, the role of labor in employee ownership, and more. The library offers hundreds of papers and research reports, on topics like labor-sponsored venture capital, employee governance, case studies, and much more.

www.nceo.org—This is the site of the National Center for Employee Ownership, a nonprofit research and membership organization that is one of the best sources for employee ownership information. Its web library features a valuable introduction to the history of Employee Stock Ownership Plans (ESOPs), plus information on open book management, stock options, and alternatives to ESOPs. An "Interactive Introduction to ESOPs" lets visitors "chat" with an expert in the same way as if they spent fifteen minutes on the phone with a lawyer. Also available are a wealth of links to related sites, plus news and statistics on employee ownership.

www.fed.org—The sponsor of this site is the Foundation for Enterprise Development—a nonprofit started by Robert Beyster, founder of employee-owned SAIC—which is an organization that aims to promote employee ownership. Its focus is not ESOPs but stock options and other forms of equity ownership. A monthly online magazine features profiles of employee ownership at specific companies, articles on developing an ownership culture, plus news. An e-mail service updates readers on headlines.

www.the-esop-emplowner.org—From the ESOP Association—a membership and lobbying organization—this site offers a resource library, news of events, reports on legislative victories, and information on legislative initiatives. The site also offers information on the ESOP Association's political action committee, which since 1988 has helped candidates for federal office who support ESOPs and ESOP law.

7. Sustainability

www.GreenBiz.com—Run by Joel Makower, editor of *The Green Business Letter*, Green Biz is the best site on progressive environmental business activities. It enables visitors to discover what companies are doing, and to access citations of countless web resources and reports, on topics like sustainable management, green auditing, EPA programs, pending legislation, clean technologies, recycling, and all things green. A new service features free job listing for environmental professionals. Get regular updates from a free e-mail newsletter, GreenBiz, published every other week.

www.rprogress.org—Run by the nonprofit Redefining Progress—which produces the Genuine Progress Indicator (as a counterpoint to GDP)—this site offers news on topics like climate change, forest-land protection, tax reform, and congressional influence peddling. Recent stories featured a proposal to promote market-based policies for reducing sprawl, a better way to return the government surplus, plus a look at Living Planet 2000—calculating the ecological footprints of the world's largest 150 countries. Numerous studies on environmental justice, tax fairness, and community indicators are available, plus links to other climate change sites.

www.sustainablebusiness.com—The monthly on-line magazine Sustainable Business offers news on the "green economy," covering recycling, product take-back, legislative developments, and so forth. Other features are a database of "Green Dream Job" openings; plus a section to help green businesses find venture capital. A library features web sites, reports, and books.

www.cleanedge.com—The new organization Clean Edge focuses on helping investors, industry, and society understand and profit from clean technology, like wind, solar, energy

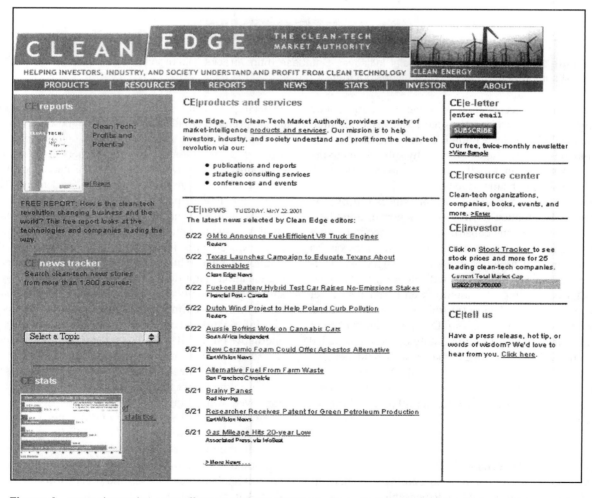

Figure 4 www.cleanedge.com offers news from 1,800 sources, stock trading information on 25 companies, plus lists of conferences, trade associations and research centers.

efficiency, and alternative fuels. The site offers news from 1,800 sources, stock trading information on 25 companies, plus lists of conferences, trade associations and research centers. The group's premier publication, "Clean Tech: Profits and Potential," reports that clean energy technologies will grow from less than $7 billion today to $82 billion by 2010.

8. Ethics

www.depaul.edu/ethics—Sponsored by the Institute for Business and Professional Ethics at DePaul University, this site offers a large compilation of ethics resources on the web, categorized by topic; educational resources for teachers and trainers, including syllabi; faculty position announcements; calls for papers; a calendar of events; a list of other ethics institutes, and much more.

www.ethics.ubc.ca—From the Center for Applied Ethics at the University of British Columbia in Canada, this site offers a particularly valuable compilation about ethics codes—featuring sample codes, guidance on writing a code, plus books and articles on the topic. Other features are links to ethics institutes, consultants, course materials, publications, and collections of articles.

www.ethics.org/businessethics.html—Sponsored by the Ethics Resource Center, this site features valuable data from several business ethics surveys 1994–2000, information on character education for youth, a compendium of codes (coming soon), plus links to many ethics centers and organizations. A research bibliography covers topics like measuring success in an ethics program, or ethics in a global economy. And a provocative "Ethics Quick Test" can be taken on-line, with results available by e-mail.

UNIT 2

Ethical Issues and Dilemmas in the Workplace

Unit Selections

Key Points to Consider

- What ethical dilemmas do *managers* face most frequently? What ethical dilemmas do *employees* face most often?

- What forms of gender and minority discrimination are most prevalent in today's workplace? In what particular job situations or occupations is discrimination more widespread and conspicuous? Why?

- Whistle-blowing occurs when an employee discloses illegal, immoral, or illegitimate organizational practices or activities. Under what circumstances do you believe whistle-blowing is appropriate? Why?

- Given the complexities of an organization, where an ethical dilemma often cannot be optimally resolved by one person alone, how can an individual secure the support of the group and help it to reach a consensus as to the appropriate resolution of the dilemma?

Student Web Site

www.mhcls.com/online

Internet References

Further information regarding these Web sites may be found in this book's preface or online.

American Psychological Association
http://www.apa.org/homepage.html

International Labour Organization (ILO)
http://www.ilo.org

LaRue Tone Hosmer, in *The Ethics of Management,* lucidly states that ethical problems in business are truly managerial dilemmas because they represent a conflict, or at least the possibility of a conflict, between the *economic performance* of an organization and its *social performance.* Whereas the economic performance is measured by revenues, costs, and profits, the social performance is judged by the fulfillment of obligations to persons both within and outside the organization.

Units 2 to 4 discuss some of the critical ethical dilemmas that management faces in making decisions in the workplace, in the marketplace, and within the global society. This unit focuses on the relationships and obligations of employers and employees to each other as well as to those they serve.

Organizational decision makers are ethical when they act with equity, fairness, and impartiality, treating with respect the rights of their employees. Organization's hiring and firing practices, treatment of women and minorities, tolerance of employees' privacy, and wages and working conditions are areas in which it has ethical responsibilities.

The employee also has ethical obligations in his or her relationship to the employer. A conflict of interest can occur when an employee allows a gratuity or favor to sway him or her in selecting a contract or purchasing a piece of equipment, making a choice that may not be in the best interests of the organization. Other possible ethical dilemmas for employees include espionage and the betrayal of secrets (especially to competitors), the theft of equipment, and the abuse of expense accounts.

The articles in this unit are broken down into seven sections representing various types of ethical dilemmas in the workplace. The initial article in this first section describes the way our personal information is being bought, sold, and sometimes stolen. The next article examines how companies have become more vigilant in the surveillance of employees with new high-tech tools.

In the subsection entitled *Organizational Misconduct and Crime,* articles explore how seniors are victimized by fraud and ways auditors can help deter bribery and kickbacks.

The selection under *Sexual Treatment of Employees* takes a close look at how women are treated in the workplace and the expansion of sex-discrimination lawsuits.

The readings in the *Discriminatory and Prejudicial Practices* section scrutinize how hiring older workers can contribute to a

Royalty-Free/CORBIS

reliable and dedicated workforce, why businesswomen are frustrated as they attempt to advance up the organizational hierarchy, and the disparities of "representatives" among three groups of blacks.

In the next subsection entitled *Downsizing of the Work Force,* articles consider why some companies are fearful of firing some types of employees and enumerates on "10 sure ways to get fired."

The selections included under the heading *Whistle-blowing in the Organization* disclose why some businesses that once feared whistleblowers are now finding new ways for employees to report wrongdoing and analyzes the ethical dilemmas and possible ramifications of whistle-blowing activities.

The article that opens the last subsection, *Handling Ethical Dilemmas at Work,* discusses how Walgreen's program trains the disabled to take on regular wage-paying jobs. The next article provides an interesting case where civil and moral law coincide. "The Parable of the Sadhu" presents a real-world ethical dilemma for the reader to ponder.

Your Privacy for Sale

Until Valentine's Day weekend 2005, Elizabeth Rosen had never heard of ChoicePoint. But ChoicePoint, it turns out, knew plenty about her.

That's when Rosen, a nurse, received a letter and found out that the Alpharetta, Ga., company had collected information about her. Among the sensitive items it had: her Social Security number, records of her insurance claims, her current and past addresses, and her employment history. Now ChoicePoint was informing her that it had inadvertently disclosed her information—and that of 165,000 other Americans—to a group of criminals. What galls Rosen more, she says, is that all along, ChoicePoint itself "was profiting by collecting and selling confidential information about me without my knowledge or consent."

ChoicePoint, which has $1 billion in annual revenues, is only one entity in a vast and secretive data industry that feeds on private information about you and millions of other Americans. Its inhabitants include corporate mastodons with access to millions of public records; swarms of private investigators, some of whom lie to obtain confidential information; and hundreds of companies selling background checks, profiles, and address lists, all to meet the surging demand from business, law enforcement, and, increasingly since 9/11, the federal government.

The data collectors say that they're not prying but speeding the retrieval of public records for both consumers and law enforcement, allowing businesses to cut their risks for fraud and helping marketers to zero in on customers who really want their products. "More than two-thirds of what we do is regulated by state and/or federal law," says Chuck Jones, a spokesman for ChoicePoint.

Federal privacy and data-security laws such as the Fair Credit Reporting Act and the Gramm-Leach-Bliley Act do guard some categories of data, including information used to determine eligibility for credit or insurance. But a 2006 investigation by the U.S. Government Accountability Office (GAO) concluded that such protections are limited and that Congress should require information resellers to safeguard all sensitive personal information.

Indeed, CR's three-month investigation found that the practices of the data collectors can rob you of your privacy, threaten you with ID theft, and profile you as, say, a deadbeat or a security risk. Worse, there's no way to find out what they are telling others about you. When our reporters requested their own records, they were told that they could not see everything that was routinely sold to businesses. The meager information they did receive was punctuated with errors.

CR Quick Take

Large data brokers have your numbers—Social Security, phone, and credit cards. They might also know about the drugs you take, what you buy, your political party, and your sexual orientation. When we investigated this secretive industry, we discovered:

- Data brokers are willing to sell even your most sensitive information to paying customers, some of them crooks.
- When CR staffers asked to see their own files, they received scant information. One report contained 31 errors.
- The federal government is a steady customer of the data collectors, but there's no way to know what it collects or exactly how much it pays.
- Pretexters, who lie to get information about you and sell it to anybody, operate largely free of regulation.

The Data Food Chain

Data and list brokers of all stripes and sizes have collected information about individuals for decades. In recent years, however, faster computers and cheaper electronic data storage have fueled the growth of giant information aggregators, such as ChoicePoint. They have put the industry on steroids by feeding on public record databases, acquiring companies with analytic software, and consolidating it all in a centralized online resource where it can be categorized, searched, and sliced into customized slabs for resale.

Among the horde of data brokers, Acxiom, LexisNexis, and ChoicePoint are some of the most prominent. Acxiom, a giant with $1.2 billion in annual revenues, processes a billion records a day. Major clients include American Express, Bank of America, Federated Department Stores—and Consumers Union, the nonprofit publisher of CONSUMER REPORTS. Acxiom officials turned down CR's request for an interview.

LexisNexis, with $2 billion a year in revenues, got its start in Dayton, Ohio, supplying data to the U.S. Air Force. It has long aggregated news, business, and legal documents, but with its acquisition last year of Seisint, which resells public records to law enforcement and private investigators, it is focusing on security. "LexisNexis products and services help to power the consumer economy, fight terrorism, and keep our streets and homes safe," says David Kurt, a company spokesman.

Her Information Sold to Crooks

WHO: Elizabeth Rosen, nurse, California
WHAT HAPPENED: Rosen learned in February 2005 that she was a victim of a large ChoicePoint data breach. Her credit report revealed no problems initially, but she recently has been hounded by calls from bill collectors who ask for other people. ID theft experts say that those calls may indicate a thief has been using her Social Security number under a different name and address—a growing trend in ID fraud.

A Murder from $150 of Data

WHO: Viola Berkeyheiser, Washington Crossing, Pa.
WHAT HAPPENED: Berkeyheiser's husband, William, was murdered in 2005 by Stanford Douglas, a mentally ill former co-worker who held a grudge against him for a joke Douglas claimed Berkeyheiser told years earlier. A civil suit filed by Viola Berkeyheiser charges that Douglas located Berkeyheiser through A-Plus Investigations, which bought his address from IRBsearch, another data broker, for a few dollars. Douglas paid A-Plus $150. IRBsearch says, "We have no proof of any of the facts." A-Plus chief executive officer John Ciaccio says that Douglas said he wanted the data for "a legal purpose."

ChoicePoint, which was spun off by Equifax, the credit bureau, in 1997, allows law enforcement to tap its data over the Internet. As the U.S. Marshals Service said in an internal document, "With as little as a first name or a partial address, you can obtain a comprehensive personal profile in minutes." ChoicePoint also keeps claims histories on your auto and homeowners policies and provides access to birth certificates and other vital records, a service it manages for many states.

What They Feed On

The big aggregators (and fleets of smaller ones, including LocatePlus and Intelius) wouldn't exist if there weren't data for them to ingest. Fortunately, for them, the richest resources—public records—are increasingly accessible. Some hire researchers to visit courthouses and county clerks' offices to retrieve information from paper records, but increasingly, state and local governments post records online, making data gathering simpler and less costly for everyone. Open access also increases the potential for misuse of sensitive information. Property deeds, tax liens, and marriage and divorce documents often contain Social Security numbers, dates of birth, and other sensitive information that are golden keys for identity thieves.

A 2004 GAO study found that up to 28 percent of counties in the U.S. posted records with Social Security numbers online. When we checked documents online for Maricopa County, Ariz., an area with the highest per-capita rate of ID theft in 2005, we found individuals' Social Security numbers on deeds, death certificates, federal tax liens, and divorce filings, one of which also included the couple's credit-card account numbers.

Consumers supply tons of data themselves, often unwittingly, because information about purchases, donations, and memberships is now widely shared. "People are surprised that their name even exists on lists," says Greg Branstetter, founder of Hippo Direct, a mailing-list broker in Cleveland. "But most of list creation comes from consumer behavior, whether it is buying from catalogs, ordering magazines, joining associations, or filling out warranty cards." Branstetter recently completed a project that required him to "track down gay-oriented business publications and Web sites" to provide mailing lists for a client who wanted to market to gay men.

Selling Your Info

Data brokers provide individual background searches for employers and others. They also take in hefty revenues from slicing and dicing your information with data-mining software to create targeted lists to appeal to marketers.

Remember all those colorful bits of detail about your ailments and hobbies that you supplied on warranty cards? In the data industry, they are combined with information drawn from other sources such as public records and credit transactions to provide what Focus USA, a data broker, describes as a "three-dimensional view." Focus's own database covers 105 million U.S. households, with labels such as "Christian Donors," who give twice the portion of their incomes that nonreligious households give to politicians and causes, and a group it calls "Hooked on Plastic," consisting of 4.2 million American families for whom "using credit cards doesn't feel like they're spending money."

Data brokers are not above selling your most sensitive information. InfoUSA, a database marketer with $400 million in sales, promises on its Web site to "find people who suffer from health conditions such as diabetes" or "search for people taking a certain medication." Clients can order a mailing list of, say, Prozac users or refine the list to include only those with incomes over $100,000 a year. Rakesh Gupta, InfoUSA's database president, says that only "legitimate companies," primarily large pharmaceutical manufacturers, are permitted to buy the lists.

Keeping Your Secrets

Federal law gives you the right to view data that will be used for certain purposes, such as background screening to determine your eligibility for insurance, a job, or an apartment rental. But there's a lot that the law doesn't cover.

Two CONSUMER REPORTS staffers requested copies of their own reports. Acxiom's report for consumers (cost: $5) provided five pages of bare-bones facts such as name, address, phone number, and age. The company included a separate sheet summarizing the range of information that consumers could not view but that the company's business clients could. Among those tidbits: e-mail address, occupation, political party, categories of retail purchases, estimated net worth, and details on their cars. ChoicePoint's free basic report was also skimpy. Only LexisNexis' "Person Report" (cost: $8) provided a little more, listing addresses and birth dates for relatives and neighbors.

The reports also contained several errors, including incorrect addresses, misspellings of names, and an incorrect Social Security number. Data brokers say, however, that they are not in the business of correcting inaccuracies. A letter accompanying the report from LexisNexis, for example, says, "We do not examine or verify our data, nor is it possible for our computers to correct or change data that is incorrect."

"It's easy to see how an ordinary consumer could fail to get a job or an apartment," says Richard Smith, a Boston Internet security consultant, "or even end up on a no-fly list, now that the government is becoming such a big client, too."

Given the sensitivity of the information that brokers distribute, ensuring its security should be a top priority. The three major data brokers have all suffered major breaches in recent years, although only ChoicePoint's thus far has led to censure by the Federal Trade Commission. It slapped the company with a $10 million fine, the largest civil penalty in agency history. It also harshly criticized the company's security and record-handling procedures. Instead of limiting access to legitimate businesses or government agencies, the company released data to crooks whose requests used commercial mail drops as business addresses, "an obvious red flag," the FTC said. As it turned out, a Nigerian fraud ring was behind the breach.

In February 2005 consumers began to learn about the data breach. To date, says Brian Hoffstadt, an assistant U.S. attorney who co-prosecuted the case against the data thieves, $600,000 worth of fraudulent credit-card charges have been documented involving an estimated 100 individual victims. "For the consumers involved, there could be a ripple effect, and we may not know the true impact for quite a while," Hoffstadt says.

Elizabeth Rosen, the nurse whose information was stolen in the ChoicePoint breach, encountered no problems initially. But more than a year later, she began to be hounded by calls from various bill collectors asking for other people. ID theft experts say that's a bad sign, indicating that a thief might have set up accounts using her Social Security number under other names and addresses—a new and growing trend in ID fraud.

In response to the FTC, ChoicePoint has tightened its security procedures, following mandates to verify the identities of businesses seeking to obtain consumer reports, even visiting some and auditing their use of those reports.

A Steady Customer

Since 2002, a rule change at the U.S. Department of Justice has allowed unrelated bits of personal data to be pieced together to target American citizens as potential threats who merit surveillance or investigation, even if no reasonable suspicion of criminal activity exists. The federal government has become a steady buyer of this kind of information. In fiscal 2005, the departments of Justice, Homeland Security, and State, and the Social Security Administration spent $30 million on data-broker contracts, according to a 2006 GAO report, which also suggested that the data-broker business was at odds with widely accepted principles for protecting personal data.

Another example: To help sell military careers to young people, the Pentagon has bought data from brokers. According to the Electronic Privacy Information Center (EPIC), they include American Student List, a company that signed a consent agreement in 2002 with the FTC promising not to distribute student data to brokers for noneducational marketing without disclosing it to students.

The Pentagon's database has accumulated information on the ethnicities, grade-point averages, intended fields of college study, phone numbers, and e-mail addresses of about 30 million Americans between ages 16 and 25. Those in the database can request by letter that the Pentagon not send direct-mail or telemarketing pitches, but they are not permitted to opt out of the database.

Activist groups, such as Leave My Child Alone, based in San Francisco, complain that recruiters repeatedly call students at home or on cell phones. Felicity Crush, the group's spokeswoman, says, "They have the money to farm this out to a private company, but when we asked the Pentagon to establish a toll-free number for opting out, they claim they didn't have money in the budget."

Finding out what the government is buying has proven impossible. When EPIC filed a request under the Freedom of Information Act in 2001 to obtain copies of records relating to federal agencies' use of data brokers, among the documents it received was a Jan. 13, 2000, PowerPoint slide presentation with the ChoicePoint and Federal Bureau of Investigation logos displayed together above the report's title: "A Partnership for the New Millennium." All other text on the slides had been blacked out, and to date, the FBI has failed to deliver 5,000 additional pages of ChoicePoint contracting documents.

"Over the past several years, we've learned about huge databases of information on law-abiding Americans being assembled by the government directly or purchased by the government from private vendors," Sen. Ron Wyden, D-Ore., recently told CR. "These reports raise serious concerns about privacy and consumer rights." In 2003, he introduced legislation to require the FBI and other federal agencies to provide detailed reports to Congress explaining their use of public and private databases. The bill failed to pass, though Wyden hopes to take up the issue again.

On a Pretext

The data industry has a shady element that includes private investigators and others who practice so-called pretexting: impersonating relatives, company officials, or even law-enforcement personnel to obtain confidential consumer information.

The results can be deadly. Case in point: Amy Boyer of Nashua, N.H., was fatally gunned down by Liam Youens, a stalker, as she left work. Youens had obtained, for less than $200, all of the information he needed to track her from Docusearch. com, an online data broker that, court papers say, hired a pre-texter to find out where she worked. A civil suit filed against the company charged that Youens maintained a Web site describing his plans to kill Boyer. The case was settled out of court. Dan Cohn, president of Docusearch, says, "Our policies and the way we do business has changed as a result."

The murder occurred in 1999, but Docusearch and similar "backgrounding" services have only grown. Rob Douglas, founder of PrivacyToday.com, information security consultants, says, "With the advent of the Internet, data brokers learned how much money could be made selling phone and bank records to customers online, and the feeding frenzy was on."

While some Web sites require that customers complete a "permissible purpose form" stating that they have a legitimate legal reason for requesting someone's confidential information, Douglas says such requirements are usually nothing more than "legal mumbo jumbo" the brokers use to cover themselves in case something goes awry later. He says faxing a fake letter-head identifying you as a member of a law firm or a potential employer usually can get you what you want.

Customers buying covertly obtained information range from large corporations tracking deadbeat customers to snoops checking up on potential mates. According to statements that some data brokers have provided to congressional investigators, their customers also include local and federal law-enforcement personnel who in this way obtain cell-phone records without subpoenas or warrants. "This illicit marriage between law enforcement and black-market information thieves deserves to be fully investigated," Douglas says.

David Gandal, a Loveland, Colo., investigator who has used pretexting to track debtors skipping out on car loans, says, "Just about every major financial institution has paid for this kind of work." He told CR that armed with a few bits of identify-ing information readily available to most investigators through large commercial databases, a pretexter calls customer service representatives at a phone company or utility. The person then tricks them into revealing account numbers, passwords, and other sensitive information by pretending to be the customer or another company employee, say, someone in tech support. "I'm a man of many voices," Gandal says. "Sometimes I would pretend to be a stroke victim having trouble getting my words out and they'd help by volunteering whatever information I needed."

While pretexting to obtain access to bank records was out-lawed in 1999 with the passage of the Gramm-Leach-Bliley Act, no federal law specifically prohibits using such deception to obtain phone, utility, or other customer records.

Fighting Back

A few fledgling efforts to combat the release of personal infor-mation have made headway. B. J. Ostergren, a former insur-ance claims supervisor, launched an effective one-woman campaign to keep her home county in Virginia from posting its

---

What You Can Do

While you have no control over much of the data collection and sharing that occurs, you can limit the amount of infor-mation circulating about you. Also, checking the accuracy of those records that you're entitled to see allows you to spot signs of ID theft and fraud.

Opt out of:

Telemarketing. Put your name on the Federal Trade Com-mission's Do Not Call registry by going to www.donotcall.gov or calling 888-382-1222.

Unwanted solicitations. Ask financial institutions, retailers, and Web sites not to share your information with other nonaffiliated companies. Contact the Direct Mar-keting Association at www.dmaconsumers.org/consumer assistance.html; for unsolicited e-mail, www.dmaconsumers. org/consumers/optoutform_emps.shtml.

Sales of your information to others. The Privacy Rights Clearinghouse lists data brokers that offer limited opt-out pol-icies at www.privacyrights.org/ar/infobrokers.htm.

Keep your information private:

Don't fill out surveys on warranty cards. Just provide your name, address, and necessary product information, and your warranty will be honored. Be careful with direct-mail surveys that don't come from companies with which you already do business.

Don't provide sensitive information on the phone, thro-ugh the mail, or over the Internet unless you've initiated the contact or you're sure that it's from an organization you trust. If in doubt, contact the organization.

Check what's on file about you:

Order your free annual report from each of the major nationwide credit-reporting companies once every 12 months at www.annualcreditreport.com.

Request your files from the major data brokers: Choi-cePoint at www.choicetrust.com and LexisNexis at www. lexisnexis.com/terms/privacy/data/obtain.asp. You can call Acxiom at 877-774-2094 or send e-mail to reference report@ acxiom.com.

Get medical information. If you've applied for individ-ual health- or life-insurance policies within the past seven years, the MIB Group keeps data that insurers use to help determine your rates. Get a report by calling MIB toll-free at 866-692-6901.

public records on the Internet. To get legislators' attention, she demonstrated the potential for harm in January 2005 by posting on her own Web site *(www.thevirginiawatchdog.com)* a few Social Security numbers for people whose records she spotted online. Among them: former CIA Director Porter Goss, former Secretary of State Colin Powell, and Florida Gov. Jeb Bush, whose number was blacked out on Dade County online records after she drew attention to it. "I understand why he'd want to black out his number," Ostergren says. "But shouldn't everyone have that right?"

Employers Look Closely at What Workers Do on Job

STEPHANIE ARMOUR

Employers have long warned their workers that company e-mail, Internet use and even phone calls are subject to monitoring.

But what many employees don't realize is that spying is going high-tech. In the spirit of James Bond wizardry, companies are tracking workers' whereabouts through Global Positioning System (GPS) satellite, implanting employees with microchips with their knowledge and hiring private investigators to check up on what employees are really doing at work.

Hewlett-Packard became embroiled in a spying scandal after being accused of hiring private eyes to spy on its directors, sending computer spyware to reporters and probing private phone records to ferret out boardroom leaks.

The developments suggest that a Brave New Workplace is here. Employers in today's highly competitive and lawsuit-driven work environment are monitoring employees with unprecedented zeal.

Marc Rotenberg, executive director and president of the Electronic Privacy Information Center, a public interest research center in Washington, says many companies have legitimate and legal reasons for such monitoring, but gumshoe tactics also can erode trust as employers become suspicious of their own staff.

"It raises questions of trust, but in fairness to employers, they have an incentive to be sure employees are doing their jobs," Rotenberg says. "We're more concerned that people are entitled to some privacy. Where do you draw the line?"

While more employers may feel they have justifiable reason to pry, others believe the practice is too corrosive to the employee-employer bond. Chuck Rauenhorst, CEO of Minneapolis-based Rauenhorst Recruiting, says monitoring employees is not something that he would do.

"Colleagues who trust one another have synergy and work better as a unit," Rauenhorst says in an e-mail. "Eavesdropping, electronic or otherwise, is always going to tear that fabric of trust."

The surveillance of employees has become increasingly commonplace, research shows. Already, 76% of companies monitor employees' website connections, and 65% block access to specific sites, up from 40% in 2001. About 35% track the content, keystrokes and time spent at the keyboard, according to the 2005 study by the American Management Association and The ePolicy Institute, a Columbus, Ohio-based training and consulting firm. More than half of employers retain and review e-mail messages.

For example:

- CityWatcher.com created a media flurry this year after the Cincinnati security company implanted microchips in some of its employees. The chips were not for tracking employees but to enable them to gain access to secure rooms, according to numerous media reports.

CityWatcher did not return repeated calls seeking comment. But the headlines about microchips, which are about the size of a grain of rice and can be implanted under the skin in the arm, raised concerns that employers could force workers to get the implants. Wisconsin this year passed legislation that would ban companies from requiring workers to be implanted with such chips. Employers who violate the law face a fine of $10,000 a day.

"It's a frightening prospect," says state Rep. Marlin Schneider, D-Wis., who sponsored the bill. "Employers would be able to monitor people wherever they go."

- Some employers require workers to use company-provided cellphones that allow whereabouts to be monitored via satellites. Xora, a Mountain View, Calif., provider of GPS-based mobile workforce management software, provides GPS technology and has sold systems to 7,000 companies representing tens of thousands of employees, mostly in construction, transportation and business services.

"Companies always want to know what's happening," says Michael Berger, manager of product marketing for Xora. "It streamlines operations."

- Some employers are scanning their employees' fingerprints or eyes to track activities or limit access to certain computers. Use of such technology is small but growing. Already, 5% of companies use fingerprint scans and 2% use facial recognition, according to the survey by the AMA and ePolicy Institute. The technology is so new that the question wasn't asked in a 2001 survey on monitoring.

At Columbus Children's Hospital in Ohio, most employees who access electronic medical data must first scan a fingerprint, a system designed to enhance security.

"From a security standpoint, it works well. You can't reproduce a fingerprint," says David Rich, medical director of clinical informatics at the hospital. "(Employees) have taken it well."

But what employees do on work equipment—even what they may do on their free time—can now cost them their jobs if their employer is watching.

Major employers such as Delta Air Lines and Google have fired employees for what they put on their own blogs. Ellen Simonetti, a Delta flight attendant, says she was fired in October 2004 after she posted pictures of herself in her uniform in suggestive poses on her blog.

"Employees should know that your employer is looking over your shoulder. If they catch you, they're canning you," says Nancy Flynn, executive director of The ePolicy Institute and author of *Blog Rules*. "You can be fired for anything, even for blogging right at home in your jammies."

Spying is Necessary

Some employers say they're not damaging trust. Instead, they say, spying on employees is necessary today in large part because technology has raised the risk that workers will goof off or do something that leaves a company vulnerable to lawsuits.

Michael Prencipe wondered what his 15 employees were really doing on work time, so the partner at HR Staffing Solutions began monitoring workers' e-mail, phone calls and where they surfed on the Internet.

He was in for some surprises.

He saw employees visit pornography sites, use e-mail to troll for other jobs and even e-mail others about him, he says. So Prencipe cracked down.

He gives each employee at the staffing company an oral warning for the first inappropriate e-mail or website visit and twice has resorted to written warnings. No one has been fired.

"You're never going to stop the e-mail jokes, but sometimes you can get an eyepopper," says Prencipe, of Springfield, Va.

Employees are "usually embarrassed and humiliated," he says. "You get a downcast look and an 'I won't do it again.'"

Workplace monitoring has become so commonplace that many employees simply take it in stride. Kim Conner, 31, of Madison, Wis., works as a contractor for LiveOps, which hires independent agents to handle call-center work from their homes. LiveOps records every call its agents take.

Conner says supervisors have listened to how she handles calls and have given her pointers on how to improve.

"Sometimes you get lost in a call. A supervisor hears it and says, 'You could have done this better or differently,'" Conner says.

"It helps me with sales."

A Breakdown of Trust

Still, some privacy advocates and employers are leery, saying that monitoring is pitting employers against their own employees. Keith Ayers is president of Integro Leadership Institute, a leadership consulting group based in West Chester, Pa. He says employees who don't feel trusted don't, in turn, trust their companies. Why, he asks, would employees work hard for a company that does not respect them? He says many employees may goof off online as a way to rebel.

"The very fact they're increasing effort to monitor people is an indication there's a lack of trust in the first place," Ayers says. "They're saying, 'I don't trust you. I have to keep an eye on you.'"

But concerns continue, in large part because technology provides workers with savvier ways to goof off, from shopping on eBay to running a blog. They can also use technology to steal company secrets, harass other employees or make employers vulnerable to lawsuits.

There may be legitimate reason for the concern. Sixty-five percent of men and 58% of women who use the Internet at work admit to accessing non-work-related websites when they're on the clock, according to a May 2006 survey by Harris Interactive for Websense, a provider of Web security and filtering software. Six percent of men and 5% of women said they had intentionally viewed pornography on the job.

Legally, employers are on safe ground monitoring their employees, especially if they notify workers beforehand, says Bill Nolan, an employment lawyer in Columbus, Ohio.

He also says employers face more risk today because employees can do more damage, such as spilling company secrets on a personal blog or using camera-phones to take pictures of products.

"Anything bad that employees could do before, they can do infinitely more because of technology. Sexual harassment, exposing trade secrets. So much information can move so quickly," Nolan says. "You've got to know what your employees are doing on their computer."

Gary Steele, CEO of Proofpoint, a Cupertino, Calif.-based messaging security company, says employers who use his e-mail-monitoring software have caught gaffes and shenanigans of all types—sharing confidential memos from the CEO with outsiders, revealing new product designs, using sexually harassing language and forwarding drafts of company earnings reports.

Business is doubling every year, he says.

At DeKalb Medical Center in Atlanta, e-mails are monitored in large part because of the need to protect patient confidentiality. About 3,300 employees have e-mail access.

Confidential information or vulgar or abusive language can be flagged, and employees are notified.

"The hospital has a policy of full disclosure. Everything is fully monitored," says Sharon Finney, information security administrator.

"Everybody signs a document that (they understand) they're monitored. The reaction has either been positive or 'OK, fine, I understand.' "

Con Artists' Old Tricks

A no-risk investment? A 'nephew' in distress? Don't believe them. Senior citizens need to be vigilant.

KATHY M. KRISTOF

W alter Kincherlow Sr., 69, never expected to retire a millionaire. But during his 29 years as a maintenance worker, he managed to sock away more than $80,000. He invested pretty well too, until an "estate planner" took a look at his portfolio while updating his living trust and clucked that Kincherlow's investment returns were paltry.

Claiming that Kincherlow could earn 20% per year safely, he persuaded the widower to pour his life savings into real estate investments with an El Segundo investment firm called Jon W. James & Associates. Kincherlow said he was assured that his principal was safe. But signs of trouble emerged when he wanted to start spending some of his savings. Then, company managers either couldn't be reached or talked him out of withdrawal, he said. Meanwhile, they tried to persuade him to secure a huge home equity loan to invest even more.

Securities regulators filed an emergency action last summer to shut down the firm, which they claimed was operating a $22-million fraud. James maintained in legal filings that the company's investments simply had insufficient time to pan out. In any event, a court-appointed receiver says investors are owed about $13 million, but the company has less than $4 million in assets to repay investors.

"They're telling me that I might end up with $6,000 or $7,000 out of all of the money I invested," said Kincherlow, who now lives in Victorville. "I wish I never had done this."

He has plenty of company. More than 200 investors are in similar straits with Jon W. James & Associates, and that's just the tip of the iceberg.

About 5 million seniors are victimized by some sort of financial fraud each year, according to the Securities and Exchange Commission. California law enforcement authorities believe that about a million of those victims live in the Golden State. Fraud against seniors is rising, experts add, but precise numbers are impossible to come by, partly because authorities believe that only 1 in 5 such frauds are ever reported.

The tragic part: Once a senior gets taken, there's little chance he or she will ever get the money back. And experts maintain that most of the fraud is easily avoided.

Karen Liebig of Torrance runs a nonprofit group called the Keep Safe Coalition. Its mission is to arm seniors with the information necessary to protect them from scams. They go everywhere: convalescent homes, senior centers, libraries, bridge clubs. Anywhere seniors gather and might want information about the hallmarks of elder abuse—financial or physical—will draw Liebig and her reams of tip sheets and little giveaways, such as pens and whistles with a message: "Blow the whistle on fraud!"

With PowerPoint presentations and gentle talks, she explains to people like Kincherlow that there is no such thing as a "safe" or "guaranteed" investment that pays 20% annually. She cajoles them to beware of "trust officers" bearing investment advice. She pulls in district attorneys and detectives to talk about salesmen who are willing to take seniors to the store and run errands for them as a way of gaining their trust before they sell them investments that could bankrupt them.

"We have a case now where the girlfriend of the grandson served as a caregiver and she's taken money out of this woman's account; she's taken home equity loans in her name," Liebig said. "The lady, who is in her late 80s or 90s, is never going to get her money back."

More than anything, Liebig urges seniors to seek help when they're being pressured to buy something and report it when someone takes advantage. And she counsels friends and family members of older folks living alone—the most vulnerable targets—to keep in close touch and look for telltale signs of trouble.

Just as you watch the people your teenagers hang out with, friends and relatives of senior citizens should be watchful when the senior takes up with new caregivers and friends. They should also worry if the family's "lost soul" takes such good care of grandma that everybody else loses contact.

"We have had immediate family members, who are in line to inherit the money anyway," said Det. Sgt. Peter Grimm of the Redondo Beach Police Department. "But the greed factor kicks in, and they say, 'I want it now.'"

That's one reason seniors are such attractive targets, officials say. Because they're embarrassed or infirm or have such a close emotional connection to the con artist, they're far less likely to report and pursue prosecution of the criminal. They're also, demographically, a wealthy group, holding billions in assets and home equity.

"It's just like Willie Sutton," said Donn Hoffman, a Los Angeles County deputy district attorney who prosecutes cases of elder abuse. Crooks "go where the money is."

Many of the crimes that affect the elderly are scams that can hit people of any age: identity theft, bogus lotteries, "free" gifts that require you to send money for shipping and Ponzi schemes that use new investor money to pay off old investors until they run out of victims and the schemes collapse.

The company that Kincherlow fell prey to didn't exclusively target seniors, just retirement assets. But he was nabbed through a "trust update," a common gambit aimed at seniors. Although living trusts can help avoid probate, state securities authorities maintain that con artists establish "trust mills" to simply get a good look at a senior's assets. They then convince the victim that their investments are either too risky or too low-yielding, and talk them into buying bogus or unsuitable investments that pay off for the broker while they impoverish the client.

The same technique is frequently used to sell seniors into variable annuities, which pay high commissions to the brokers, but can lock the investor's money up for decades.

Although these investments arguably are viable for younger individuals, they're almost always unsuitable for the over-70 set, to whom they're often sold, Hoffman said.

Riffling through pending investigations on his desk, Hoffman pulled out three involving the sale of annuities to elderly individuals and couples.

In one, a 74-year-old woman who told her agent she needed regular income from her investments was sold an annuity that provided no regular income. If she pulls money out during the next 10 years, she'll lose 20% of her principal to "surrender" penalties.

A similar case involved a couple in their late 60s who were both in ill health with diabetes and heart disease. Instead of an investment that would generate the income they needed to buy medications, they got an annuity that doesn't provide access to their savings until the husband turns 98.

In the third, a 71-year old woman with Alzheimer's was befriended by an agent who talked her into transferring her

Signs of Trouble

About 5 million seniors are victims of financial fraud each year, according to the Securities and Exchange Commission. California authorities estimate that 1 million of those victims live in the Golden State. Red flags include:

"Guaranteed" Investments That Pay Double-digit Returns

Any investment that promises to pay more than a certificate of deposit or Treasury bill bears substantial risk. Most "guarantees" offered on high-return investments aren't worth the paper they're written on.

Living-trust Officers Bearing Investment Advice

Regulators maintain that many companies that update living trusts are really just seeking a close look at a senior's portfolio to sell them high-cost and, often, inappropriate investments. Buy legal advice and investment advice separately. Not sure if you need a trust? Contact Healthcare and Elder Law Programs Corp., a nonprofit education and counseling group, at (310) 533-1996 or http://www.help4srs.org.

Free Lunch Seminars

Securities regulators say seminars offering seniors a free meal are too often come-ons for high-pressure salespeople to pitch annuities that can lock up your assets for decades, while paying huge fees to the salesperson. You can go to lunch, but don't invest until you've had a savvy friend or impartial investment advisor review the prospectus or offering circular. If the salesperson says the "opportunity" can't wait for you to examine the details, pass it up.

"Free Gifts" and Foreign Lottery Winnings

If you need to send a payment for "postage" or "taxes," you haven't won a "free gift" or a foreign lottery, you're being reeled in on a scam. Your winnings won't arrive; and you'll lose the amount you sent—or more. Some crooks use these scams to steal your banking information.

E-mailed Bank "Updates," IRS Refund Notices and "Account Warnings"

Your banker, the federal government and even PayPal are not going to ask you to update your account information by clicking on a link in an e-mail, but a con artist wanting your credit card numbers or Social Security number to commit identity theft will. Don't click through. If you think your banker needs to update your account information, call your bank directly. If you're wondering about a federal tax refund, contact the Internal Revenue Service at (800) 829-1040 or http://www.irs.gov.

Relatives and Caregivers Who Take Your Mail or Isolate You

Relatives and caregivers are often a tremendous help, but some bad apples take advantage of their trusted positions to commit identity theft and steal from seniors' bank accounts. Beware of anyone who discourages you from seeing others or who won't let you see your mail.

Call for Help

Seniors who are concerned about a caregiver, or friends or neighbors who worry that a senior may be in trouble, should call their county's adult protective services agency.

investments into annuities. She lost $30,000 to surrender fees on the first transfer and lost access to her money.

"I didn't dig through the complaints looking for the good ones," Hoffman said. "These are just typical."

Some frauds are tailor-made to ensnare senior citizens.

Consider, for example, the "nephew scam" that hit dozens of South Bay seniors. Someone would call with a friendly greeting such as, "Hi, Auntie! It's your favorite nephew. You remember me, don't you?"

The older person, often hard of hearing and not wanting to admit he or she might have forgotten a relative, would volunteer something along the lines of, "Is that you, Johnny?," giving the con artist a name to work with, Liebig said.

The bogus nephew then says he's at a local airport on his way to a business meeting but just got robbed and doesn't even have cab fare. The "favorite aunt" is asked to lend him a substantial sum, which will be picked up by one of the nephew's associates and repaid promptly. Naturally, neither the money nor the "nephew" is ever seen again.

Although this "nephew" is a bogus one, Liebig said, too often seniors are taken by their own relatives. Adult children, grandchildren, nieces and nephews can perpetrate identity fraud or mortgage fraud or simply raid the senior's bank account.

Although experts can tell seniors to be cautious of telemarketers and strangers offering investment advice, it's difficult to warn them about their own families.

"We tell people that we're not trying to scare them, but if someone is attempting to isolate them from other friends and family members—if they take your mail—you've got to be cautious no matter who they are," Liebig said.

On the bright side, regulators of all stripes are paying more attention to fraud against seniors.

Many states, including California, have passed laws to stiffen penalties for defrauding seniors, whether through Ponzi schemes or simply recommending unsuitable investments. Police departments and district attorney's offices in many major cities all over the country have launched units focused solely on senior abuse.

California insurance regulators are contemplating new rules that would impose stricter standards on the sale of variable annuities to anyone over age 65. The Securities and Exchange Commission has been investigating companies offering "free lunch" seminars, which are often used to lure elderly investors. And the SEC has teamed up with the National Assn. of Securities Dealers and AARP to host a "senior summit" next month aimed at getting regulators, law enforcement and community groups in the same room to find ways to combat senior fraud.

In the meantime, Liebig said, seniors need nosy neighbors to protect them.

"If there was somebody that used to sit on the porch and waive at you every day and you don't see them for a while, you need to knock on the door and check on them," she said.

If you suspect there's something wrong, call local law enforcement or adult protective services, she added.

kathy.kristof@latimes.com

Corruption: Causes and Cures

Auditors can help detect and deter bribery and kickbacks.

Joseph T. Wells

"You'll never catch Burgin," television investigative reporter Marsha Halford said to me during an off-camera interview regarding rumors of bribery in the Mississippi senate. "He is the smartest and most corrupt politician in the state."

The Federal Bureau of Investigation had Senator William G. Burgin Jr., chairman of the Mississippi State Senate Appropriations Committee, under scrutiny. As the agent in charge of the case, I wasn't allowed to answer her. But I knew something that Halford and even Burgin didn't know: We'd just about nailed him, and he wasn't very smart after all.

Within a month of that interview, Burgin was indicted for pocketing at least $83,000 in bribes. He later was convicted and served three years in federal prison. The Burgin investigation illustrates a checklist of classic lessons that CPAs can apply when confronted with allegations or suspicions of bribery.

Rumors Often Are True

Those who accept illegal payments usually have a motive for doing so. For most people, it is debt; but once they pay their debts, they end up spending the rest of the loot. Coworkers often notice extravagances and report them; CPAs should be alert to rumors or complaints about employees who seem to live beyond their means.

Burgin's lifestyle. For years Burgin—a part-time legislator—had one of the most successful solo law practices in Mississippi and lived the life of a wealthy plantation owner. Because of his visibility as a politician, people noticed his ostentatious wealth, and it was one of them who tipped the FBI off to his illegal scheme. Evidence later showed that one of the principal reasons for his "success" was that his firm served as a conduit for the lucre of corruption.

Look to the Top

At some point, regardless of internal controls or safeguards, a person at the top of an organization has the ultimate authority to decide how it spends its money; lower-level employees must contend with restrictions. This means that within an entity the chief purchasing agent or similar officer would be the most likely suspect for corruption. CPAs therefore should satisfy themselves that controls over purchasing managers are adequate and are not being overridden.

Burgin's opportunity. As chairman of the Mississippi Senate Appropriations Committee, Burgin was the state's chief purchasing agent of sorts. The state neatly divided its finances according to revenue and appropriations. While the Senate Revenue Committee raised money to fund state programs, Burgin's committee was in charge of spending it. Every check the state wrote was within his powerful domain. There were controls, of course—but none the enterprising politician couldn't bypass.

The "Sniff Test"

In theory, any employee authorized to spend an organization's money is a possible candidate for corruption. Those paying the bribes tend to be commissioned salespeople or intermediaries for outside vendors. The following players usually are present in a corruption scheme.

The gift bearer. Illegal inducements often begin when a businessperson routinely offers inappropriate gifts or provides lavish entertainment to an employee with purchasing authority or otherwise tries to ingratiate himself or herself for the purpose of influencing those in charge.

The odd couple. When a purchasing agent becomes the "friend" of an outside vendor, beware. A key technique bribe-givers use is to befriend their targets. They go to lunch together, take trips and engage in other social outings. But often the pair has nothing in common except for an illegal scheme.

The too-successful bidder. A supplier who consistently wins business without any apparent competitive advantage might be providing under-the-table incentives to obtain the work. Be alert to sole-source contracts and to bidders who nearly always win, who win by thin margins and who bid last. These are indicators someone at the company is supplying the winning bidder inside information.

The one-person operator. Some suppliers, rather than directly engage in payoffs, hire someone—called a bagman—to do the dirty work. Be alert to independent sales representatives, consultants or other middlemen, as they are favored conduits for funneling and concealing illegal payments.

Once an employee crosses the line and accepts kickbacks, he or she hardly is in a position to complain to the vendor about goods or services. The vendor knows this and often reacts by supplying items of poor quality and raising prices for purchases.

When a corrupt employee takes bribes, the underlying business arrangement usually is flawed. For instance, the products or services the dishonest worker contracted for, besides being substandard, are often unneeded, purchased from remote or vague sources, bought at odd times or from odd places or make little economic sense. To help uncover fraudulent transactions, CPAs should employ skepticism when examining the rationale for material purchases by the company.

Burgin's scheme. My investigation of Bill Burgin had commenced a year earlier when a confidential banking source alerted me to a contract between the state of Mississippi and Learning Development Corp. (LDC). Because the document was public record, I went down to the secretary of state's office to take a look.

I discovered there were two contracts under which the state would pay LDC a total of $860,000, purportedly to provide "educational services for disadvantaged youths in the state of Mississippi." In examining the details of the agreements, three items jumped out at me. First, they were sole-source contracts—ones with no competitive bids. The second oddity: LDC was headquartered in Nashville. With the pressure on politicians to create jobs in their own states, I wondered why the contracts didn't go to a Mississippi service provider. And there was one other thing—it was hard to decipher what the contract said and what LDC actually had to do for its money.

Under-the-Table Payments

Being the conduit or bagman for bribe money is a profession of sorts; learning to pass bribes and get away with it takes experience and know-how. This particular profession tends to attract a small cadre of sleazy people. They typically are one-person operations and pass bribes for a variety of "clients." For example, during the Pentagon procurement scandals of the 1980s, just one bagman represented some of America's largest defense contractors. And when I investigated corruption in the private sector, I found the same trend. CPAs therefore should be alert to shadowy "consultants" on the payroll.

Burgin's "consultant." Burgin's bagman was D. Flavous Lambert, a lobbyist and former politician with a questionable reputation. On the surface the two men seemed to have little in common. I theorized that if Burgin's job was to see that the state approved the LDC contract, Lambert's task was to work with LDC to ensure the twosome got their take.

Since the contracts didn't pass the sniff test, I decided to take the investigation to the next level by examining LDC's books. The odor got worse. In tracing the corporation's receipts and disbursements, a pattern emerged. LDC received its state payments in monthly installments of $65,000 Each time LDC deposited a state check, it would immediately disburse $32,500—exactly half of the deposit amount—to Developmental Associates, a Georgia concern. The disbursement code identified it as a "finder's fee."

Development Associates turned out to be nothing more than a bank account in Atlanta with only one name on the signature card: D. Flavous Lambert. The following business day, Lambert would send a share of the money to the bank account of Burgin's law firm. Believe it: Burgin was accepting bribes by check. The only reason I could figure for his flagrancy was that he had been corrupt for so long that he felt immune to discovery.

The Bribe-Taker Gets Involved

Anyone who takes a bribe makes a pact with the devil. Since the employee is committing a crime, he or she will go to extreme lengths to avoid discovery; that means keeping the bribe-giver happy. Corrupt employees must frequently intercede to resolve problems for the vendor, such as demanding that payments be expedited or requesting that substandard work be accepted. CPAs should look for these anomalies.

Burgin's downfall. No physical evidence linked Burgin to the crime until he interceded directly for LDC. In fact, Burgin didn't even sign the contract between the state of Mississippi and LDC. Instead, welfare commissioner Fred St. Clair signed it. Later, before a federal grand jury, St. Clair admitted he had been pressured by Burgin to approve the deal. St. Clair also told the grand jury that problems with LDC led to the checks from the state being delayed. But shortly before the holidays, Burgin showed up at the welfare commissioner's office demanding he be given LDC's overdue $65,000 check at once. Otherwise, the senator lamented, "Employees of LDC are not going to have a Christmas." It was obvious to St. Clair that LDC or Lambert had pressured the senator to intercede. Burgin, on the other hand, denied the incident ever occurred. Evidence to incriminate Burgin would be so important that, wearing surgical gloves in order not to contaminate any fingerprints on the check, I spent two days in the bowels of the dusty state archives examining canceled checks. Once I located the "Christmas check" the FBI lab found Burgin's thumbprint right in the middle of it. Sure enough, the check had been deposited to the LDC bank account.

Auditing Vendors

If an employee in your company is taking bribes, the illegal payment will not be reflected in your client's books, but rather it will be in those of the bribe-giver. The payments often are disguised in the vendor's records as consulting or finder's fees, commissions or similar expenses.

To help keep your vendors honest, you should insist that major suppliers agree to let you audit their books if necessary. Here is a sample of the way such an agreement could be worded.

"Vendor grants to purchaser the right to audit vendor's books and records, and to make copies and extracts, to the extent the books or records relate to the performance of this contract."

Book 'Em, Dan-O

As corruption schemes progress, conspirators usually get careless.

Frauds—including bribes and kickbacks—normally are not onetime events, but continuous crimes that occur over extended time periods. The Association of Certified Fraud Examiners' 2002 *Report to the Nation: Occupational Fraud and Abuse* concluded the average fraud lasted about 17 months and corruption schemes typically took about two years to be discovered.

The perpetrator's modus operandi tends to change over time. Initially, the crooked employee carefully covers his or her tracks. But as the crime progresses without being uncovered, perpetrators look for ways to accomplish the same illegal goals with less hassle. In the beginning the suspect may make sure all of the documents appear in order. Later, he or she may not even bother with any phony paperwork.

CPAs should consider major deficiencies in contract documentation to be a significant red flag. Moreover, many fraudsters don't continue to conceal their ill-gotten gains very well. In short, they get sloppy. In fact, most of the time, the bribe-taker will deposit the illicit funds in his or her own bank account.

Burgin's last stand. Burgin's trial, held in Gulfport, Mississippi, lasted about two weeks. The government presented its case against the senator. In his defense Burgin took the stand and claimed he had no idea the money in his firm's bank account came from LDC. His story—and he stuck to it—was that he had represented Lambert in a legal matter 20 years ago and that Lambert finally was paying the bill.

During the dramatic closing of the trial, Burgin looked directly at the jury and said, "There is no way I would ever deprive the citizens of this great state of their hard-earned tax money." He then pulled a large red bandana from his breast pocket, dabbed his eyes and honked loudly into the handkerchief.

For the FBI agent in charge of the investigation, the scene was too much; without thinking, I burst out laughing. Then the jurors started guffawing. Burgin's defense lawyer was immediately on his feet shouting, "Mistrial!" The prosecutor glared at me. The trial recessed for about 15 minutes so the judge could chew me out. Then he sent the case to the jury.

In less than half a day, the jury convicted Burgin and Lambert. A reporter later asked one of the jurors about the strength of the government's evidence. In his soft Mississippi drawl, the juror said: "Well, when we saw the paper trail, we were convinced. The only way the case could have been stronger was if the checks to Burgin would've had the word *bribe* written on the description line."

JOSEPH T. WELLS, CPA, CFE, is founder and chairman of the Association of Certified Fraud Examiners and a professor of fraud examination at the University of Texas at Austin. Mr. Wells is a member of the AICPA Business and Industry Hall of Fame. He won the Lawler Award for the best *JofA* article in 2000. Mr. Wells' e-mail address is joe@cfenet.com.

Gender Issues

Sex-discrimination lawsuits are on the rise. Is your company at risk?

JENNIFER GILL

For large corporations, the news has been grim: Last July, Boeing agreed to pay as much as $72.5 million to settle a class-action lawsuit by female employees. That same month, Morgan Stanley paid $54 million to settle a similar suit.

Sex-discrimination suits against small companies don't make headlines but they are just as common. In fact, nearly half of all sex-discrimination charges—running the gamut from sexual harassment to gender-related firing—filed with the Equal Employment Opportunity Commission last year were aimed at firms with 200 or fewer employees. And claims could surge in the years ahead as more women gain confidence from high-profile cases in the news, according to Cari Dominguez, chairperson of the EEOC. Many female baby boomers are entering their 50s and are "looking to leave a legacy," Dominguez says. "Women are taking on the role of whistleblower."

Smaller companies are particularly vulnerable because they tend to have less structured atmospheres and are less likely to have formal sex-discrimination policies in place, Dominguez adds. "A lack of infrastructure and awareness of the issues can lead a small business to run afoul of the law," she warns.

Donna Salyers, founder and president of Donna Salyers's Fabulous Furs, a faux-fur retailer based in Covington, Ky., learned that lesson three years ago. Back then, the retailer—which has 35 full-time employees, an online store, a retail shop in Covington, and celebrity clients such as longtime *Cosmopolitan* editor Helen Gurley Brown—was struggling to recover from the economic impact of the 9/11 terrorist attacks. Then Salyers received more shocking news: The EEOC was suing Fabulous Furs for sexual harassment on behalf of four temporary employees in the company's distribution center who claimed that their supervisor made offensive remarks to them. The women, who had been let go after the company's busy season, also claimed that they were fired in retaliation for their complaints. Salyers soon found herself consumed with the lawsuit, watching as her legal bills skyrocketed to $100,000. Finally, last fall, she decided to settle. Her company, which admitted no wrongdoing in the case, paid $45,000 in damages to the plaintiffs and agreed to implement a new sexual-harassment policy. "Small businesses like ours aren't equipped to handle these claims," says Guy van Rooyen, CEO of Fabulous Furs. "It's like a smack in the face."

Salyers, who founded Fabulous Furs in 1989, is determined that this never happen again. Before the lawsuit, her company's sex-discrimination policy consisted of little more than the standard guidelines in an employee handbook. After the suit was filed, however, she hired a full-time human resources director to develop and review her company's employee policies. As part of the settlement, she also created a complaint hot line for workers and began holding annual sex-discrimination seminars for managers. By being up-front about what is and is not permissible, Salyers hopes to limit her company's exposure to any future claims.

The EEOC's Dominguez wishes more privately owned companies would follow suit. Until recently, the commission's efforts have been focused on large corporations. But now, smaller companies are the top priority, says Dominguez, who has launched an aggressive outreach program to educate small and midsize businesses. "They're the brave new world for us," she says. "That's where the growth opportunities are for the country's economy, but I see liability potential, as well."

Federal antidiscrimination laws apply to businesses with 15 or more employees, and state or local statutes often cover even smaller ones. In Chicago, for instance, companies with just a single employee can be sued for discrimination. To find out where your company stands, call the small-business liaison at your local EEOC field office (see www. eeoc.gov for a list of offices). The liaison will explain the law, provide educational materials for your staff, and even make free presentations at your workplace.

Next, spell out your firm's antiharassment and equal-opportunity policies in an employee handbook. Most companies follow a standard template, which can be found on the website of the Employment Law Information Network (www.elinfonet.com). In the handbook, tell employees whom to contact in the event of a complaint. Be sure to name someone besides the employee's direct manager, in case the issue involves that person. Merely providing the information in a handbook may not be enough, so follow Salyers's lead by posting your policy in areas frequented by employees, such as the kitchen or the restroom.

Many female baby boomers are entering their 50s and are looking to leave a legacy. They're taking on the role of whistleblower.

Bear in mind that guidelines written in legalese can be difficult to understand. For instance, an employee may realize that telling a dirty joke is a no-no. But he may not be aware that asking a female subordinate about her childcare arrangements is a bad idea. One comment isn't an actionable offense, and federal law does not prohibit simple teasing, offhand comments, or isolated incidents that aren't extremely serious. But there could be trouble if the conduct is frequent and severe enough to create a hostile work environment or results in a tangible employment action, such as firing or demotion. To help clarify the law for your staff, hire an employment lawyer to hold annual sex-discrimination seminars. Some trade associations and chambers of commerce also offer workshops for members.

Finally, be sure to keep a written record of your employees' shortcomings, advises Susan Stahlfeld, a partner at law firm Miller Nash's Seattle office. In a surprising number of cases, managers criticize employees verbally during reviews but give them high marks on written evaluations. Such evaluations can be critical to your company's defense if, say, an employee claims she was fired based solely on her sex. "It comes down to what you have in that person's file," Stahlfeld says.

Of course, even if you take every precaution, sex-discrimination complaints may arise. To prevent them from snowballing into lawsuits, investigate each one immediately. "Putting your head in the sand is never a good idea," says Jill

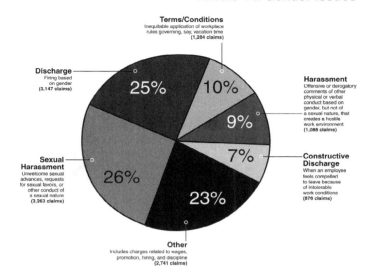

Figure 1 Discrimination Decoded. Last year, 12,399 sex-discrimination claims were filed against U.S. companies with between 15 and 100 workers. Here is a breakdown of the types of claims filed.

Schwartz, of Jill S. Schwartz & Associates, an employment law firm in Winter Park, Fla. For instance, if a female worker questions why she's being paid $10,000 less than her male counterpart, go over performance reviews and take her tenure into consideration. If there's a reason other than gender for the pay difference, explain it to her. If not, fix the discrepancy. As the recent spate of high-profile lawsuits has proved, granting a raise will cost much less than going to court.

Toyota's Sex-Harassment Lawsuit Could Set Standard

JAYNE O'DONNELL AND CHRIS WOODYARD

Toyota (TM) says it has settled a $190 million sexual-harassment lawsuit that squeezed out the automaker's top U.S. official.

The settlement, announced Friday without details, should get the attention of executives at other international businesses, because it resulted in a new policy for reporting harassment allegations against the top executive, as well as changes in Toyota's training and employment procedures.

Other companies "will see it and say, 'If Toyota's doing this, it's going to be the industry practice and we need to make sure we're doing whatever everyone else is doing,'" says New York-based employment discrimination lawyer Douglas Wigdor.

All companies "could stand to take a look at what they would do if the top person in charge is (accused) of sex harassment," says Lisa Guerin, legal editor at book publisher Nolo and a lawyer specializing in employment law.

In Toyota's case, plaintiff Sayaka Kobayashi said she complained to Toyota Motor North America's then-senior vice president Dennis Cuneo, who was in charge of human resources, but nothing was done. That's despite her allegation that former Toyota North America CEO Hideaki Otaka was not just making off-color comments but trying to force her to have sex.

Otaka has denied wrongdoing, but he left his U.S. post and returned to Japan earlier than planned. He now is retired.

Cuneo no longer oversees the Toyota HR department, the car company said Monday. Human resources now reports to Patricia Salas Pineda, a group vice president. She is a member of the task force headed by former Labor secretary Alexis Herman that Toyota formed to review its sexual-harassment policies. Toyota said Monday that the task force's work would continue for several more months.

"Japan is getting more serious about the subject" of sexual harassment, says Los Angeles-based executive Yasuo "Mike" Nakamura. The Japanese businessman has spent 24 years in the USA working for companies including Panasonic and Quasar.

"Most of the businessmen are as well aware in Japan" of harassment issues as they are in the USA, he says.

The U.S. lawsuit was filed May 1 by Kobayashi, 42. She said that sexual harassment by Otaka escalated over three months. She alleged that the harassment included trying to force her into a sex act in Central Park and in a Washington, D.C., hotel room. The lawsuit charged that Toyota officials knew—or should have known—Otaka had "the reputation of repeatedly engaging and/or attempting to engage in extramarital sexual relationships."

Toyota has refused to comment on the specific allegations. After the lawsuit was filed, Toyota said it was "focused on moving ahead and learning from this experience."

Toyota and Kobayashi, in a joint statement, said Friday, "We are very pleased to have resolved this matter in a way that all parties have agreed is fair, appropriate and mutually satisfactory."

Toyota says that as a result:

- U.S. executives are being trained to "enable them to better recognize, prevent and handle any instances of inappropriate behavior." The training will be repeated periodically.
- Company policy has changed so that allegations of misconduct against an executive must be investigated immediately and reported to the executive's superior.

If the executive being accused happens to be the chairman, CEO or president, a report has to be made directly to the company's board of directors.

John Malott, president of the Japan-America Society of Washington, says it is unusual for a Japanese-born woman to go public with the allegations Kobayashi has. In an interview before the settlement, Kobayashi's attorney, Christopher Brennan, agreed it was difficult for her to come forward.

"If you take somebody who has devoted half of her working career to a company, it's a tremendous betrayal to be put in a position where she had to publicly come forward," Brennan said.

Experts on cultural differences in the workplace consider the Toyota trouble an aberration.

"Generally speaking, dealing with the Japanese is like dealing with any American," says Douglas Erber of the Japan-America Society of Southern California.

The sexual-harassment allegations were part of a string of embarrassing developments.

Toyota has recalled large numbers of vehicles lately, threatening its image as a maker of premium-quality vehicles. Japanese authorities have launched a criminal investigation into three Toyota officials suspected of failing to disclose that some vehicles might have had a faulty steering part. That is suspected of causing a 2004 head-on accident in Japan that injured five.

The U.S. government is investigating 2004-05 Toyota Sienna minivans because of complaints that the lift-gate door failed to stay open and dropped onto owners.

Hiring Older Workers

Unique skills, values come through the experience of age.

Stephen Bastien

anted: Employees who are honest, responsible, dependable, loyal, focused, organized and mature. Is this too much to ask?

American employers spend millions of hours each year placing ads, prescreening, interviewing, hiring and training workers, only to find that many of the new hires work for only a few months and then decide they don't want to be "just a clerk" anymore or feel something better has come along as they work their way up the corporate ladder.

Where can American employers find dependable, steady employees who have no plans to move up and out? Employees who are dedicated to the job at hand and take pride in their work? Employees who cost less to hire, train and maintain?

The answer, I have found in many of my own business ventures, is senior citizens, or, for the purposes of this article, older workers.

Here are 10 advantages of hiring older workers that may solve managers' difficulties with maintaining a reliable, dedicated work-force and result in significant cost savings in both the short and long term.

1. Dedicated workers produce better quality work, which can result in significant savings. Stories abound of highly committed older workers finding others' potentially costly mistakes in everything from incorrect zip codes and misspelling of client names to pricing errors and accounting mistakes.

2. Punctuallty seems to be a given for older workers. They look forward to going to work each day, so they arrive on time and ready to work.

3. Honesty is common among many older workers, whose values include personal integrity and a devotion to the truth.

4. Detail-oriented, focused and attentive workers add an intangible value that rubs off on all employees and can save thousands of dollars. One business owner described a case in which one of his older workers saved the company more than $50,000 on one large mailing

job. His 75-year-old clerical worker recognized that all of the zip codes were off by one digit. Neither his mailing house nor his degreed and highly paid marketing manager had noticed it.

5. Pride in a job well done has become increasingly scarce among employees. Younger workers want to put in their time at work and leave, while older employees willingly stay later to get a job done because of their sense of pride in the final product.

6. Organizational skills among older workers mean employers who hire them are less likely to be a part of this startling statistic: More than a million staff hours are lost each year due to workplace disorganization.

7. Efficiency and the confidence to share their recommendations and ideas make older workers ideal employees. Their years of experience in the workplace give them superior understanding of how jobs can be done more efficiently, which saves companies money. Their confidence, built up over their years in the workforce, means they'll not hesitate to share their ideas with management.

8. Maturity comes from years of life and work experience and makes for workers who get less "rattled" when problems occur.

9. Setting an example for other employees is an intangible value many employers appreciate. Older workers make excellent mentors and role models, so training other employees is less difficult.

10. Reduced labor costs may be a benefit when hiring older workers. Most already have insurance plans from prior employers or have an additional source of income. They understand that working for a company can be about much more than just collecting a paycheck.

Employers who are hesitant to hire older workers should consider these benefits. Older workers' unique skills and values make hiring them a simple matter of rethinking the costs of high turnover in a more youthful workforce versus the benefits of experience and mature standards that older workers bring to the mix. So the next time you need to make a hiring decision, seriously consider older workers. Their contribution could positively impact the bottom line for years to come.

STEPHEN BASTIEN is an author and authority on entrepreneurship. His current venture, Bastien Financial Publications (www.usbj.biz), offers businesses the latest developments through daily newsletters. To contact him, call 1-800-407-9044 or send an e-mail to steve@creditnews.com.

Where Are the Women?

Not in the corner office, even after all these years. Not now. Maybe not ever. So what happened?

LINDA TISCHLER

Brenda Barnes knows what it takes to hold a top job in a highly competitive company. As president and chief executive of the North American arm of PepsiCo, a place famous for its driven culture, she set a fast pace. Rising at 3:30 A.M., she would blitz through a few hours of work before waking her three children at 7 A.M., then dash off to the office, where she'd grind through an 11- or 12-hour day crammed with meetings, conference calls, and strategy sessions. Then it was home for dinner and bedtime stories before finishing up with phone calls or email before falling into bed. Three nights a week, she was on the road. Seven times, she relocated when the company wanted her in another office. For eight years, she and her husband lived in separate cities, trying valiantly to juggle both job demands and those of marriage and family. And all the effort was paying off: Barnes was widely considered a real contender for the top job at PepsiCo when CEO Roger Enrico retired. But in September 1997, at 43, she suddenly stepped down when the toll of the job began, in her mind, to outstrip its rewards.

Unlike some women executives who have famously dropped out, Barnes did not go home to write her memoirs or devote herself to charity and her children's soccer schedules. She just chose what is for her, a less demanding path: She serves on the board of six major companies, among them Sears, Avon, and The New York Times; she's taught at the Kellogg School of Management, and stepped in as interim president of Starwood Hotels and Resorts in early 2000. Although she's had many offers for other enticing jobs, she's unwilling to consider another gig at the top. "When you talk about those big jobs, those CEO jobs, you just have to give them your life," she says. "You can't alter them to make them accommodate women any better than men. It's just the way it is."

Six years after the fact, Barnes is still happy with her decision. But she admits that despite her considerable post-PepsiCo accomplishments, she's been forever branded as The Woman Who Walked Away. Small wonder. In a workplace where women CEOs of major companies are so scarce that they can be identified, like rock stars, by first name only—Carly and Martha and Andrea and Oprah and Meg—it's shocking each time a contender to join their august ranks steps down.

It wasn't supposed to turn out this way. By 2004, after three decades of the women's movement, when business schools annually graduate thousands of qualified young women, when the managerial pipeline is stuffed with capable, talented female candidates for senior positions, why are there still so few women at the top?

In part, the answer probably still lies in lingering bias in the system. Most women interviewed for this story say that overt discrimination is rare; still, the executive suites of most major corporations remain largely boys' clubs. Catalyst, the women's business group, blames the gap on the fact that women often choose staff jobs, such as marketing and human resources, while senior executives are disproportionately plucked from the ranks of those with line jobs, where a manager can have critical profit-and-loss responsibility. Others fault the workplace itself, saying corporations don't do enough to accommodate women's often more-significant family responsibilities.

All those things are true. But there may be a simpler—and in many ways more disturbing—reason that women remain so underrepresented in the corner office: For the most part, men just compete harder than women. They put in more hours. They're more willing to relocate. They're more comfortable putting work ahead of personal commitments. And they just want the top job more.

Let's be clear: Many, many individual women work at least as hard as men. Many even harder. But in the aggregate, statistics show, they work less, and as long as that remains true, it means women's chances of reaching parity in the corner office will remain remote. Those top jobs have become all-consuming: In today's markets, being CEO is a global, 24-hour-a-day job. You have to, as Barnes says, give it your life. Since women tend to experience work-life conflicts more viscerally than their male peers, they're less likely to be willing to do that. And at the upper reaches of corporate hierarchy, where the pyramid narrows sharply and the game becomes winner-take-all, a moment's hesitation—one important stint in the Beijing office that a woman doesn't take because of a sick child or an unhappy husband—means the odds get a little worse for her and a little better for the guy down the hall.

And let's be clear, too, that we're not talking about women who simply opt out. They've been getting a lot of press and sparking a lot of controversy lately—those young women investment bankers and lawyers who are quitting to become stay-at-home moms (and, really, they're still using those MBA skills on the board of the PTA). That's still a fringe phenomenon affecting relatively few privileged women with high-earning husbands.

Many, many women work at least as hard as men. But the disturbing truth is that most women don't compete as hard as most men.

No, the women we're talking about here work, want to work, want to continue to work. But not the way you have to work in order to reach the top these days. That's the conclusion that Marta Cabrera finally came to four years ago. By 1999, Cabrera was a vice president at JP Morgan Chase, one of only two women on the emerging-markets trading desk. True, the demands were steep—12-hour days were the norm. But the rewards, at the peak of the boom, were pretty delicious, too: an apartment in Manhattan, a country home, and the chance for an artist husband to pursue his vocation.

Not only was Cabrera at the top of her game, but she had, by all measures, managed to pull off the career woman's trifecta—a great job, a happy marriage, and two beautiful, healthy little daughters—all by age 43. But in October of that year, as she watched her second-grader blow out the candles on her birthday cake, Cabrera had an unsettling realization: She didn't know her own child as well as most of the friends and family who had gathered to celebrate the big event. "I realized seven years had gone by, and I had only seen her and my five-year-old on weekends," she says. No first words. No school plays. No class trips. "I asked myself, 'What the hell am I doing?'" Then she thought about her job. To walk away would mean upheaval. Plus, there was a principal at stake: "I had the sense I was letting down my sex by leaving."

It took another seven months, and much soul-searching, to reach her decision, but in May of 2000, Cabrera quit. Like Barnes, she did not opt out. No 180-degree turn to a life of play dates or book groups. No reconnecting with her inner tennis-lady. Instead, she became executive director of EMPower, a microlender in developing countries. Facing a precipitous drop in income, she and her husband rented out their Manhattan place and moved to the country. Now she works from home three days a week, and is in the city the other two, an arrangement that lets her do rewarding work and still spend time with her kids.

And what did her experience at JP Morgan Chase teach her? "There's a different quality of what men give up versus what women give up" when they attempt to reconcile the demands of a senior job with those of family responsibilities. "The sacrifices for women are deeper, and you must weigh them very

consciously if you want to continue," she says. "I didn't want to be the biggest, best, greatest. I didn't feel compelled to be number one."

She was doing what women often do: scaling back on work for the sake of family, with a clear-eyed realization that she was, simultaneously, torpedoing her chances for a climb up the ladder. What's more, she didn't care. It's a choice women often make, with no particular social sanctions. For some, it's even an easy and convenient way to escape an increasingly hostile and unfriendly work world, an out that men simply don't have. But it's also the reason women may continue to be stalled at the lower rungs in organizations and men may continue to rule.

Charles A. O'Reilly III, professor of organizational behavior at Stanford Graduate School of Business, has been particularly interested in women's career attainment and the problem of why, despite notable gains in education and experience, women are still so woefully underrepresented in the top ranks of American corporations. In 1986, he began following a group of University of California, Berkeley MBAs to see if he could isolate those qualities that led to a corner office. His conclusion is starkly simple: Success in a corporation is less a function of gender discrimination than of how hard a person chooses to compete. And the folks who tend to compete the hardest are generally the stereotypical manly men.

Think of careers as a tournament, he says. In the final rounds, players are usually matched pretty equally for ability. At that point, what differentiates winners from losers is effort—how many backhands a tennis player hits in practice, how many calls a sales rep is willing to make. "From an organization's perspective," he says, "those most likely to be promoted are those who both have the skills and are willing to put in the effort. Individuals who are more loyal, work longer hours, and are willing to sacrifice for the organization are the ones who will be rewarded."

Today's women, he says, are equal to their male counterparts in education, experience, and skill. But when it's a painful choice between the client crisis and the birthday party, the long road trip and the middle schooler who needs attention, the employee most likely to put company over family is the traditional, work-oriented male. Interestingly, the women in O'Reilly's study reported levels of career satisfaction equal to those of their more-driven male peers, even if they were not as outwardly successful. In other words, women may be happier not gunning for power positions if it means they can work less and have a life.

After seven years with the big computer leasing company Comdisco, Diane Brandt, for example, left to form a small investment banking firm with two male colleagues. She decided to leave that job, too, when the growing business's hours increased and the moment approached when her only son would leave for college. Recently, she launched a small company, Captio Corp., that offers budgeting and scheduling tools for college students. "I've made choices all through my career," she says from her home in Menlo Park, California, days before heading to Germany to visit her son, who's studying abroad. "I've not pursued promotions in the same way I might have had I not been trying to balance other things in my life. It's been important to me to be home and have dinner with my family. You can't do that and move up the ladder."

Beth Johnson, a banker in Chicago, describes herself as "very ambitious," and says she has always loved business: the deal making, the challenge, the money. But she still remembers when her son was a baby, calculating the percentage of his waking hours that she could, if all went well, actually be present. "I doubt that his father was doing the same," she says dryly.

Recently, when the fund she was managing fell victim to the stock market, she decided to take some time off to help her son negotiate his final precollege year. Her brief attempt to be a "golf lady" didn't pan out. "I just couldn't do it," she confesses. She's now mulling various job offers. While she will go back to work, she knows there are sacrifices she and most other women are less willing to make than men. "People may get mad if I describe women as a group," she says, "but we are relational family beings. We do not have a world that's structured to understand that, to know how to account for it, and I don't know that we ever will."

There's a scene near the end of the 1956 movie *The Man in the Gray Flannel Suit* in which Fredric March, who plays a work-obsessed network president, turns on Gregory Peck, who plays his conflicted speechwriter. "Big, successful companies just aren't built by men like you, nine-to-five and home and family," March says. "They're built by men like me, who give everything they've got to it, who live it body and soul." March, of course, has sacrificed his own happiness to the company, a choice that Peck is unwilling to make.

Not much has changed in 48 years, says David Nadler chairman of Mercer Delta Consulting. Nadler, who advises senior managers, says that because top jobs are typically crushing in their demands, they require a certain psychological type. "I've worked closely with 20 CEOs over the past two decades—both men and women," he says. "All of them are characterized by being driven. Something in them says, 'This is important enough for me to make the sacrifices that are inherent with the job.' "

Certainly, there are women willing and able to compete by those draconian rules. A 2003 Catalyst study found that more than half of the women not yet in senior leadership positions within their companies aspired to be there (although 26% also said they weren't interested.) And some women want nothing less than a full-throttle engagement with work. "I don't seek balance. I want to work, work, work," Ann Livermore, executive vice president of Hewlett-Packard, told Karin Kauffmann and Peggy Baskin for their book, *Beyond Superwoman* (Carmel,

2003). Or as Kim Perdikou, CIO of Juniper Networks, told the author, "I'm wired 24 hours a day."

But such decisions continue to have consequences that thoughtful women are all too aware of. Asked what advice she would give to a daughter, M.R.C. Greenwood, chancellor of the University of California at Santa Cruz, warns, "Remember that the assumption that one's marriage will remain intact as she moves up is a false assumption. You really have to know yourself and know it will take a toll."

Conversely, there are plenty of men who would like the option to lead saner lives. A recent study of 101 senior human-resource managers found that men are also starting to leave big companies to try to improve the balance between their home lives and their worklives. Still, many more men than women seem to get an adrenaline rush from work that allows them to log long hours, zoom through time zones, and multitask savagely.

As a nation, we now clock more time on the job than any other worker on earth, some 500 hours a year more than the Germans, and 250 hours per year more than the British. But the true heavy lifters in the productivity parade are American men. According to the Bureau of Labor Statistics, men work longer hours in every industry, including those traditionally identified with women. In financial fields, for example, men worked an average of 43.8 hours per week compared with women's 38.7; in management, it was men 47.2, women 39.4; in educational services, men 39.2, women 36.0; in health services, men 43.1, women 36.4.

The same pattern holds true in professions whose elaborate hazing rituals are designed to separate potential chiefs from the rest of the tribe. Young associates at prestigious law firms, for example, often put in 60- to 70-hour weeks for long periods of time. "It's almost an intentional hurdle placed by the firms to weed out those who simply don't have the drive and ambition to do it," says Stanford University economist Edward Lazear. "It may be excessive, but you select out a very elite few, and those are the ones who make it to partner and make very high salaries."

Women are as scarce in the upper reaches of the legal profession as they are in top-tier corporate offices. According to the National Directory of Legal Employers and Catalyst, women represented only 15.6% of law partners nationwide and 13.7% of the general counsels of Fortune 500 companies in 2000 (even though they have accounted for at least 40% of enrollments at top law schools since 1985 and nearly 50% since 2000). Women in these firms say personal or family responsibilities are the top barrier to advancement, with 71% of women in law firms reporting difficulty juggling work and family, and 66% of women in corporate legal departments citing the same struggle.

Depending on the specialty, medical practices can be similarly pitiless. Among doctors, women work 45 hours per week compared with men's 50. Male physicians also see 117 patients per week, compared with 97 for women. And, as with the law, the top rungs of the medical ladder are populated by men who are willing to put work ahead of family, with women doctors concentrated in lower-paying positions in hospitals, HMOs, and group practices.

Table 1   Average Hours Worked per Week

	Men	Women
Lawyers*	47.5	43.0
Management, business, and financial operations occupations*	46.1	40.4
Doctors (primary care physicians)**	50.0	45.0

Sources: *Bureau of Labor Statistics, Current Population
Survey 1989 (lawyers), 2002 (business); **Medical Economics, 2003

Meanwhile, back in the executive suite, researchers at Catalyst say some progress has been made. Women made up 15.7% of corporate officers in the *Fortune* 500 in 2002, up from 8.7% in 1995. In 2003, they held 13.6% of board seats in the same companies, up from 12.4% in 2001. But their actual numbers, compared to the percentage of women in the workforce, are still minuscule. This has occasioned much hand-wringing among business organizations and women's advocacy groups. But maybe all that angst is misplaced.

"The higher up you go, jobs get greedier and greedier," says one researcher. "The idea that if only employers would reshape jobs they would be perfectly easy for women to do is just nonsense."

"When a woman gets near the top, she starts asking herself the most intelligent questions," says Warren Farrell, the San Diego-based author of *The Myth of Male Power* (Simon & Schuster, 1993). The fact that few women make it to the very top is a measure of women's power, not powerlessness, he maintains. "Women haven't learned to get their love by being president of a company," he says. "They've learned they can get respect and love in a variety of different ways—from being a good parent, from being a top executive, or a combination of both." Free of the ego needs driving male colleagues, they're likelier to weigh the trade-offs and opt for saner lives.

Mary Lou Quinlan has seen the view from the top and decided it's not worth the price. In 1998, she stepped down as CEO of the big advertising agency N.W. Ayer when she realized she was no longer enjoying a life that had no room for weekends, vacations, or, often, sleep. She went on to found Just Ask a Woman, a New York-based consulting firm that helps big companies build business with women. The decision wasn't driven by guilt over giving family responsibilities short shrift (Quinlan has no children); it was about calibrating the value of work in one's life. Quinlan thinks that calculation is different for women. "The reason a lot of women aren't shooting for the corner office is that they've seen it up close, and it's not a pretty scene," she says. "It's not about talent, dedication, experience, or the ability to take the heat. Women simply say, 'I just don't like that kitchen.' "

Catalyst and other groups have suggested that the heat can be turned down in that kitchen—that senior jobs can be changed to allow for more flexibility and balance, which will in turn help more women to the top of the heap. Catherine Hakim thinks that is bunk. Hakim, a sociologist at the London School of Economics, has been investigating the attitudes toward work among European men and women, and says reengineering jobs won't solve two fundamental problems: First, many women have decidedly mixed feelings about working, and second, top jobs by their very nature will remain relentlessly demanding. In surveys of 4,700 workers in Britain and Spain, she found that only 20% of women considered themselves "work-centered"—they made their careers a primary focus of their lives, and said they would work even if they didn't have to. By contrast, 55% of men said they focused primarily on work. Given those numbers, most top jobs will continue to go to men, she says, despite the equal-opportunity movement and the contraceptive revolution.

That's because work-centered employees are most likely to leap to the tasks that are most disruptive to life. "That's the bottom line, and it's not a sexist bottom line," Hakim says. "Of course, you could say jobs shouldn't be so greedy, but in practice, the higher up you go, by and large, jobs get greedier and greedier. The idea that some people have, that if only employers would reshape jobs they would be perfectly easy for women to do, is just nonsense."

Not surprisingly, the suggestion that the fault lies with women and not with the system drives many women nuts. Margaret Heffernan, the outspoken former CEO of the CMGI company iCast, for example, goes apoplectic at what she calls the perennial "little black dress stories"—tales of how various women have stepped down from their big jobs to spend more time with their families. Their implicit message, she says, is that women can't cut it and would prefer to be back in the kitchen. Indeed, she says, the conclusion we should be drawing is, "Another company just f****d up big time. Another company just trained somebody and made them incredibly skilled and still couldn't keep them."

Heffernan says the hordes of women refusing to play the career-advancement game aren't doing so because they can't hack it, but because they've lost faith in the institutions they've worked for and are tired of cultures driven by hairy-chested notions of how companies must function. Instead, they are founding businesses where they can use the experience in an environment they can better control. "They leave to create companies where they don't have to be the change agents, where they can start from scratch without the fights, without the baggage, and without the brawls," she says.

Stanford's Lazear so envisions a different scenario for women, one in which they wouldn't have to leave corporate America to get the jobs they want. Given the coming labor shortage, which the U.S. Department of Labor predicts will hit by 2010, companies maybe forced to redesign jobs to a talented workers. And that, combined with technology that will let people work from a variety of locations, he says, will make it possible

Table 2 Percentage of Workers in Top Jobs

	Men	Women
Lawyers (partner)*	84.4%	15.6%
Corporate officers in the *Fortune* 500**	84.3%	15.7%
Top-earning doctors***	93.4%	6.6%

Sources: *National Directory of Legal Employers, NALP 2000, and 2000 Catalyst Census of Women Corporate Officers and Top Earners; **2002 Catalyst; ***Medical Economics: cardiology, gastroenterology, and orthopedic surgery are top-earning specialities. Percentages of women in those fields calculated from data on doctors (by gender and specialty), from American Medical Association.

for more women to reach the top. He predicts that 20% of CEOs in top organizations will be women in 15 to 20 years. But total parity? "I don't expect it ever to be equal—ever," he says.

Brenda Barnes thinks as today's business-school students gain power in companies, they will force changes that benefit men and women. When she taught at Kellogg, she asked her students to write a paper describing how they saw their careers playing out. "They were far more focused on having a life than my generation was," she says. "And it wasn't just a female thing. They grew up seeing their parents killing themselves and then being downsized despite their loyalty. How much this generation is willing to give to any enterprise is a totally different ballgame."

We can hope so. Unfortunately, her students' desire for more balance could be one more form of youthful idealism. As a 24-hour global economy makes it ever more difficult to turn off the office, it's hard to imagine a day when the promotions won't go to the worker who makes just a little more effort, who logs on just a little longer. Or to envision a day when there won't be plenty of contenders—maybe most of them men—who will be willing to do just that.

LINDA TISCHLER (ltischler@fastcompany.com) is a FAST COMPANY senior writer.

Crippled by Their Culture

Race doesn't hold back America's 'black rednecks.' Nor does racism.

THOMAS SOWELL

For most of the history of this country, differences between the black and the white population—whether in income, IQ, crime rates, or whatever—have been attributed to either race or racism. For much of the first half of the 20th century, these differences were attributed to race—that is, to an assumption that blacks just did not have it in their genes to do as well as white people. The tide began to turn in the second half of the 20th century, when the assumption developed that black-white differences were due to racism on the part of whites.

Three decades of my own research lead me to believe that neither of those explanations will stand up under scrutiny of the facts. As one small example, a study published last year indicated that most of the black alumni of Harvard were from either the West Indies or Africa, or were the children of West Indian or African immigrants. These people are the same race as American blacks, who greatly outnumber either or both.

If this disparity is not due to race, it is equally hard to explain by racism. To a racist, one black is pretty much the same as another. But, even if a racist somehow let his racism stop at the water's edge, how could he tell which student was the son or daughter of someone born in the West Indies or in Africa, especially since their American-born offspring probably do not even have a foreign accent?

What then could explain such large disparities in demographic "representation" among these three groups of blacks? Perhaps they have different patterns of behavior and different cultures and values behind their behavior.

There have always been large disparities, even within the native black population of the U.S. Those blacks whose ancestors were "free persons of color" in 1850 have fared far better in income, occupation, and family stability than those blacks whose ancestors were freed in the next decade by Abraham Lincoln.

What is not nearly as widely known is that there were also very large disparities within the white population of the pre-Civil War South and the white population of the Northern states. Although Southern whites were only about one-third of the white population of the U.S., an absolute majority of all the illiterate whites in the country were in the South.

The North had four times as many schools as the South, attended by more than four times as many students. Children in Massachusetts spent more than twice as many years in school as children in Virginia. Such disparities obviously produce other disparities. Northern newspapers had more than four times the circulation of Southern newspapers. Only 8% of the patents issued in 1851 went to Southerners. Even though agriculture was the principal economic activity of the antebellum South at the time, the vast majority of the patents for agricultural inventions went to Northerners. Even the cotton gin was invented by a Northerner.

Disparities between Southern whites and Northern whites extended across the board from rates of violence to rates of illegitimacy. American writers from both the antebellum South and the North commented on the great differences between the white people in the two regions. So did famed French visitor Alexis de Tocqueville.

None of these disparities can be attributed to either race or racism. Many contemporary observers attributed these differences to the existence of slavery in the South, as many in later times would likewise attribute both the difference between Northern and Southern whites, and between blacks and whites nationwide, to slavery. But slavery doesn't stand up under scrutiny of historical facts any better than race or racism as explanations of North-South differences or black-white differences. The people who settled in the South came from different regions of Britain than the people who settled in the North—and they differed as radically on the other side of the Atlantic as they did here—that is, before they had ever seen a black slave.

Slavery also cannot explain the difference between American blacks and West Indian blacks living in the United States because the ancestors of both were enslaved. When race, racism, and slavery all fail the empirical test, what is left?

Culture is left.

The culture of the people who were called "rednecks" and "crackers" before they ever got on the boats to cross the Atlantic was a culture that produced far lower levels of intellectual and economic achievement, as well as far higher levels of violence and sexual promiscuity. That culture had its own way of talking, not only in the pronunciation of particular words but also in a loud, dramatic style of oratory with vivid imagery, repetitive phrases and repetitive cadences.

Although that style originated on the other side of the Atlantic in centuries past, it became for generations the style of both religious oratory and political oratory among Southern whites and among Southern blacks—not only in the South but in the Northern ghettos in which Southern blacks settled. It was a style used by Southern white politicians in the era of Jim Crow and later by black civil rights leaders fighting Jim Crow. Martin Luther King's famous speech at the Lincoln Memorial in 1963 was a classic example of that style.

While a third of the white population of the U.S. lived within the redneck culture, more than 90% of the black population did. Although that culture eroded away over the generations, it did so at different rates in different places and among different people. It eroded away much faster in Britain than in the U.S. and somewhat faster among Southern whites than among Southern blacks, who had fewer opportunities for education or for the rewards that came with escape from that counterproductive culture.

Nevertheless the process took a long time. As late as the First World War, white soldiers from Georgia, Arkansas, Kentucky and Mississippi scored lower on mental tests than black soldiers from Ohio, Illinois, New York and Pennsylvania. Again, neither race nor racism can explain that—and neither can slavery.

The redneck culture proved to be a major handicap for both whites and blacks who absorbed it. Today, the last remnants of that culture can still be found in the worst of the black ghettos, whether in the North or the South, for the ghettos of the North were settled by blacks from the South. The counterproductive and self-destructive culture of black rednecks in today's ghettos is regarded by many as the only "authentic" black culture—and, for that reason, something not to be tampered with. Their talk, their attitudes, and their behavior are regarded as sacrosanct.

The people who take this view may think of themselves as friends of blacks. But they are the kinds of friends who can do more harm than enemies.

MR. SOWELL, the Rose and Milton Friedman Senior Fellow at the Hoover Institution, is author, most recently, of "Black Rednecks and White Liberals," by Encounter Books.

Fear of Firing

How the threat of litigation is making companies skittish about axing problem workers.

MICHAEL OREY

Would you have dared fire Hemant K. Mody? In February, 2003, the longtime engineer had returned to work at a General Electric Co. (GE) facility in Plainville, Conn., after a two-month medical leave. He was a very unhappy man. For much of the prior year, he and his superiors had been sparring over his performance and promotion prospects. According to court documents, Mody's bosses claimed he spoke disparagingly of his co-workers, refused an assignment as being beneath him, and was abruptly taking days off and coming to work late.

But Mody was also 49, Indian born, and even after returning from leave continued to suffer a major disability: chronic kidney failure that required him to receive daily dialysis. The run-ins resumed with his managers, whom he had accused flat out of discriminating against him because of his race and age. It doesn't take an advanced degree in human resources to recognize that the situation was a ticking time bomb. But Mody's bosses were fed up. They axed him in April, 2003.

The bomb exploded last July. Following a six-day trial, a federal court jury in Bridgeport, Conn., found GE's termination of Mody to be improper and awarded him $11.1 million, including $10 million in punitive damages. But the award wasn't for discrimination. The judge found those claims so weak that Mody wasn't allowed to present them. Instead, jurors concluded that Mody had been fired in retaliation for complaining about bias. GE is seeking to have the award overturned, and a spokesman said, "We feel strongly there is no basis for this claim." Through his attorney, Mody declined to discuss the case with *BusinessWeek*.

If this can happen to GE, a company famed for its rigorous performance reviews, with an HR operation that is studied worldwide, it can happen anywhere. It has never been easier for U.S. workers to go to court and allege that they've been sacked unfairly. Over the past 40 years federal, state, and local lawmakers have steadily expanded the categories of workers who enjoy special legal protection—a sprawling group that now includes women, minorities, gays, whistleblowers, the disabled, people over 40, employees who have filed workers' compensation claims, and workers who have been called away for jury duty or military service, among others. Factor in white men who believe that they are bias victims—so-called reverse-discrimination lawsuits—and

"it's difficult to find someone who doesn't have some capacity to claim protected status," observes Lisa H. Cassilly, an employment defense attorney at Alston & Bird in Atlanta.

These workers wield a potent weapon. They can force companies to prove in court that there was a legitimate business reason for their termination. And once a case is in court, it's expensive. A company can easily spend $100,000 to get a meritless lawsuit tossed out before trial. And if a case goes to a jury, the fees skyrocket to $300,000, and often much higher. The result: Many companies today are gripped by a fear of firing. Terrified of lawsuits, they let unproductive employees linger, lay off coveted workers while retaining less valuable ones, and pay severance to screwups and even crooks in exchange for promises that they won't sue. "I've seen us make decisions [about terminations] that in the absence of this litigious risk environment, you'd have a different result," acknowledges Johnny C. Taylor, Jr., head of HR at IAC/InterActiveCorp (IACI), the conglomerate that runs businesses such as Match.com and Ticketmaster.

Managers often fail to build a case for firing by shying away from regular and candid evaluations.

The fear of firing is particularly acute in the HR and legal departments. They don't directly suffer when an underperformer lingers in the corporate hierarchy, but they may endure unpleasant indirect consequences if that person files a lawsuit. Says Dick Grote, an Addison (Tex.) talent management consultant: "They don't get their bonuses based on the number of lawsuits they win. They get their bonuses based on the number of lawsuits they don't get involved in."

This set of divergent incentives puts line managers in a tough position. When they finally decide to get rid of the underperforming slob who plays PC solitaire all day in her cubicle, it can be surprisingly tough to do. And that, in turn, affects productive workers. "Few things demotivate an organization faster than tolerating and retaining low performers," says Grant Freeland, a regional leader in Boston Consulting Group's organization practice.

But it's often the supervisors themselves who bear much of the blame when HR says someone can't be shown the door. That's because most fail to give the kind of regular and candid evaluations that will allow a company to prove poor performance if a fired employee hauls them into court. Honest, if harsh, reviews not only offer legal cover, but they're also critical for organizations intent on developing top talent. "There were definitely a lot of situations where a supervisor got fed up with somebody and wanted to terminate them, but there's no paperwork," says Sara Anderson, who worked in HR at Perry Ellis International (PERY) and Kenneth Cole Productions Inc. (KCP) in New York. Frequently, the work that the manager suddenly claims is intolerable is accompanied by years of performance evaluations that say "meets expectations." Says Anderson: "You look in the file, and there's nothing there to prove [poor performance], so it's like it didn't happen."

W hen Mody Signed GE's Job application in 1998, the form said his employment was "at will" and "the Company may terminate my employment at any time for any reason."

Well, not exactly.

The notion that American workers are employed "at will"— meaning, as one lawyer put it, you can be fired if your manager doesn't like the color of your socks—took root in the laissez-faire atmosphere of the late 19th century, and as an official matter is still the law of the land in every state, save Montana. The popular conception of at-will employment is exemplified by the television show *The Apprentice,* which features Donald Trump pointing a finger at an underling and ousting him or her on the spot. That dramatic gesture makes great television, but it isn't something that happens very frequently anymore in the American workplace.

The rise of unions was the first development to put a check on summary dismissal. Collective-bargaining agreements outlined the specific kinds of infractions that could lead to termination, and set up procedures for discipline and review that a company must follow before a worker can be fired. But unions generally didn't deal with the problem of discrimination, and in some cases perpetuated it.

For most American workers now, their status as at-will employees has been transformed by a succession of laws growing out of the civil rights movement in the 1960s that bar employers from making decisions based on such things as race, religion, sex, age, and national origin. This is hardly controversial. Even the legal system's harshest critics find little fault with rules aimed at assuring that personnel decisions are based on merit. And most freely acknowledge that it is much easier to fire people in the U.S. than it is in, say, most of Western Europe. Mass layoffs, in fact, are a recurring event on the American corporate scene. On Apr. 17, for example, Citigroup Inc. (C) announced it will shed some 17,000 workers.

Yet even in these situations, RIFs (for "reduction in force") are carefully vetted by attorneys to assess the impact on employees who are in a legally protected category. And these days the

---

Untouchable Nation

Fired workers who fall into a protected category have special legal status. These days, it's harder than you might imagine to find an American worker who wouldn't fall into one—or sometimes several—of these categories.

Total Labour Force: 151.4 million

- Minorities (31%)
- 40 and over (52%)
- Female (46%)
- Unprotected*: White males under 40 (16%)

*But not if the employee is: Disabled, gay, a whistle-blower, a veteran, foreign-born, called for jury duty, a workers' compensation claimant.

Data: U.S Bureau of Labour Statistics, 2006.

---

majority of American workers fall into one or more such groups. Mody, for example, belonged to three because of who he was (age, race, and national origin) and two more because of things he had done (complained of discrimination and taken medical leave). That doesn't mean such people are immune from firing. But it does mean a company will have to show a legitimate, non-discriminatory business reason for the termination, should the matter ever land in court.

As it happens, the judge in Mody's case tossed out his discrimination claims. But the retaliation allegation did go to the jury—a development that is increasingly blindsiding businesses. Plaintiffs are winning large sums not because a company discriminated against them, but because the company retaliated when they complained about the unproven mistreatment.

The rules surrounding retaliation may sound crazy, but they are one of the big reasons why the fear of firing is so prevalent. Retaliation suits are a hot growth area in employment law. In 2005 and 2006, retaliation claims represented 30% of all charges individuals filed with the Equal Employment Opportunity Commission, a required first step before most discrimination cases can go to federal court. That's up from about 20% just 10 years ago. "Even if there isn't a good discrimination claim, the employee has a second bite at the apple," notes Martin W. Aron of defense firm Edwards Angell Palmer & Dodge in Short Hills, N.J. Last year the U.S. Supreme Court increased the legal risk to business by ruling that improper retaliation can involve acts far short of firing or demoting someone. So even excluding an employee from meetings, relocating his or her office, or other intangible slights could lead to liability.

Of course, prohibitions against retaliation exist for a good reason. Without them, many workers would find it too risky to come forward with even legitimate complaints. Yet defense attorneys are deeply suspicious that some workers abuse the protection. Fearing their jobs may be in jeopardy, they may quickly contact HR with an allegation of discrimination or call a corporate hotline to report misconduct, thereby cloaking themselves in the protection of anti-retaliation law. "That's a fairly common fact scenario," says Mike Delikat of Orrick Herrington & Sutcliffe in New York, a law firm that represents businesses. "The best defense is a good offense."

After 1991, when Congress allowed punitive damages and jury trials in job discrimination cases, litigation in the area exploded. In 2006, 14,353 employment cases were filed in federal court, up from 8,273 in 1990, though down from a peak of 20,955 in 2002. It should be noted that these statistics, which include both unlawful termination cases and other types of claims, dramatically understate the frequency with which companies deal with these issues. For every case that's filed in court, several more are quietly settled well beforehand.

Many of the lawsuits may seem ridiculous. IBM (IBM) is currently defending a case filed by James C. Pacenza, a plant worker it dismissed for visiting an adult Internet chat room while on the job. In his lawsuit, Pacenza claims that his propensity to such behavior stems from post-traumatic stress disorder, which he suffers as a result of military service in Vietnam, and that IBM violated the Americans with Disabilities Act. He also alleges that two other employees who had sex on an IBM desk were "merely transferred," so he was treated with undue harshness. Pacenza's attorney, Michael D. Diederich Jr., says his client "didn't violate any of IBM's policies regarding computer usage."

Even when employers beat back silly suits, it often doesn't feel like much of a victory. That's because meritless cases can still tie up companies in burdensome and expensive proceedings for years. In October, 2002, Southview Hospital in Dayton fired Karen Stephens, a nurse who worked in a unit for premature babies and other at-risk newborns. Six other nurses had reported that Stephens was abusive to infants, according to court filings, spanking them when they were fussy, wagging their noses until they screamed in pain, pinching their noses shut to force-feed them, and calling them "son of a bitch." Stephens, who was 60 at the time, sued Kettering Adventist Healthcare Network, which operates Southview, denying "inappropriate" conduct and alleging that the real reason she was let go was age discrimination.

Only after a year and a half of legal dueling did a federal district judge in Dayton toss out Stephens' claims in April, 2005. But then she appealed, and it took another year—and an additional round of legal briefing—before the U.S. Court of Appeals for the Sixth Circuit upheld the dismissal, noting that "Stephens has offered no evidence to indicate that she did not mistreat the infants," or that Kettering did not have a "legitimate, nondiscriminatory reason for discharging her." Kettering declined to comment on the case. "I never lost a baby in 25 years," Stephens said in an interview.

The cost and distraction of lawsuits lead many employers to engage in contortional, and at times perverse, litigation avoidance. Defense attorney Cassilly offers the story of one of her clients, a hospital in the Southeast forced to reduce its ranks because of budget cuts. The head of one department elected to let go a female employee in favor of keeping a more junior male, whom he had spent a great deal of effort to recruit and whom he felt was more valuable. But the hospital overrode that choice and laid off the man out of concern that it would be more exposed in a lawsuit by the woman.

Another of Cassilly's clients, a manufacturer, acquired a new facility and quickly identified one worker as having "a variety of performance problems." But the woman, an African American, had nothing in her personnel file indicating prior trouble, which made firing her a risky bet. So the company put her on a six-month "performance improvement program" to document her deficiencies—and to find out if she could mend her ways. She couldn't, and, Cassilly notes, her client "had to suffer through her poor performance during the whole period."

Early this year, Cassilly got a call from the client. They had just discovered that the woman, an office administrator, had stolen thousands of dollars from the company, and they promptly dismissed her. "It was almost a case where the company was delighted to find out they were the victim of theft," Cassilly says, as opposed to having to defend far more subjective performance evaluations.

Even in the face of theft, Revolution Partners, a small investment banking advisory firm in Boston, balked before showing one of its employees the door. The woman had used her company credit card for a personal shopping spree and plane ticket, but Revolution retained an employment attorney, got the woman to sign a form waiving her right to sue for wrongful dismissal, and after she was fired took no legal action to recover the amounts improperly charged. "We're a little firm, and the last thing I need is to spend a lot of time on a lawsuit, whether it's warranted or not," says Peter Falvey, one of Revolution's co-founders.

Falvey isn't alone. A number of defense attorneys and HR managers said companies they work for prefer to buy themselves peace of mind over facing the prospect of being sued. "They don't want the publicity or the expense," says Robert J. Nobile, an attorney at Seyfarth Shaw in New York. "Some of them say, Hey, we'll swallow our pride and pay 10 grand now rather than 100 grand later." That's an approach that makes IAC's Taylor shudder. "If that becomes your norm, then you train the plaintiffs' bar and your departing employees that they should expect something on the way out, no matter how poorly they perform," he says.

Many observers put much of the blame for fear of firing on HR. "The problem is much more with HR managers being nervous Nellies than it is a problem in actual legal exposure," says consultant Grote. The bigger risk is retaining poor performers, not terminating them, he says, provided the firing is done properly.

Indeed, at most companies HR is essentially a support function that gets called in only when a personnel problem has reached the crisis stage. At that point, the best they may be able to do is suggest the kind of risk-avoidance measures that drive managers crazy—such as requiring that an employee's deficiencies actually be documented in writing for an extended period before he or she is fired. This can be avoided, says Amy Rasner, a former HR manager in the fashion industry, if human resources personnel are teamed with line managers, working with them on an ongoing basis to develop and communicate specific, measurable performance objectives to employees.

In interview after interview, attorneys and HR execs say the biggest problem they confront in terminations is the failure of managers to have these kinds of conversations. In a 2005 Hewitt

For Every 10,000 Lawsuits, Few Losses, but High Cost

The maneuvering companies engage in to avoid wrongful-termination lawsuits is out of proportion to the risk of actually losing in court. One big reason: the high cost of litigating claims, even the ones that end up with the company winning.

Out of 10,000 employment suits	Stage of lawsuit	Cumulative cost for a company to defend a single lawsuit
	Filing	
7,000	Settle (most settlements are for nuisance value)	$10,000
	Summary Judgment	
2,400	Get resolved by summary judgement and other pretrial rulings	$100,000
	Start of Trial	
600	Go to trial	$175,000
	End of Trial	
186	Trials are won by plaintiffs	$250,000*
	Appeal	
13**	Plaintiffs victories survive appeal	$300,000

Sources: Cornell Law School; Hofstra Labor & Employment Law Journal; BW reporting
* Assumes a five-day trial
** Out of 22 trial losses typically appealed by companies

Associates (HEW) survey of 129 major U.S. corporations, 72% said managers' ability to carry out performance management discussions and decisions effectively was the part of their personnel evaluation process most in need of improvement.

The reasons for this, of course, are varied. Some managers simply see the whole review process as a bureaucratic waste of time. It's also not easy to do. Many supervisors have been promoted into their jobs because they excelled in operations, not because they are skilled as managers. What's more, they've often spent a lot of time working alongside the very people they now oversee, so giving candid feedback to friends and former peers may be awkward. Managers in this position are "the biggest chickens on earth," says Fred Kiel, an executive-development consultant at KRW International Inc. in Minneapolis.

Ironically, when it came to handling personnel issues involving Mody, GE managers appear to have done most things right, offering regular and candid performance appraisals and involving HR and legal personnel at an early stage when matters began to sour. In trial exhibits and testimony, Mody's GE supervisors described him as a talented but prickly worker. Performance reviews and other documents faulted both his people and leadership skills.

But in the trial against GE, Mody's attorney, Scott R. Lucas of Stamford, Conn., laid out the details of what he labeled a campaign of retaliation against his client. Following a July, 2002, memo in which Mody accused the company of discrimination, Lucas told jurors, Mody's boss began complaining that he was absent and tardy too often. In a court filing, Lucas called this "a contrived performance issue," and says Mody was also "falsely criticized for lack of output."

What's more, just six weeks after having given Mody a "very favorable review," his boss gave Mody a "very poor and critical evaluation," according to the filing. Mody was excluded from various conferences and removed from "meaningful contribution" to projects. At one point, Mody's boss allegedly told him: "There are things I can ask you to do that if I asked you to do them, you would just quit." The last straw for Mody came when he returned from medical leave and was asked to do an assignment that he alleged was low-level and intentionally demeaning.

On July 18, jurors awarded Mody about $1.1 million in back pay and compensatory damages and—in one of several aspects of the case being challenged by GE—a tidy $10 million in punitive damages. Even for a company as big as GE, an $11.1 million verdict is plenty of cause to justify a fear of firing. But Mark S. Dichter, head of the employment practice at Morgan Lewis & Bockius in Philadelphia, thinks that's the wrong lesson to draw from the Mody case and other similar lawsuits. "I can design HR policies that can virtually eliminate your risk of facing employment claims, but you'll have a pretty lousy workforce," says Dichter. "At the end of the day, you have to run your business."

OREY is a senior writer for *BusinessWeek* in New York

Workplace Abuses That Guarantee Trouble

KEVIN SMITH

Want to get fired?
You could start by using illegal drugs or consuming alcohol on the job. And if that doesn't do the trick, try arriving late for work every day.

These are definite no-nos for any work environment that's run in a professional manner. But there are plenty of other ways to get the ax and some are more serious than you might think, according to Steffan & Co. Inc., a permanent-placement employment agency.

Experience is the best teacher, and you can learn from the mistakes of others. In that spirit, Steffan & Co. Inc. has compiled a list of "10 Sure-Fire Ways to Get Fired."

They include:

Using e-mail excessively for personal reasons. Most people have access to e-mail through their company's systems. Chances are, your boss isn't providing the e-mail so you can shop online or keep in touch with your college friends.

Sending or receiving inappropriate materials via e-mail or putting sensitive company information in e-mail messages.

Abusing the Internet. A survey by the ePolicy Institute, the American Management Association and U.S. News & World Report found that 35 percent of companies have disciplined or terminated employees for visiting restricted or unauthorized Web sites. Think your company isn't tracking your Internet use? Think again.

Consistently showing up late for work and then making sure you leave early. That sends a clear message that you just don't care.

Being disrespectful or politically incorrect in the workplace. Political correctness is a hot topic in today's modern workplace and most companies have zero tolerance for offensive remarks and actions.

Doing the bare minimum—nothing more. Employees like this get passed over for promotions and place themselves on the top of the "dispensable" list.

Consistently handling personal business at work. While most managers understand that personal business comes up from time to time during work hours, this business should be kept to a minimum.

Using illegal substances or drinking alcohol during the workday. This one sounds too obvious to mention, but drinking during the day or using illegal substances are habits that will send you back to the job search market.

Treating the workplace like it's your own personal social club. It's great to make new friends at work and be involved in the company's social scene. But it becomes a problem if you're spending more time at other people's desks than at your own.

Blatantly looking for other jobs. Think it's a good idea to fax your resume out from work and do phone interviews for other positions from your desk? Your manager will beg to differ.

Gary Kaplan, president of Gary Kaplan & Associates, an executive search firm based in Pasadena, said many companies monitor employee Internet use.

"They have software that gives them ability to look in on what you're doing," he said. "A fail-safe way, if you want to get rid of someone, is to do an oversight of their computer usage. There are very few people who don't use it for personal reasons."

Employees can also be shown the door for falsifying their academic credentials or past work experience, he said.

"If you get caught in terms of falsifying your background and got hired because of inaccurate information, or if you have a criminal record (and hid it) . . . these are all grounds for termination," Kaplan said.

In a broader sense, employees can also find themselves on thin ice because they don't fit in with a particular workplace culture, he said.

"I find that more people are terminated because of that than because of a lack of some technical competence," Kaplan said. "It's all about chemistry. If someone has a bad attitude or is difficult to work with, that can contribute to a toxic or hostile work environment."

Morris & Berger, a Glendale executive search firm that deals strictly in the not-for-profit world, has its own sexual harassment policy, according to partner Jay Berger.

"We established guidelines for what is appropriate to say and what's not appropriate to say," he said. "Things that used be considered joking might now be overheard and offend someone."

Employees who send or receive e-mail jokes or other material that's not work related also need to exercise some caution, Berger said.

"Common sense should prevail," he said.

Birth of the Ethics Industry

JAMES C. HYATT

Board of directors resigning,
My auditor's front page news.
My CFO's calling in from Rio,
I got the Sarbanes-Oxley blues.
　　　　　—posting by a Denver banking firm.

A lot of companies are singing the compliance blues these days, as they struggle to cope with the complexities of Sarbanes-Oxley legislation, passed in 2002 in the wake of financial scandals. Complaints about the cost and time involved are common, but there's another effect of Sarbanes-Oxley less remarked upon. Corporations are rushing to learn ethics virtually overnight, and as they do so, a vast new industry of consultants and suppliers has emerged. The ethics industry has been born.

Consider a few examples of recent mushrooming attention to ethics. At Goldman Sachs, CEO Hank Paulson will moderate 20 forums this year on ethics, for the bank's entire staff of managing directors. Citigroup is adding annual ethics training for all 300,000 employees, and The New York Times Co. is doing likewise.

Where do such firms turn for help? The New York Times signed a multi-year agreement with LRN, an 11-year-old Los Angeles-based firm that helped advise the U.S. Sentencing Commission on effective compliance programs. LRN will provide a legal and ethics education program, including a customized course on the company's business ethics policy. LRN CEO Dov Seidman says his business has at least doubled in the last two years. Growth is also rapid at EthicsPoint, a five-year-old Portland, Ore. firm that is one of three leading providers of ethics hotline services. Section 301 of Sarbanes-Oxley (SOX, as it's often called) requires board audit committees to create a reporting system to receive complaints and tips. In the past, nearly two out of three companies used internal systems, says EthicsPoint CEO David Childers. "But in the last year, there has been a dramatic wave of going to outside providers," he adds. Studies have found employees are 50 percent more likely to use a hotline managed out of house. "People are afraid of retaliation and that anonymity can be breached," he says. Among EthicsPoint's clients are Ceridian, First Federal Bankshares Inc., and Syracuse University.

The faces behind these ethics services include people like Kevin Kelton, 48, who spent 24 years writing TV scripts for *Saturday Night Live* and *Night Court*, and now is a "content author manager" for LRN. Kelton directs six in-house writers to prepare lessons on a variety of ethical and legal issues for LRN, which offers a web-based education platform with more than 200 modules.

Kelton's new job isn't that different from his old one, he insists. The challenge is to engage audiences, "not so much as entertainment as to keep the user emotionally involved." Thus, the ethics writers might prepare a script on how an executive ran afoul of conflict-of-interest rules, illustrating how such behavior didn't square with ethics rules.

Julie, 24, a recent college graduate, works in a West Coast call center for EthicsPoint, fielding hotline inquiries over the phone and the web, on issues ranging from suspected fraud to sexual harassment. (Her last name remains confidential due to the nature of her job.) "My boss describes it more as 911 dispatch," Julie said. Most calls aren't ethics related, and only 9 to 10 percent are SOX-related. More than half involve human resource issues such as complaints about harassment or workplace conditions.

Callers, she finds, are often upset or angry, not able to tell the full story. It may take her two hours to elicit enough information to forward to a client (while protecting the caller's identity). The hardest part of her job: "Not giving advice."

R ecruiting for the ethics army is vigorous. Craigslist—the free community search engine—recently listed 64 jobs in San Francisco and 50 in Boston that included the word "Sarbanes." Monster.com—a broader job search engine—tallies more than 1,000 and, on a recent check, 158 posted in "the last 24 hours."

Not all new "Sarbanes" jobs are directly tied to ethics, since the legislation focuses on accounting control systems, creating a boom in accounting positions. The Public Company Accounting Oversight Board, created by SOX, has a $136 million budget and should have 450 employees by the end of this year.

At major firms, there has been a boom in new ethics officer positions, with such positions being filled recently at the New York Stock Exchange, Marsh & McLennan, Nortel Networks, and Computer Associates International, among many others.

Kerry D. Moynihan, a managing partner at recruiting firm Christian & Timbers, reports "more and more work" helping companies find executives to handle compliance issues, with job titles ranging from chief compliance officer or general counsel to vice president of human relations. At financial companies, in particular, such officials are called upon to be "much more accountable to boards and to federal regulators." And more companies "are creating offices around things like corporate social responsibility officer."

There was a time, he says, when compliance duties landed in the lap of "the green eyeshade people you didn't want as front men. Now they are much more front of the house, three doors down from the chief executive." Wall Street compliance officers that used to make $350,000 to $450,000 a year now can command $750,000 or a million dollars in salary, he reports. And he expects demand to continue. He predicts hedge funds, for instance, will be subject to SEC regulations by 2006. And mutual funds will need help "coming up to speed."

Ethics officers often wear more than one hat. At Lubrizol Corp., in Wyckliffe, Oh., Mark Meister has been vice president for human relations as well as chief ethics officer since 1994. He finds the duties have expanded substantially over the years. Currently, two people work with him on ethics part-time, helping with tasks like posting ethics guidelines in seven languages, and overseeing 27 regional ethics leaders around the world whom employees can contact with questions. The company currently is rolling out its ethics program to 3,000 new employees who've joined Lubrizol, a specialty chemicals company, through an acquisition.

To convince employees it's serious about ethics, Lubrizol frequently notes the experience of CEO James Hambrick. When he oversaw business in the former Soviet Union, "he came back and said basically we can have our business plan or our ethics policy, but not both. We walked away from business as a result," Meister says. The story "lets people know you can make ethical decisions and be successful in this organization."

Venture capital money is flowing into the ethics industry these days, as a result of the boom. The training business Midi Corp. of Princeton, N.J., was acquired a year ago with $7 million in venture capital and "more money has been guaranteed when we need it," said CEO Bette Tomaszewicz. In one year, company employees have grown from 20 to nearly 70.

Midi has developed more than 50 different courses on legal and ethical topics, and is adding 20 courses a year. The material, available as online videos, is designed to "have a long mental shelf life," said Jeffrey M. Kaplan, a Midi vice president. "Nobody ever asks an employee to commit a crime three days after training," he says. "The devil on your shoulder is always pretty big: your boss or a customer in your face. The question is, what is your little angel going to say? We want our training to give the devil a run for his money."

Kaplan says what's driving the ethics boom is not so much the SOX legislation, as the increased tendency of prosecutors and regulators to take ethics programs into account when considering charges. Midi also sees demand for training on the Foreign Corrupt Practices Act, antitrust issues, and harassment.

One Sarbanes-related script Midi produced depicts a sales executive persuading a customer to help inflate sales numbers by accepting goods that can be returned later. The sales person, in turn, asks another employee to help cover up the arrangement. The second employee considers reporting the problem, but doesn't, lies to an FBI agent, threatens a whistleblower, and eventually goes to prison—a chain of events "you're likely to remember for a long time," Kaplan says. Midi's sales, about $2 million last year, are projected to balloon to $8 to $10 million this year, possibly $20 million next year.

In this new era of growth, established ethics-related businesses are re-creating themselves. Global Compliance Services, in Charlotte, N.C.—the largest hotline provider—traces its business to AlertLine, set up in 1981 to help defense contractors identify fraud. The business eventually became part of the Pinkerton security company, and it now provides services to half of the Fortune 500. In 2003, two Pinkerton businesses were purchased in a management buyout, and the new company has embarked on a drive to expand in the current receptive climate. CEO Dennis Muse says AlertLine gets 25,000 calls a month, with topics ranging from ethics charges to a manager's behavior.

Reaching out beyond ethics, Pinkerton recently launched a service called "Stakeholder," providing a way for stakeholders like shareholders, customers, or contractors to voice concerns.

Software companies have found a bonanza in Sarbanes-Oxley. "Last year (2004), we more than tripled our revenue," declares Ed Thomas, product marketing manager for OpenPages, Waltham, Mass., a maker of governance, risk, and compliance management software. He expects similar growth this year.

The company's SOX Express software helps companies automate the compliance process of documenting internal financial controls, a SOX requirement. Next on the horizon: expanding to general risk management issues such as manufacturing and human resources. "Sarbanes is risk management for your financial department," he says.

EMC Corp., the $8 billion-revenue information storage company in Hopkinton, Mass., is also finding opportunities in what a spokesman calls the "emerging trend of records management." In 2003 the firm spent nearly $3 billion to acquire two software companies serving that market. Fueled in part by SOX demands, revenues at those two companies rose more than 20 percent in first quarter 2005. "A lot of the Sarbanes-related activity ended up being about protection and management of information," says Andrew Cohen, director and senior counsel at EMC.

At Iron Mountain Inc., the big Boston record management company, the impact of the current ethics era "has been profound," says Ken Rubin, executive vice president for corporate marketing. The collapse of Arthur Andersen and Enron moved records management "from the back room to the boardroom," he says. "How companies manage records became linked to corporate ethics and, ultimately, to brand reputation and share price." In the new atmosphere, clients "began to treat records as information assets, as footprints of action or inaction."

The price of all this new activity is enormous. AMR Research estimates that organizations this year will spend $6.1 billion on Sarbanes-Oxley; others estimate twice that amount. Large companies dealing with one of the big four accounting firms have seen their annual fees double. Technology research firm Aberdeen Group of Boston reported earlier this year that "for many mid-tier firms, the cost of complying with SOX is temporarily spelling the difference between profit and loss."

The collapse of Arthur Andersen and Enron moved records management from the back room to the boardroom. Companies now treat records as footprints of action or inaction.

At its best, though, the ethics evolution underway is about more than complying with expensive and detailed rules. It's about shifting how firms are managed, to incorporate an ethics focus. Dov Seidman, LRN's founder and CEO, likes to say he was in the ethics business "BE—Before Enron." He began LRN 10 years ago doing legal research for Fortune 500 companies, "putting out fires through expert analysis." But he soon developed a notion of "ethical capitalism as a long-term driver of business success," and launched training programs to establish "do it right cultures." LRN has worked with companies like Johnson & Johnson, Pfizer, and DuPont for years. "Ethics isn't about games," Seidman says. "Integrity is either there or it's not."

David Gebler, president of Working Values Ltd., a decade-old Boston-based business ethics consulting firm, says in the new climate, "it's often hard for organizations to make the leap to an ethical culture because they are unsure of where to start."

He adds: "It is not enough to merely ask whether controls are in place or if everyone has attended a class or signed a code. The organization has to understand what the drivers of behavior are," and how those align with integrity goals.

Brian Gontarski, director of business development at Working Values, says an organization's code of conduct, its values, and its business goals may be created by separate units. "We strive to find the point where they all intersect," so ethics is seen "as a way of doing business, not just following the company line."

Over time, as boards get more involved, the new focus on ethical behavior will only expand, says Mary Ann Jorgenson, a partner in Cleveland-based Squire, Sanders & Dempsey LLP. "What's changed dramatically is that CEOs are moving away from the inclination to control board discussions," becoming willing to hear other points of view, she says. Her job as an advisor is to "make people comfortable with the exercise of independent judgment and to understand what constructive skepticism is."

It may all be working. There are indications that the focus on ethics is bearing fruit.

The National Benchmark Study by the University of Michigan and research firm Employee Motivation & Performance Assessment looks at a variety of working condition measures, and it found that among 1,000 major companies, the only statistically significant change in 2004 was a jump in companies' scores for "ethics and fairness."

Surveying financial executives, Oversight Systems Inc., Atlanta found that most have seen bottom-line benefits from SOX compliance. Nearly half, 49 percent, say SOX compliance reduced the risk of fraud and errors, and 48 percent say it made financial operations more efficient.

There are always critics, of course, and they're making a buck as well. CafePress, selling customized merchandise online, is offering mugs priced at $15.99 that are emblazoned with the words, "Sox Stinks!"

JAMES C. HYATT (jchyatt@yahoo.com), a Princeton, N.J., freelance writer, formerly was a reporter and editor for *The Wall Street Journal*.

Learning to Love Whistleblowers

Some businesses that once feared whistleblowers are now giving workers new ways to report wrongdoing.

DARREN DAHL

Marvin windows and doors is a family-owned business in Warroad, Minnesota, and one of the world's largest custom manufacturers of wooden windows and doors. In 2005, the company grossed an estimated $500 million. As sales have increased, so has Marvin's work force, which now tops 5,500 employees spread among a dozen plants, including one in Honduras. To keep track of all these workers, the company recently implemented what software makers call a whistle-blowing system. It allows workers to anonymously submit tips, suggestions, and complaints to top executives in either English or Spanish about anything from safety conditions to bad managers to fraud and theft. "We want to demonstrate that we are serious about establishing an ethical culture," says senior vice president and general counsel Steve Tourek.

Marvin Windows is not alone in setting up a system that encourages whistle-blowing. An industry has sprung up to make it easy for employees to alert their bosses to trouble, and vendors report that clients include businesses of all sizes. One company with just nine workers recently signed up with EthicsPoint, a vendor that sets up toll-free 24-hour call centers and websites. Systems vary in price, but most start at about $12,000 per year, plus a sign-up fee.

The systems can also be used by companies to keep an eye on their top executives. Many systems will automatically route to a designated outside board member any tip that implicates a member of the management team like the CEO or the CFO.

The popularity of whistle-blowing systems is due in large part to the Sarbanes-Oxley Act of 2002, which compels public companies to establish procedures for identifying wrongdoing. Whistle-blowing software had been around for at least a decade, but after Congress passed the law, software firms created a lot of new applications, thinking that companies covered by the law would want them. To the surprise of many people in the industry, sales of whistle-blowing systems to private companies, which are not covered by Sarbanes-Oxley, are also on the rise. By using their employees as an early-warning system, employers seek to head off problems before they spiral out of control.

What Exactly Is an Internal Control?

The idea of companies soliciting whistleblowers would have seemed ridiculous a decade ago, when many executives viewed them as troublemakers and attention-seekers. Corporate scandals changed that. This year, 88 percent of respondents to a survey of public and private companies agreed that encouraging whistleblowers is good for business, according to Tatum Partners, a financial consulting firm based in Atlanta.

These results contrast with the conventional hatred of Sarbanes-Oxley, which bas been blamed repeatedly for a range of corporate maladies from overzealous auditing to the torpid market for initial public offerings. One requirement in particular—that companies establish adequate "internal controls"—has been held up for criticism because the law doesn't spell out what an internal control is. Software companies have positioned whistleblower software as a suitable control.

To some extent, this sales pitch has worked. Many public companies have purchased whistleblower systems in the past few years. So have some privately held businesses that are compelled to adopt Sarbanes-Oxley-related policies by publicly held joint venture partners or customers or lenders. Then there are private firms that install these systems simply because they see real value in them. In a recent survey, PricewaterhouseCoopers found that 60 percent of private companies that have voluntarily adopted the regulations did so because they thought they were the "best business practices," while 59 percent felt that they would help a company address potential problems.

A Way to Avoid Jail Time

Some evidence suggests that it's wise for employers to implement any kind of system that encourages workers to speak up. In a 2004 study of 508 companies where occupational fraud occurred, the Association of Certified Fraud Examiners found that companies that uncovered troubling activity were more likely to find out about it from a co-worker's tip than from an internal or external audit. Moreover, organizations that bad anonymous reporting systems in place suffered less than half

Table 1   Quiz: Name the Famous Whistleblowers

Many corporate and government truthtellers have enjoyed 15 minutes of fame, movie deals included.

1971	1974	1984	1993	2001	2002	2002	2003
a. This State Department officer slipped the **Pentagon Papers** to *The New York Times.*	**b.** This blue-collar worker raised **Plutonium plant safety concerns** before her untimely death.	**c.** She alleged **sexual harassment** at the "North Country" coal mine where she worked.	**d.** This ex-Brown & Williamson "insider" alleged that the **tobacco industry** made cigarettes more addictive.	**e.** He kicked off the most recent wave of corporate scandals when he alleged fraud at telecom **Global Crossing.**	**f.** One of *Time's* persons of the year, she detailed accounting irregularities at **Enron.**	**g.** This **WorldCom** auditor, another of *Time's* heroes, investigated $3.8 billion in accounting irregularities.	**h.** This Army Corps of Engineers official criticized **no-bid contracts** received by a Halliburton subsidiary in Iraq.

Quiz Answer Key

a. Daniel Ellsberg b. Karen Silkwood c. Lois Jensen
d. Jeffrey Wigand e. Roy Olofson f. Sherron Watkins
g. Cynthia Cooper h. Bunnatine H. Greenhouse

the financial losses from fraud sustained by companies without such systems.

There are other incentives for encouraging whistle-blowing. Sections 301 and 404 of Sarbanes-Oxley, which compel companies to maintain an ethical culture and a system of internal controls, have roots in the Federal Sentencing Guidelines for corporate crime and fraud that were established in 1991. These guidelines provide federal judges with a set of standards to use in doling out punishment for all companies, public or private, that are convicted of a crime. If a company can demonstrate that it has tried to develop an ethical culture, such as by adopting a whistleblower system, a judge may be lenient in handing out fines and jail time.

Fears of False Accusations

Nonetheless, there is one risk that most managers think long and hard about before they sign up. What happens if employees swamp the system with petty grievances? What if a worker fabricates an allegation? These were Gerald Massey's initial concerns. Massey is the CEO of Fios, a Portland, Oregon, company that lawyers hire to inspect computer equipment for information pertaining to a lawsuit. Because his firm was in the business of uncovering the misdeeds of companies involved in litigation or under investigation, Massey was predisposed to see the benefits of whistle-blowing software. And Fios had

long since outgrown its trusty employee suggestion box, with 120 employees spread out among offices in four states. Even so, Massey says, "my board and I were worried that we would be opening a Pandora's box."

Massey's system went live in the fall of 2004, and some of his fears were certainly justified: Fios' 120 workers submitted more than 30 suggestions in the first 18 months. This usage was high. Most vendors say that the average annual volume of tips is a manageable four per every 100 employees. And, says Massey, all but two of these complaints were minor. This is typical. Vendors estimate that only about 3 percent of all tips involve a serious disclosure. For workers to trust the system to work, however, little gripes cannot be ignored, experts say. Every report must be taken seriously, and there can be no retaliation. Still, most managers are happy to field minor complaints about HR issues (which they should probably address anyway) in return for added vigilance about crucial legal and financial issues.

The enduring legacy of Sarbanes-Oxley and the recent scandals may be a change in the way companies look at employees who are unafraid to raise red flags. "We want the company to do the right thing," says Marvin Windows' Steve Tourek. "And we want to give our employees a place to tell us when we aren't."

DARREN DAHL can be e-mailed at DDahl@inc.com.

On Witnessing a Fraud

Saying no to the scam was easy, but deciding whether to report it was harder.

Don Soeken

Skiers in bright parkas swooshed by on the slopes as Joe pushed open the gleaming silver doors of the Highland Ski Club, ready to begin another day as computer technician. It was expensive living in the tourist town of Bastcliff, Colo., but Joe loved it. Little did he know, on this fine November morning, of the emotional storm that approached just inside the doors.

The nightmare began innocently enough, when a supervisor tapped Joe on the shoulder and murmured, "We've had an energy surge in the computer system. Will you check out the damage and report to the club manager?"

"Sure thing," said Joe. "I'll get right on it."

He found a relatively minor problem. The surge had fried a few underground wires and computer circuits, which would have to be replaced at a cost of about $15,000. When Joe reported this to the supervisor and the club manager, their response surprised him. They asked him to dig up nearly all the underground wire and cable, then dispose of it before the insurance adjuster arrived. If that were done, the cost of the repair job paid by the insurance company would come to $600,000.

"Wow, I don't think that's something I want to do," Joe told them. But his superiors assured him that if the scam were discovered, the company would be liable rather than him personally. They also noted the plan would allow the club to install a new computer system, which Joe had been asking for.

"I'm sorry," Joe said. "It's fraud, and I refuse to be part of it."

The club manager scowled angrily, and then shrugged as Joe left the room. Minutes later Joe was dismayed to learn that his fellow employee Todd was on his way to dig up the good wiring and stash it in a dumpster far removed from the clubhouse.

To clear his head, Joe stepped out into the cold bright air. Should he report the scam, he asked himself, or let it go? What should he do?

C. Fred Alford, Professor of Government and Politics, University of Maryland, College Park

Ever since my book on whistleblowing (Whistleblowers: Broken Lives and Organizational Power) was published, I've been contacted once a month from would-be whistleblowers asking what they should do. Usually the cases are complex, both factually and ethically. The first part of this case isn't. Joe is being asked to go along with felony fraud, and he has no choice but to say no. The second part is harder: Should he inform the insurance company and possibly get his friend Todd in trouble?

My advice is yes, he should make that phone call. You can't let something like this go—it's like seeing a traffic accident and not reporting it.

Joe will no doubt be fired, and will have to find new work. But he's in field with a lot of jobs, unlike the field of nuclear engineering, for example, where whistleblowers have little chance to start over. I assume Joe has not been working at the ski club for years and years, since most of these jobs are staffed by young people looking for adventure.

If some or all of this is true, I recommend Joe move to another state, come up with a convincing explanation for the gap in his employment record, and get on with his life. Most whistleblowers want vindication—they want to fight a lawsuit for reinstatement. But it's enough to have done the right thing and move on.

Here my advice is practical rather than moral. Rather than explaining why he was fired, I'm suggesting Joe leave that job out of his resume and make something up to fill the gap. I recommend he lie. Not about having done something bad, but about having done something moral.

Don Soeken's Comments

Even at the risk of losing his job, Joe behaved with the ethical integrity he had been taught to value during childhood: he refused to be part of a fraud. Joe did what too many of us are afraid to do, in standing up for what's right.

As for reporting the fraud, I agree that Joe must call the insurance company. Prof. Alford introduces a surprising twist, in suggesting that when Joe loses his job, he should lie to smooth out his employment record. This is a question on which I think good people will disagree. I recommend that Joe keep the resume correct and list someone at the ski club who could help him get another job.

What Actually Happened

Joe reported the $600,000 attempted fraud to the insurance company, and admitted to his bosses he was the whistleblower. He was fired. The ski club received money from the insurance company, which was slow to investigate, and the outcome of that investigation is unknown. No negative consequences happened to Joe's coworker who dug up the cable. Joe later discovered the ski club had defrauded insurance companies on several occasions.

Joe found it hard to get another job, since his personnel file held a negative assessment of his job performance. Several evaluations said he had "problems with authority." Before the whistleblowing, similar evaluations had described Joe's work as superior. Soon, Joe was struggling with clinical depression.

He filed a lawsuit to seek various kinds of compensation— including lost wages. After years of legal wrangling, the judge ordered both mediation and settlement talks. Joe settled for an undisclosed payment. The company did not admit wrongdoing.

DON SOEKEN (helpline@tidal wave.net) is director of Integrity International, which provides counseling support and expert witness testimony for whistleblowers. See www.whistleblowing.us.

All cases in What Would You Do? are real, though disguised.

From *Business Ethics,* Summer 2004, vol. 18, pp. 14. Copyright © 2004 by Business Ethics Magazine. Reprinted by permission.

Erasing 'Un' from 'Unemployable'

Walgreen program trains the disabled to take on regular wage-paying jobs.

AMY MERRICK

L ike many people with autism, Harrison Mullinax, a pale, redheaded 18-year-old with a serious expression, speaks in a monotonous, halting voice and sometimes struggles to concentrate on tasks. Unlike most who are autistic, he now has a real job.

Mr. Mullinax works eight hours a day at a new Walgreen Co. distribution center, where he wields a bar-code scanner, checking in boxes of merchandise bound for the company's drugstores. From his paycheck, he tithes to his church and sometimes treats his mother to dinner at Kenny's, a local buffet restaurant.

An innovative program at the distribution center is offering jobs to people with mental and physical disabilities of a nature that has frequently deemed them "unemployable," while saving Walgreen money through automation.

"It answered a prayer," says Mr. Mullinax's mother, Vikki, who gets him up for work at 5 each morning, before sending him off to the bus for work. "It's given us the hope that at some point Harrison can live with minimal assistance."

A number of large employers, such as McDonald's Corp. and Wal-Mart Stores Inc., recruit people with disabilities to be cashiers, maintenance workers or store greeters. At Home Depot Inc., developmentally disabled workers stock shelves, clean displays and help customers find items. Home Depot has been working with a nonprofit organization called Ken's Kids, which was formed a decade ago by a group of parents seeking employment opportunities for their young-adult children, and has placed more than 100 people in 54 stores. In addition, smaller businesses around the nation have made a goal of employing workers passed over by other companies.

Still, executives at Walgreen and the social-services agencies working with it believe the company's program has a larger number of disabled employees, doing more-sophisticated work, than is typically available to people with mental and physical challenges.

Mr. Mullinax, like many of Walgreen's employees with disabilities, learned his job in a large metal-clad shed 15 minutes down the road from the distribution center. There, trainees learn how to work in one of three departments: "case check-in," where workers initially receive merchandise; "de-trash," where they unpack the goods; and "picking," where they sort the products into tubs based on individual store orders.

The distribution center opened in January at a cost of $175 million. It currently employs 264 people, more than 40% of whom have various disabilities, and it is 20% more efficient than the company's older facilities. On some days, disabled employees are its most productive workers.

"One thing we found is they can all do the job," says Randy Lewis, a senior vice president of distribution and logistics at Walgreen, which is based in Deerfield, Ill. "What surprised us is the environment that it's created. It's a building where everybody helps each other out."

When they make the transition to the distribution center, disabled employees at first have a job coach. Those needing it learn social skills, from the importance of wearing deodorant to finding appropriate conversation topics.

The idea began four years ago, when Mr. Lewis was evaluating new technology that could make Walgreen's next round of distribution centers far more automated than in the past. Mr. Lewis asked: Could Walgreen make the work simple enough to employ people with cognitive disabilities?

For him, the question was personal. His 19-year-old son, Austin, has autism. "I'm keenly aware of the lack of opportunities for kids like that," he says. Among people with the disability, the unemployment rate can be as high as 95%, according to social-service agencies.

Because employing disabled people wasn't expected to affect the distribution center's costs or efficiency, it wasn't difficult for Mr. Lewis to persuade the Walgreen board and David Bernauer, then the company's chief executive and now its chairman, to try the project. "The fact that we can use disabled people for this was a great plus," Mr. Bernauer says. "It didn't move the needle on the business decision."

As part of the program, Walgreen converted its computer displays from lines of type to touch screens with a few icons. It persuaded vendors to include more information in bar codes on merchandise, so that employees wouldn't have to enter so much data themselves. It redesigned work stations so that people don't have to stretch as far, and it added help buttons to summon assistance. Instead of posting printed cards to remind workers about having their bags inspected, Walgreen shows a video of someone opening a bag.

Angela Campbell, the facility's career-outreach coordinator, suggested adding pictures to numbered work stations. In the "de-trash" area, where workers remove merchandise from boxes and prepare it to be sorted for individual stores, there are images of farm animals.

Ms. Campbell, who has cerebral palsy and carefully maneuvers the building's many flights of stairs, tells employees they should feel comfortable asking her awkward questions about why someone looks or behaves a certain way. "I know what it's like to fight your whole life to have an employer look past your disability," she says.

All workers are constantly monitored to track whether they're meeting productivity goals. One day, workers with disabilities topped the productivity list in three major departments, says Keith Scarbrough, the distribution center's manager.

Many trainees volunteer their time to learn, sometimes spending as much as a year without pay. Anderson County arranges transportation for many employees to get to work. Walgreen estimates that if it reaches its goal of employing 200 workers with disabilities, the value of the government benefits it receives will be about $3.5 million.

Starting pay at the distribution center is $10.85 an hour, climbing to $13.80 an hour after two years.

The disabilities of workers at the center run the gamut and present the supervisory staff with a variety of challenges. Desiree Neff, 43, struggles with her balance and uses a walker, her 26-year-old son and co-worker, Troy Mayben, is legally blind. Recently, Ms. Neff wanted to learn how to operate a forklift so she could expand her skills, but she didn't have a place to put her walker. An engineer devised a clamp that attaches the walker to the forklift.

In another case, managers didn't know what to do about a disruptive employee who screamed "Hello!" every morning. Some argued that the behavior was part of the worker's disability. But Deb Russell, the career-outreach manager for Walgreen, reasoned, "We don't allow anyone else to do that." She instructed workers to ignore his shouting. Within two days, she says, he stopped.

As for Vikki Mullinax, she says now that Harrison is working, she can spend more time with her husband and 16-year-old daughter. Harrison "has improved tremendously," she says.

Harrison Mullinax says he has made friends, and he likes being paid. Working at Walgreen, he says, has taught him how to offer help to others and "not to cuss anybody out."

The Ethics of Edits

When a crook changes the contract.

Shel Horowitz

When Richard fired Susan for insubordination, she was a department head who had worked her way up from an entry-level finance job. Richard asked Susan to sign a document that released the company from any claims related to her termination. She signed without protest and left the company. Once Susan was gone, things got weird. Something wasn't right with the audits, previously handled by Susan. A thorough investigation led to the discovery that Susan had embezzled more than $800,000 from Richard's company. Richard also learned she had been prosecuted for stealing thousands of dollars from a previous employer and was sentenced to three years' probation.

And when Richard sued her to regain the money, he received another shock: Susan had edited the termination contract, adding a clause that eliminated the company's ability to recover any claims against her. She had not told the company about the changes she made, which were not initialed on the document. But she freely admitted that she had doctored it. Richard had prepared the original document and did not realize Susan had changed it. And, because he was not aware of her previous conviction for large-scale fraud, he signed it without re-reading it—and without catching the alteration.

It is unfortunate that Richard did not exercise due diligence and check the document for unilateral changes before signing it. Software exists that would have surfaced these changes instantly.

Richard was clearly negligent and erred in not thoroughly reading the version of the document Susan signed. But it seems reasonable to conclude that the more grievous offense, likely to reach to fraud, is the cloaked change made by Susan, which protected her against any claims against her. Richard should consult counsel to explore ways to seek a legal remedy.

In the meantime, this case offers an interesting moment in which civil and moral law coincide. At its core is the principle of disclosure. Often at the heart of legal breaches, such as accounting irregularities, is the absence of disclosure. Similarly, a lack of disclosure is often the hallmark of moral and ethical lapses. Even a two-year-old child recognizes Randall as the villain in the film Monsters, Inc. Why? Because Randall operates in darkness and often appears in a slithering fashion, unannounced. The bottom line: If an issue is "on the table," it is more likely to be ethical; if it is "under the table" and cloaked, there is more likelihood of a legal and/or ethical lapse.

What Actually Happened

This case is still in the courts, and the laws in Richard's state are, unfortunately, ambiguous. Richard's lawyers argue that the document he signed was not the document he had prepared, and because he was not made aware of the changes, his signature was fraudulently obtained. Susan's lawyers say that he should have read the entire contract through again, and that the signature is binding.

All of this begs the question: How did Susan gain so much trust that she was able to embezzle that much money so easily? Here's Richard's analysis: "She was easy to manage. I got lulled to sleep. She always took direction, never complained, was compliant with all requests, and was very good at being a friend to everyone. She invited her department to her home each year, treated them well and in a nurturing way, and was their trusted advisor. When it came to tenure, this department, finance, had the best. It is very hard to figure this out when you are being manipulated by a master. Her every move was calculated and I was dealing from the perspective of trust and reasonableness."

Lessons Learned

Susan's betrayal caused a major wake-up call for Richard and for his company. Richard accepts responsibility for both failing to require adequate back-ground checks as Susan worked her way up to positions of greater authority, and for neglecting to re-read the contract after Susan re-turned it. These days, everyone who works for Richard, even a model employee (as Susan had appeared to be) undergoes rigorous screening before hiring or promotion. "We do credit checks, criminal checks, call every reference and check every previous employer."

SHEL HOROWITZ, author of *Principled Profit: Marketing That Puts People First,* initiated the Business Ethics Pledge movement at www.business-ethics-pledge.org.

The Parable of the Sadhu

**After encountering a dying pilgrim on a climbing trip
in the Himalayas, a businessman ponders the differences
between individual and corporate ethics.**

Bowen H. McCoy

Last year, as the first participant in the new six-month sabbatical program that Morgan Stanley has adopted, I enjoyed a rare opportunity to collect my thoughts as well as do some traveling. I spent the first three months in Nepal, walking 600 miles through 200 villages in the Himalayas and climbing some 120,000 vertical feet. My sole Western companion on the trip was an anthropologist who shed light on the cultural patterns of the villages that we passed through.

During the Nepal hike, something occurred that has had a powerful impact on my thinking about corporate ethics. Although some might argue that the experience has no relevance to business, it was a situation in which a basic ethical dilemma suddenly intruded into the lives of a group of individuals. How the group responded holds a lesson for all organizations, no matter how defined.

The Sadhu

The Nepal experience was more rugged than I had anticipated. Most commercial treks last two or three weeks and cover a quarter of the distance we traveled.

My friend Stephen, the anthropologist, and I were halfway through the 60-day Himalayan part of the trip when we reached the high point, an 18,000-foot pass over a crest that we'd have to traverse to reach the village of Muklinath, an ancient holy place for pilgrims.

Six years earlier, I had suffered pulmonary edema, an acute form of altitude sickness, at 16,500 feet in the vicinity of Everest base camp—so we were understandably concerned about what would happen at 18,000 feet. Moreover, the Himalayas were having their wettest spring in 20 years; hip-deep powder and ice had already driven us off one ridge. If we failed to cross the pass, I feared that the last half of our once-in-a-lifetime trip would be ruined.

The night before we would try the pass, we camped in a hut at 14,500 feet. In the photos taken at that camp, my face appears wan. The last village we'd passed through was a sturdy two-day walk below us, and I was tired.

During the late afternoon, four backpackers from New Zealand joined us, and we spent most of the night awake, anticipating the climb. Below, we could see the fires of two other parties, which turned out to be two Swiss couples and a Japanese hiking club.

To get over the steep part of the climb before the sun melted the steps cut in the ice, we departed at 3:30 A.M. The New Zealanders left first, followed by Stephen and myself, our porters and Sherpas, and then the Swiss. The Japanese lingered in their camp. The sky was clear, and we were confident that no spring storm would erupt that day to close the pass.

At 15,500 feet, it looked to me as if Stephen were shuffling and staggering a bit, which are symptoms of altitude sickness. (The initial stage of altitude sickness brings a headache and nausea. As the condition worsens, a climber may encounter difficult breathing, disorientation, aphasia, and paralysis.) I felt strong—my adrenaline was flowing—but I was very concerned about my ultimate ability to get across. A couple of our porters were also suffering from the height, and Pasang, our Sherpa sirdar (leader), was worried.

Just after daybreak, while we rested at 15,500 feet, one of the New Zealanders, who had gone ahead, came staggering down toward us with a body slung across his shoulders. He dumped the almost naked, barefoot body of an Indian holy man—a sadhu—at my feet. He had found the pilgrim lying on the ice, shivering and suffering from hypothermia. I cradled the sadhu's head and laid him out on the rocks. The New Zealander was angry. He wanted to get across the pass before the bright sun melted the snow. He said, "Look, I've done what I can. You have porters and Sherpa guides. You care for him. We're going on!" He turned and went back up the mountain to join his friends.

I took a carotid pulse and found that the sadhu was still alive. We figured he had probably visited the holy shrines at Muklinath and was on his way home. It was fruitless to question why he had chosen this desperately high route instead of the safe, heavily traveled caravan route through the Kali Gandaki gorge. Or why he was shoeless and almost naked, or how long he had been lying in the pass. The answers weren't going to solve our problem.

Stephen and the four Swiss began stripping off their outer clothing and opening their packs. The sadhu was soon clothed from head to foot. He was not able to walk, but he was very much alive. I looked down the mountain and spotted the Japanese climbers, marching up with a horse.

When I reached them, Stephen glared at me and said, "How do you feel about contributing to the death of a fellow man?"

Without a great deal of thought, I told Stephen and Pasang that I was concerned about withstanding the heights to come and wanted to get over the pass. I took off after several of our porters who had gone ahead.

On the steep part of the ascent where, if the ice steps had given way, I would have slid down about 3,000 feet, I felt vertigo. I stopped for a breather, allowing the Swiss to catch up with me. I inquired about the sadhu and Stephen. They said that the sadhu was fine and that Stephen was just behind them. I set off again for the summit.

Stephen arrived at the summit an hour after I did. Still exhilarated by victory, I ran down the slope to congratulate him. He was suffering from altitude sickness—walking 15 steps, then stopping, walking 15 steps, then stopping. Pasang accompanied him all the way up. When I reached them, Stephen glared at me and said: "How do you feel about contributing to the death of a fellow man?"

I did not completely comprehend what he meant. "Is the sadhu dead?" I inquired.

"No," replied Stephen, "but he surely will be!"

After I had gone, followed not long after by the Swiss, Stephen had remained with the sadhu. When the Japanese had arrived, Stephen had asked to use their horse to transport the sadhu down to the hut. They had refused. He had then asked Pasang to have a group of our porters carry the sadhu. Pasang had resisted the idea, saying that the porters would have to exert all their energy to get themselves over the pass. He believed they could not carry a man down 1,000 feet to the hut, reclimb the slope, and get across safely before the snow melted. Pasang had pressed Stephen not to delay any longer.

The Sherpas had carried the sadhu down to a rock in the sun at about 15,000 feet and pointed out the hut another 500 feet below. The Japanese had given him food and drink. When they had last seen him, he was listlessly throwing rocks at the Japanese party's dog, which had frightened him.

We do not know if the sadhu lived or died.

For many of the following days and evenings, Stephen and I discussed and debated our behavior toward the sadhu. Stephen is a committed Quaker with deep moral vision. He said, "I feel that what happened with the sadhu is a good example of the breakdown between the individual ethic and the corporate ethic. No one person was willing to assume ultimate responsibility for

the sadhu. Each was willing to do his bit just so long as it was not too inconvenient. When it got to be a bother, everyone just passed the buck to someone else and took off. Jesus was relevant to a more individualistic stage of society, but how do we interpret his teaching today in a world filled with large, impersonal organizations and groups?"

I defended the larger group, saying, "Look, we all cared. We all gave aid and comfort. Everyone did his bit. The New Zealander carried him down below the snow line. I took his pulse and suggested we treat him for hypothermia. You and the Swiss gave him clothing and got him warmed up. The Japanese gave him food and water. The Sherpas carried him down to the sun and pointed out the easy trail toward the hut. He was well enough to throw rocks at a dog. What more could we do?"

"You have just described the typical affluent Westerner's response to a problem. Throwing money—in this case, food and sweaters—at it, but not solving the fundamentals!" Stephen retorted.

I asked, "Where is the limit of our responsibility in a situation like this?"

"What would satisfy you?" I said. "Here we are, a group of New Zealanders, Swiss, Americans, and Japanese who have never met before and who are at the apex of one of the most powerful experiences of our lives. Some years the pass is so bad no one gets over it. What right does an almost naked pilgrim who chooses the wrong trail have to disrupt our lives? Even the Sherpas had no interest in risking the trip to help him beyond a certain point."

Stephen calmly rebutted, "I wonder what the Sherpas would have done if the sadhu had been a well-dressed Nepali, or what the Japanese would have done if the sadhu had been a well-dressed Asian, or what you would have done, Buzz, if the sadhu had been a well-dressed Western woman?"

"Where, in your opinion," I asked, "is the limit of our responsibility in a situation like this? We had our own well-being to worry about. Our Sherpa guides were unwilling to jeopardize us or the porters for the sadhu. No one else on the mountain was willing to commit himself beyond certain self-imposed limits."

Stephen said, "As individual Christians or people with a Western ethical tradition, we can fulfill our obligations in such a situation only if one, the sadhu dies in our care; two, the sadhu demonstrates to us that he can undertake the two-day walk down to the village; or three, we carry the sadhu for two days down to the village and persuade someone there to care for him."

"Leaving the sadhu in the sun with food and clothing—where he demonstrated hand-eye coordination by throwing a rock at a dog—comes close to fulfilling items one and two," I answered. "And it wouldn't have made sense to take him to the village where the people appeared to be far less caring than the Sherpas, so the third condition is impractical. Are you really saying that, no matter what the implications, we should, at the drop of a hat, have changed our entire plan?"

The Individual Versus the Group Ethic

Despite my arguments, I felt and continue to feel guilt about the sadhu. I had literally walked through a classic moral dilemma without fully thinking through the consequences. My excuses for my actions include a high adrenaline flow, a superordinate goal, and a once-in-a-lifetime opportunity—common factors in corporate situations, especially stressful ones.

Real moral dilemmas are ambiguous, and many of us hike right through them, unaware that they exist. When, usually after the fact, someone makes an issue of one, we tend to resent his or her bringing it up. Often, when the full import of what we have done (or not done) hits us, we dig into a defensive position from which it is very difficult to emerge. In rare circumstances, we may contemplate what we have done from inside a prison.

Had we mountaineers been free of stress caused by the effort and the high altitude, we might have treated the sadhu differently. Yet isn't stress the real test of personal and corporate values? The instant decisions that executives make under pressure reveal the most about personal and corporate character.

As a group, we had no process for developing a consensus. We had no sense of purpose or plan.

Among the many questions that occur to me when I ponder my experience with the sadhu are: What are the practical limits of moral imagination and vision? Is there a collective or institutional ethic that differs from the ethics of the individual? At what level of effort or commitment can one discharge one's ethical responsibilities?

Not every ethical dilemma has a right solution. Reasonable people often disagree; otherwise there would be no dilemma. In a business context, however, it is essential that managers agree on a process for dealing with dilemmas.

Our experience with the sadhu offers an interesting parallel to business situations. An immediate response was mandatory. Failure to act was a decision in itself. Up on the mountain we could not resign and submit our résumés to a headhunter. In contrast to philosophy, business involves action and implementation—getting things done. Managers must come up with answers based on what they see and what they allow to influence their decision-making processes. On the mountain, none of us but Stephen realized the true dimensions of the situation we were facing.

One of our problems was that as a group we had no process for developing a consensus. We had no sense of purpose or plan. The difficulties of dealing with the sadhu were so complex that no one person could handle them. Because the group did not have a set of preconditions that could guide its action to an acceptable resolution, we reacted instinctively as individuals. The cross-cultural nature of the group added a further layer of complexity. We had no leader with whom we could all identify and in whose purpose we believed. Only Stephen was willing to take charge, but he could not gain adequate support from the group to care for the sadhu.

Some organizations do have values that transcend the personal values of their managers. Such values, which go beyond profitability, are usually revealed when the organization is under stress. People throughout the organization generally accept its values, which, because they are not presented as a rigid list of commandments, may be somewhat ambiguous. The stories people tell, rather than printed materials, transmit the organization's conceptions of what is proper behavior.

For 20 years, I have been exposed at senior levels to a variety of corporations and organizations. It is amazing how quickly an outsider can sense the tone and style of an organization and, with that, the degree of tolerated openness and freedom to challenge management.

Organizations that do not have a heritage of mutually accepted, shared values tend to become unhinged during stress, with each individual bailing out for himself or herself. In the great takeover battles we have witnessed during past years, companies that had strong cultures drew the wagons around them and fought it out, while other companies saw executives—supported by golden parachutes—bail out of the struggles.

Because corporations and their members are interdependent, for the corporation to be strong the members need to share a preconceived notion of correct behavior, a "business ethic," and think of it as a positive force, not a constraint.

As an investment banker, I am continually warned by well-meaning lawyers, clients, and associates to be wary of conflicts of interest. Yet if I were to run away from every difficult situation, I wouldn't be an effective investment banker. I have to feel my way through conflicts. An effective manager can't run from risk either; he or she has to confront risk. To feel "safe" in doing that, managers need the guidelines of an agreed-upon process and set of values within the organization.

After my three months in Nepal, I spent three months as an executive-in-residence at both the Stanford Business School and the University of California at Berkeley's Center for Ethics and Social Policy of the Graduate Theological Union. Those six months away from my job gave me time to assimilate 20 years of business experience. My thoughts turned often to the meaning of the leadership role in any large organization. Students at the seminary thought of themselves as antibusiness. But when I questioned them, they agreed that they distrusted all large organizations, including the church. They perceived all large organizations as impersonal and opposed to individual values and needs. Yet we all know of organizations in which people's values and beliefs are respected and their expressions encouraged. What makes the difference? Can we identify the difference and, as a result, manage more effectively?

The word *ethics* turns off many and confuses more. Yet the notions of shared values and an agreed-upon process for dealing with adversity and change—what many people mean when they talk about corporate culture—seem to be at the heart of the ethical issue. People who are in touch with their own core beliefs and the beliefs of others and who are sustained by them can be more comfortable living on the cutting edge. At times, taking a tough line or a decisive stand in a muddle of ambiguity

When Do We Take a Stand?

I wrote about my experiences purposely to present an ambiguous situation. I never found out if the sadhu lived or died. I can attest, though, that the sadhu lives on in his story. He lives in the ethics classes I teach each year at business schools and churches. He lives in the class-rooms of numerous business schools, where professors have taught the case to tens of thousands of students. He lives in several casebooks on ethics and on an educational video. And he lives in organizations such as the American Red Cross and AT&T, which use his story in their ethics training.

As I reflect on the sadhu now, 15 years after the fact, I first have to wonder, What actually happened on that Himalayan slope? When I first wrote about the event, I reported the experience in as much detail as I could remember, but I shaped it to the needs of a good classroom discussion. After years of reading my story, viewing it on video, and hearing others discuss it, I'm not sure I myself know what actually occurred on the mountainside that day!

I've also heard a wide variety of responses to the story. The sadhu, for example, may not have wanted our help at all—he may have been intentionally bringing on his own death as a way to holiness. Why had he taken the danger-ous way over the pass instead of the caravan route through the gorge? Hindu businesspeople have told me that in trying to assist the sadhu, we were being typically arrogant West-erners imposing our cultural values on the world.

I've learned that each year along the pass, a few Nepali porters are left to freeze to death outside the tents of the unthinking tourists who hired them. A few years ago, a French group even left one of their own, a young French woman, to die there. The difficult pass seems to demonstrate a perverse version of Gresham's law of currency: The bad practices of previous travelers have driven out the values that new travelers might have followed if they were at home. Perhaps that helps to explain why our porters behaved as they did and why it was so difficult for Stephen or anyone else to establish a different approach on the spot.

Our Sherpa sirdar, Pasang, was focused on his respon-sibility for bringing us up the mountain safe and sound. (His livelihood and status in the Sherpa ethnic group depended on our safe return.) We were weak, our party was split, the porters were well on their way to the top with all our gear and food, and a storm would have separated us irrevocably from our logistical base.

The fact was, we had no plan for dealing with the contin-gency of the sadhu. There was nothing we could do to unite our multicultural group in the little time we had. An ethical dilemma had come upon us unexpectedly, an element of drama that may explain why the sadhu's story has contin-ued to attract students.

I am often asked for help in teaching the story. I usu-ally advise keeping the details as ambiguous as possible. A true ethical dilemma requires a decision between two hard choices. In the case of the sadhu, we had to decide how much to sacrifice ourselves to take care of a stranger. And given the constraints of our trek, we had to make a group decision, not an individual one. If a large majority of students in a class ends up thinking I'm a bad person because of my decision on the mountain, the instructor may not have given the case its due. The same is true if the majority sees no problem with the choices we made.

Any class's response depends on its setting, whether it's a business school, a church, or a corporation. I've found that younger students are more likely to see the issue as black-and-white, whereas older ones tend to see shades of gray. Some have seen a conflict between the different ethi-cal approaches that we followed at the time. Stephen felt he had to do everything he could to save the sadhu's life, in accordance with his Christian ethic of compassion. I had a utilitarian response: do the greatest good for the greatest number. Give a burst of aid to minimize the sadhu's expo-sure, then continue on our way.

The basic question of the case remains, When do we take a stand? When do we allow a "sadhu" to intrude into our daily lives? Few of us can afford the time or effort to take care of every needy person we encounter. How much must we give of ourselves? And how do we prepare our organiza-tions and institutions so they will respond appropriately in a crisis? How do we influence them if we do not agree with their points of view?

We cannot quit our jobs over every ethical dilemma, but if we continually ignore our sense of values, who do we become? As a journalist asked at a recent conference on eth-ics, "Which ditch are we willing to die in?" For each of us, the answer is a bit different. How we act in response to that ques-tion defines better than anything else who we are, just as, in a collective sense, our acts define our institutions. In effect, the sadhu is always there, ready to remind us of the tensions between our own goals and the claims of strangers.

is the only ethical thing to do. If a manager is indecisive about a problem and spends time trying to figure out the "good" thing to do, the enterprise may be lost.

Business ethics, then, has to do with the authenticity and integrity of the enterprise. To be ethical is to follow the busi-ness as well as the cultural goals of the corporation, its owners, its employees, and its customers. Those who cannot serve the corporate vision are not authentic businesspeople and, there-fore, are not ethical in the business sense.

At this stage of my own business experience, I have a strong interest in organizational behavior. Sociologists are keenly studying what they call corporate stories, legends, and heroes as a way organizations have of transmitting value systems. Corporations such as Arco have even hired consultants to perform an audit of their corporate culture. In a company, a leader is a person who understands, interprets, and manages the corporate value system. Effective managers, therefore, are action-oriented people who resolve conflict, are tolerant of ambiguity, stress, and change, and have a strong sense of purpose for themselves and their organizations.

If all this is true, I wonder about the role of the professional manager who moves from company to company. How can he or she quickly absorb the values and culture of different organizations? Or is there, indeed, an art of management that is totally transportable? Assuming that such fungible managers do exist, is it proper for them to manipulate the values of others?

What would have happened had Stephen and I carried the sadhu for two days back to the village and become involved with the villagers in his care? In four trips to Nepal, my most interesting experience occurred in 1975 when I lived in a Sherpa home in the Khumbu for five days while recovering from altitude sickness. The high point of Stephen's trip was an invitation to participate in a family funeral ceremony in Manang. Neither experience had to do with climbing the high passes of the Himalayas. Why were we so reluctant to try the lower path, the ambiguous trail? Perhaps because we did not have a leader who could reveal the greater purpose of the trip to us.

Why didn't Stephen, with his moral vision, opt to take the sadhu under his personal care? The answer is partly because Stephen was hard-stressed physically himself and partly because, without some support system that encompassed our involuntary and episodic community on the mountain, it was beyond his individual capacity to do so.

I see the current interest in corporate culture and corporate value systems as a positive response to pessimism such as Stephen's about the decline of the role of the individual in large organizations. Individuals who operate from a thoughtful set of personal values provide the foundation for a corporate culture. A corporate tradition that encourages freedom of inquiry, supports personal values, and reinforces a focused sense of direction can fulfill the need to combine individuality with the prosperity and success of the group. Without such corporate support, the individual is lost.

That is the lesson of the sadhu. In a complex corporate situation, the individual requires and deserves the support of the group. When people cannot find such support in their organizations, they don't know how to act. If such support is forthcoming, a person has a stake in the success of the group and can add much to the process of establishing and maintaining a corporate culture. Management's challenge is to be sensitive to individual needs, to shape them, and to direct and focus them for the benefit of the group as a whole.

For each of us the sadhu lives. Should we stop what we are doing and comfort him; or should we keep trudging up toward the high pass? Should I pause to help the derelict I pass on the street each night as I walk by the Yale Club en route to Grand Central Station? Am I his brother? What is the nature of our responsibility if we consider ourselves to be ethical persons? Perhaps it is to change the values of the group so that it can, with all its resources, take the other road.

BOWEN H. MCCOY retired from Morgan Stanley in 1990 after 28 years of service. He is now a real estate and business counselor, a teacher and a philanthropist.

Editor's Note: This article was originally published in the September–October 1983 issue of HBR. For its republication as an HBR Classic, Bowen H. McCoy has written the commentary "When Do We Take a Stand?" to update his observations.

Academic Values and the Lure of Profit

DEREK BOK

John Le Carré's latest novel, *The Constant Gardener*, tells of the murder of a young woman in Africa and her husband's valiant efforts to avenge her death. It soon appears that these events all grow out of a major pharmaceutical company's campaign to develop a new drug for combating tuberculosis. Discovered in a Polish laboratory, the drug looks promising at first, raising hopes of earning hundreds of millions of dollars. As tests on human subjects begin in Kenya and other African countries, however, problems start to surface. There are side effects. Patients die.

One of the scientists who discovered the drug has second thoughts and threatens to go public. Frantic, the company tries to suppress the unfavorable evidence and to buy off or intimidate critics. To bolster its case, the company uses money to get help from universities. It contrives to have several well-known professors publish favorable reports about the drug in leading journals without disclosing that the reports were actually written by the company itself and that the purported authors are beneficiaries of lucrative research contracts from the same source. A distant medical school is persuaded to offer the disaffected discoverer of the drug an amply funded post where she can be watched and induced to keep silent. When she finally speaks out, she is quickly vilified and ostracized by colleagues at her university and its affiliated hospital, which just happen to have been promised large donations by . . . that's right, the drug's manufacturer.

Le Carré takes care to point out that his book is a work of imagination. He makes no claim that pharmaceutical companies resort to beatings and killings to get new drugs to the market. Still, the author does say that his account "draws on several cases, particularly in the North American continent, where highly qualified medical researchers have dared to disagree with their pharmaceutical paymasters and suffered vilification and persecution for their pains."

Is Le Carré correct? Just how far have industrial sponsors actually gone in seeking to use higher-education institutions and professors for their own commercial ends? How willing have universities been to accept money at the cost of compromising values central to the academic enterprise?

To understand what lies behind Le Carré's book, one must appreciate the predicament in which universities find themselves. Now more than ever, they have become the principal source of the three most important ingredients of progress in a modern, industrial society: expert knowledge, highly educated people, and scientific discoveries. At the same time—in a depressed economy, with the federal budget heavily in deficit and state governments cutting investments in higher education—campus officials are confronting a chronic shortage of money to satisfy the demands of students, faculty members, and other constituencies.

As a result, university administrators are under great pressure to become more entrepreneurial. They feel compelled to search more aggressively for novel ways of making profits that can help meet pressing campus needs. Increasingly, one reads of new lucrative ventures launched by one university or another: medical-school consortia to test drugs for pharmaceutical companies; highly advertised executive courses to earn a tidy surplus for their business-school sponsors; alliances with venture capitalists to launch for-profit companies producing Internet courses for far-flung audiences.

The "entrepreneurial university" is the subject of a growing body of scholarly literature and media commentary. Led by resourceful executives, these institutions are often portrayed in books and articles as constantly looking out for new and ingenious ways to serve society's needs while reaping profits with which to scale new pinnacles of excellence and prestige. Reading such accounts, skeptics are quick to assume that such institutions have turned their backs on their academic missions and to criticize them for attempting to bring such businesslike ways into the academy.

Yet profit seeking has undoubtedly helped in some instances to improve academic work and to enhance higher education's value to society. Before Congress made it easy for universities to patent government-financed scientific discoveries and license them to corporations, administrators made little effort to scour campus laboratories for advances that could be turned to practical use to benefit consumers. Today, several hundred institutions have active technology-transfer offices to perform that function, and the number of patents issued to universities has grown more than tenfold. The lure of profit has likewise brought about keener competition to produce more and better-quality training programs for business executives than would have existed otherwise. Similar incentives could conceivably spur a more rapid development of Internet courses that will allow universities to make excellent educational programs available to distant audiences.

But, in their pursuit of moneymaking ventures, universities also risk compromising their essential academic values. To earn a handsome profit from a company, business schools may divert assistant professors from their on-campus duties so that they can teach elementary material to entry-level executives. To win at football, colleges may admit students with grades and scores far below the normal requirements. To profit from the Internet, universities may offer gullible students overseas a chance to take inferior courses that will earn them a dubious certificate of business studies. Once such compromises are made, competitive pressures can cause the questionable practices to spread and eventually become so deeply rooted as to be well nigh irreversible. One can imagine a university of the future tenuring professors because they bring in large amounts of patent royalties, seeking commercial advertisers to sponsor courses on the Internet, and admitting undistinguished students on the quiet understanding that their parents will make substantial gifts.

To avoid those pitfalls, universities need to examine the process of commercialization with greater care than in the past. Otherwise, they may gradually alter their essential character in ways that could eventually forfeit the respect of students and faculty members, and erode the trust of the public.

History offers several lessons about commercialization that are well worth pondering. One conclusion that emerges repeatedly is that rewards from profit-seeking ventures seldom are as great as their university sponsors hoped at the beginning. High-profile athletics teams—the academy's first big commercial venture—have certainly produced revenues. But their costs have risen at least as rapidly, to the point where very few institutions consistently make money from their sports programs. Likewise, patent licensing has brought substantial revenues to a handful of universities, but most institutions do not earn much more than the cost of operating their technology-transfer offices.

Internet courses have been recently touted as the latest El Dorado in the long history of commercial ventures. Not long ago, newspapers were filled with accounts of exciting new schemes offering large potential profits. In the last two years, however, New York and Temple Universities have both shut down for-profit Internet ventures, and Columbia University in January announced the demise of its widely publicized Fathom program after losing millions of dollars in the enterprise.

Commercialization has already taken a toll on the quality of educational programs.

If disappointing profits were the only problem with moneymaking activities, there would be little reason to lose much sleep over growing commercialization. But profit seeking has already shown disturbing tendencies to get out of hand and threaten far more important matters than expected revenues. In high-profile sports, for example, the prior grades and test scores of freshman athletes and their subsequent academic performance in college have fallen further and further below

the levels of their classmates, and scandals have continued to erupt periodically in one university after another.

While athletics may be dismissed as an extracurricular activity peripheral to the main academic enterprise, other commercial ventures have begun to strike closer to the core of research and education. In their zeal to build financial support from industry, many universities have signed research agreements with companies that allow more secrecy than is needed to protect the legitimate interests of their sponsors. Many campuses have failed to impose strict conflict-of-interest rules to prevent their scientists from performing experiments on human subjects for companies to which they have significant financial ties. Echoing the events described by John Le Carré, some universities have failed to protect their scientists from corporate pressure to suppress unfavorable research findings. Thomas Bodenheimer, a clinical professor of family and community medicine at the University of California at San Francisco, has even reported that as many as 10 percent of published reports by university researchers on the efficacy of products manufactured by the commercial sponsors of the research are actually ghostwritten by company personnel. As practices of this kind become more widely known, the public's confidence in the credibility and objectivity of university research is bound to suffer.

Commercialization has also taken a toll on the quality of educational programs. Many institutions, seeking to profit from their continuing-education divisions, follow practices in those areas that they would never tolerate in their regular degree programs. They typically offer little or no financial aid, while paying salaries to instructors that are well below the normal university scale. As a result, access to such programs has suffered, along with the quality of teaching.

In medical schools, administrators hoping to extract a greater surplus from continuing-education programs accept substantial subsidies from pharmaceutical companies in exchange for agreeing to choose instructors from company-approved lists and allowing the sponsor to prepare the slides and teaching notes that are used in the lectures. Further harm could result from commercializing Internet programs if universities (and their venture-capital partners) try to maximize profits by attracting large audiences of unwary students with flashy lecture courses taught by famous professors who do not take full advantage of the (more expensive) interactive power that new technology allows to improve the effectiveness of teaching and learning.

How significant are the questionable practices that many universities already tolerate? Because they involve values as well as money, the costs are impossible to quantify. But that does not mean they are unimportant. Far from it. It is vital to uphold admissions standards, preserve the integrity of evaluating faculty scholarship and student papers, maintain the openness and objectivity of scientific inquiry, and sustain other important academic values. These values are essential to maintaining the public's trust in student transcripts and published faculty research. They preserve professors' faith in the academic enterprise and help ensure that they will continue to regard their work as a calling rather than merely a way to make a living.

University officials may insist that they can keep commercial activity from getting out of hand. Yet the long, sorry history of intercollegiate sports clearly shows how far the erosion of values can proceed. Through a series of small steps, many prominent institutions have come to sacrifice the most basic academic standards in their quest for added athletics revenue and visibility. Left unchecked, the chronic need for money could drive universities to similar extremes in more-central programs of education and research.

What can universities do to protect themselves against that danger? Five steps seem especially important.

First, universities should not rely upon presidents alone to protect the institution and its values from the pitfalls of commercialization. Presidents are under enormous pressure to find the money not only to balance the budget but to improve financial aid, build new buildings and laboratories, increase faculty salaries, launch new programs, and hire star professors to enhance the institution's reputation. Trustees judge presidential performance in substantial part by the amount of money that the chief executive raises. Faculty members hold presidents accountable for finding the means to fulfill intellectual ambitions. Students want better residence halls. Boosters insist on winning teams.

In the face of these pressures, if presidents are left by themselves to preserve academic values, questionable compromises are likely to occur. Though none may be glaring by itself, their accumulation will gradually threaten the integrity of the institution. The values of a college or university can be preserved only if boards of trustees make upholding academic standards an integral part of evaluating presidents—and insist on reviewing conflict-of-interest rules, admissions practices for athletes, and other standards that are at risk from commercialization.

The second principle to observe is not to consider commercial opportunities on a case-by-case basis. Rather, institutions should insist on promulgating general rules to govern matters such as secrecy provisions in corporate-research agreements, admissions standards for athletes, and conflicts of interest for scientists. Ad hoc decisions are bound to lead to a gradual erosion of academic values; the cards are almost always stacked in favor of allowing moneymaking schemes to proceed.

When such opportunities present themselves, interested faculty members and administrators are typically those with a stake in having the project move forward; the risks are usually too diffuse to generate opposition. The potential rewards seem tangible and very tempting at the outset, while the dangers will be speculative and hard to quantify. The hoped-for benefits are, for the most part, immediate, whereas the risks loom far in the future.

In addition, the benefits accrue to the institution and its members, but the costs often involve matters, such as a loss of trust in the objectivity of research, that are shared by all universities. Similarly, the blame for turning a project down falls squarely on identifiable university officials, but the responsibility for undermining academic standards and squandering public trust can never be traced to any specific decision or institution. Under such circumstances, in the absence of clear, well-publicized rules, the path of least resistance will almost always lie in approving the questionable project.

A third important principle is to involve the faculty in developing and enforcing all rules that protect academic values. Many administrators have a dangerous habit of regarding the faculty as an irritating obstruction to discussions of commercial ventures. The entrepreneurial university, it is said, must be able to move quickly. It cannot wait for windy faculty debates to run their course lest valuable opportunities be lost in the fast-moving corporate world in which we live.

In fact, there is remarkably little evidence to support this view. Looking back over the checkered history of commercial activity on campuses, one can much more easily point to examples of costly unilateral decisions by impatient administrators, such as ill-advised Internet ventures or grandiose athletics projects, than to valuable opportunities lost through inordinate faculty delays.

That is not to say that existing processes of faculty governance are perfect, or even nearly so. New and streamlined procedures may be needed, with smaller committees staffed by carefully chosen, well-respected, highly knowledgeable professors, in order to deal with conflicts of interest, secrecy, and other complex issues created by emerging commercial opportunities. Still, the essential fact remains that faculty members have the greatest stake in preserving academic values—and hence have a critical role to play in making sure that the quest for revenue does not impair the basic intellectual standards of the institution.

Universities should ponder the sorry history of intercollegiate athletics.

A fourth useful step in safeguarding academic standards is to look for opportunities for universities to agree among themselves on basic rules governing matters such as conflicts of interest in research, the length of time that results can be kept secret under commercially sponsored research agreements, or conference-wide rules protecting academic standards in athletics. The Ivy League agreement setting minimum admissions requirements for athletes is a case in point.

Without such agreements, competition works to erode academic standards. In the struggle for revenue or competitive advantage, a few institutions are bound to succumb to the temptation to undertake highly questionable commercial ventures. Once a few agree, competitive pressures on other universities will cause them to do likewise. Before long, what began as suspect behavior will become accepted practice. Uniform rules, by agreement or by legislation, are often the only defense against such corrosive pressures (although universities need to take pains to avoid the sort of restrictive agreements without a redeeming public purpose that could run afoul of antitrust laws).

Finally, reasonably stable government support is the ultimate guarantee of high academic standards. Faced with a choice between sacrificing academic values and enduring serious cuts in programs, most universities will find a way to choose the former. Fortunately, government support for higher education has been relatively generous over the years. That is one important reason why American universities have achieved such a place of eminence in the world. My point is not to complain or to urge massive increases in public support for higher education. I simply want to make clear that sudden, major cuts, or steady erosion of support over an extended period of time, will put intolerable pressure on universities to sacrifice important academic standards in the hope of gaining badly needed revenue through dubious commercial ventures.

Above all, university leaders, faculty members, and trustees need to recognize the risks involved in pursuing more and more commercial ventures and begin to build sturdier safeguards. To be sure, setting proper limits and providing supportive structures will take a lot of work. Entrepreneurial professors may resist new rules. Boosters may protest athletics reforms. Corporations may balk at strict secrecy limits and refuse to enter into lucrative research contracts.

Meanwhile, the temptation to push ahead will frequently be great. Most profit-seeking ventures start not with obvious violations of principle but with modest compromises that carry few immediate costs. The problems tend to appear so gradually that their link to commercialization may not even be perceived. Like adolescents experimenting with drugs, campus officials may believe that they can proceed without serious risk.

Before succumbing to such temptations, university leaders should recall the history of intercollegiate athletics and ponder the sobering lessons that it teaches. Once the critical compromises have been made and tolerated long enough, universities will find it hard to rebuild the public's trust, regain the faculty's respect, and return to the happier conditions of earlier times. In exchange for ephemeral gains in the constant struggle for prestige, universities will have sacrificed essential values that are very difficult to restore.

Derek Bok is a university professor and president emeritus of Harvard University. His latest book, *Universities in the Marketplace: The Commercialization of Higher Education,* was published April 2003 by Princeton University Press.

UNIT 3

Business and Society: Contemporary Ethical, Social, and Environmental Issues

Unit Selections

Key Points to Consider

- How well are organizations responding to issues of work and family schedules, day care, and telecommuting?

- Should corporations and executives face criminal charges for releasing unsafe products into the marketplace, creating or allowing dangerous working conditions, or allowing illegal levels of industrial pollution? Why or why not?

- What ethical dilemmas will management likely face when conducting business in foreign environments?

Student Web Site

www.mhcls.com/online

Internet References

Further information regarding these Web sites may be found in this book's preface or online.

National Immigrant Forum
http://www.immigrationforum.org

Workopolis.com
http://sympatico.workopolis.com

United Nations Environment Programme (UNEP)
http://www.unep.ch

United States Trade Representative (USTR)
http://www.ustr.gov

Both at home and abroad, there are social and environmental issues that have potential ethical consequences for management. Incidents of insider trading, deaths resulting from unsafe products or work environments, AIDS in the workplace, and the adoption of policies for involvement in the global market are a few of the issues that need to be seriously addressed by management.

This unit investigates the nature and ramifications of prominent ethical, social, and environmental issues facing management today. The unit's articles are grouped into three sections. The first article, "Does It Pay to Be Good" covers why corporate citizenship is a diffuse concept for many. The next article scrutinizes the importance of companies gaining and maintaining trust in the marketplace. The last three articles in this subsection provide some thoughtful insight on ways companies are embracing customer service practices, how executives and their Human Resource teams are attempting to find better ways to deal with workplace romances, and how Starbucks is reaching out to both employees and customers with disabilities.

The first article in the second subsection addresses ways to keep identity thieves from stealing your name and your money. The second article in this subsection examines the dark side of online advertising.

The subsection *Global Ethics* concludes this unit with readings that provide helpful insight on ethical issues and dilemmas inherent in multinational operations. They describe adapting ethical decisions to a global marketplace and offer guidelines for helping management deal with product quality and ethical issues in international markets. The articles also examine the complex social issues faced by professional women in Japan, and reveal how some large corporations are using their clout to improve working conditions around the world.

Does It Pay to Be Good?

Yes, say advocates of corporate citizenship, who believe their time has come—finally.

A.J. VOGL

Corporate citizenship: For believers, the words speak of the dawning of a new era of capitalism, when business, government, and citizen groups join forces for the greater good, to jointly tackle such problems as water shortages and air pollution, to do something about the 1.2 billion people who live on less than a dollar a day.

Corporate citizenship: For critics of today's capitalism, the words smack of hypocrisy, big business' cynical response to charges of greed and corruption in high places, intended to mollify those who say corporations have too much power and that they wield it shamelessly. Critics charge that corporate citizenship is a placebo to the enemies of globalization, a public-relations smoke screen, capitalism's last-ditch attempt to preserve itself by co-opting its opposition.

Corporate citizenship: For many, it remains a diffuse concept, but generally it speaks to companies voluntarily adopting a triple bottom line, one that takes into account social, economic, and environmental considerations as well as financial results. Though some associate corporate citizenship with charity and philanthropy, the concept goes further—it embraces a corporate *conscience* above and beyond profits and markets. David Vidal, who directs research in global corporate citizenship at The Conference Board, comments, "Citizenship is not, as some critics charge, window dressing for the corporation. It deals with primary business relationships that are part of a company's strategic vision, and a good business case can be made for corporate citizenship."

Whether you are a critic or believer, however, there is no question that corporate citizenship—a term that embraces corporate social responsibility (CSR) and sustainability—is no longer a concept fostered by idealists on the fringe. It has entered the mainstream.

But why *now*? Though the era of corporate citizenship was ushered in with the fall of the Berlin Wall and the rise of market capitalism worldwide, current sentiment against big business has given new weight to the cause. Virtually every opinion survey shows that people think corporations have too much power, and that they will do anything in the pursuit of profits. And now, to add to public distrust, we have a flagging

economy, a shambolic stock market, and what have been called "pornographic" CEO salaries. These circumstances have given citizenship's champions new planks for their platform, such as accounting and compensation practices. At the same time, attacks on the very nature of business have sent corporate leaders searching for a bright spot, and that spot may very well be the concept of corporate citizenship.

But that makes corporate enthusiasm for citizenship sound like a calculated, even cynical stance that is likely to last only as long as the environment remains hostile. There are grounds for believing that it is more than that, that it speaks to deeper changes in the greater world that make it *necessary* for large corporations to do good. Some of these changes include:

Tightening regulatory pressures. France, for instance, requires all companies listed on the Paris Stock Exchange to include information about their social and environmental performance within their financial statements; the Johannesburg Stock Exchange requires compliance with a CSR-based code of conduct; and the United Kingdom (the first nation with a minister for corporate social responsibility) requires pension-fund managers to disclose the degree to which social and environmental criteria are part of their investment decisions.

Will there be more national legislation? "If you had asked me that three or four years ago, I would have answered, 'Unclear, or probably not,'" says Allen White. White is acting chief executive of Global Reporting Initiative, an Amsterdam-based organization that has developed uniform guidelines for CSR reporting. "But in 2002 we've seen developments that could not have been anticipated several years ago, developments that have challenged companies to reconstruct or restore credibility, challenges to markets to demonstrate to investors that available information is accurate. Governments have taken note and are considering legislative and regulatory action."

Changing demographics. A socially engaged and better-educated population demands that the companies with which they do business—as consumers, employees, or investors—conform to higher standards. Both consumers and employees tell researchers that they prefer to purchase from and work for a company that is a good corporate citizen. On the investor front,

Investors Are Listening

For companies in sectors not considered exemplars of corporate citizenship—munitions, pornography, gambling, and tobacco (yes); liquor (probably); and oil (maybe)—there's good news: The market hasn't penalized them for their supposed lack of citizenship. For companies at the opposite end of the spectrum, there's also good news: Investors haven't penalized them for their expenditures on social causes.

On balance, the better news is for the socially responsible companies, who have long labored under the assumption that the investor automatically pays a price for investing in a socially responsible company or mutual fund—the price, of course, being a company or fund that doesn't perform as well as its peers that don't fly the socially-responsible banner.

Investors appear to be listening. According to Financial Research Corp., investors added $1.29 billion of new money into socially responsible funds during the first half of 2002, compared to $847.1 million added during all of 2001. Over the year ending July 31, the average mutual fund—including stock, bond, and balanced funds—was down 13 percent, while comparable socially responsible funds were down 19 percent. But advocates point out that different indices—particularly the Domini Social Index, a capitalization-weighted market index of 400 common stocks screened according to social and environmental criteria, and the Citizen's Index, a market-weighted portfolio of common stocks representing ownership in 300 of the most socially responsible U.S. companies, have outperformed the S&P 500 over the last one, three, and five years.

While the $13 billion invested in socially responsible funds (according to Morningstar) comprises only about 2 percent of total fund assets, advocates expect this percentage to climb to 10 percent by 2012, says Barbara Krumsiek, chief executive of the Bethesda, Md.-based Calvert Group, a mutual-fund complex specializing in socially responsible investing. And others' tallies are far higher: The nonprofit Social Investment Forum counts more than $2 trillion in total assets under management in portfolios screened for socially concerned investors, including socially screened mutual funds and separate accounts managed for socially conscious institutions and individual investors.

Plus, recent corporate scandals may have raised many investors' consciousness: In the first half of 2002, socially responsible mutual funds saw their assets increase by 3 percent, while conventional diversified funds lost 9.5 percent in total assets. People may have decided that if their mutual-fund investments were going to lose money, it might as well be for a good cause.

—A.J.V.

activists—including individuals, socially responsible mutual funds, public pension funds, and religious groups—submitted 800 resolutions in 2002, according to Meg Voorhes, director of the social-issues department at Investor Responsibility Research Center, a Washington, D.C.-based organization that tracks proxies.

More opportunity for investors to back their convictions with money. Socially aware investors can choose among some 230 mutual funds, and, according to Steven J. Schueth of the nonprofit Social Investment Forum, more than 800 independent asset managers identify themselves as managers of socially responsible portfolios for institutional investors and high-net-worth individuals. (See "Investors Are Listening,") Indexes of social and environmental performance—like the Dow Jones Sustainability World Indexes and FTSE4Good—are becoming significant market factors in screening for good citizenship. These indexes have teeth in them: They will and do drop companies that fail to meet social-responsibility standards.

Pressure from nongovernmental organizations. Not only are international NGOs growing in number—at last count, there were 28,000 worldwide—their visibility and credibility are on the rise. Last year, PR executive Richard Edelman told the World Economic Forum, "NGOs are now the Fifth Estate in global governance—the true credible source on issues related to the environment and social justice." While Americans generally trust corporations more than NGO "brands," the opposite is true in Europe. A study conducted by Edelman's firm found that Amnesty International, the World Wildlife Fund, and Greenpeace outstripped by a margin of nearly two to one the four highest-rated corporations in Europe: Microsoft, Bayer, Shell, and Ford. As in other areas, it appears, European public opinion affirming social responsibility is ahead of that of the United States.

The most prominent corporate citizens rarely receive commensurate rewards.

Greater transparency. If good news travels fast, bad news moves faster. The Internet has given a platform to critics who, if they existed before, could be ignored; now they will be heard. There is the by-now-classic story of MIT graduate student Jonah Peretti, who submitted the word *sweatshop* to Nike's personalize-your-shoes iD program. Nike refused the order, terming the word "inappropriate slang." Peretti replied, "I have decided to order the shoes with a different iD, but I would like to make one small request. Could you please send me a color snapshot of the ten-year-old Vietnamese girl who makes my shoes?" His e-mail correspondence was forwarded around the world and picked up by the mass media. Nike, in its first annual "corporate responsibility report," responded convincingly to charges that it exploited workers—indeed, the company is generally known as a CSR innovator—but inevitably sounded defensive.

Bringing Standards up to Code

In May 2000, the International Chamber of Commerce counted more than 40 codes, existing or in preparation, intended to govern the activities of global corporations; among the most prominent are those of the OECD, the U.N. Global Compact, and the International Labor Organization.

Companies may be forgiven for having been confused over which set of guidelines to follow.

That confusion appears to be on the way to being lifted through the "2002 Sustainability Reporting Guidelines," introduced at the World Summit in Johannesburg by the Global Reporting Initiative. The guidelines are not another code. Rather, they are an attempt to create a generally accepted reporting framework for social responsibility. The outcome of two years of work by GRI, the guidelines are a rejoinder to the "deep scepticism" that "the creation of new wealth . . . will do anything to decrease social inequities," as the document's introduction states. In nearly 100 pages, the guidelines cover such issues as transparency, sustainability, auditability, and comparability.

The last of these issues is critical, argues Eric Israel, a partner at BearingPoint, the consultancy formerly known as KPMG Consulting. "The meaning of citizenship for one particular company can be completely different than for another," he says. "So how do you benchmark an organization and compare it to others in the same industry? Up to now, there's been no equivalent of GAAP for social responsibility. That's where GRI comes in with its guidelines."

How does one verify that GRI guidelines have been met? Since the advent of CSR codes, companies have hired organizations, ranging from consultancies like BearingPoint to single-issue nonprofits, to verify their compliance for onlookers' eyes. Some monitor the companies themselves and attest that standards are being met—for instance, Chiquita Brands International has partnered with the Rainforest Alliance, which sends inspectors to each farm and offers its Better Bananas seal of approval to products from those farms that pass muster.

Other firms simply verify companies' CSR reports, the public face of compliance with codes. Considering the many codes in circulation and the range of organizations hired to verify compliance, it's not easy to put any particular report in broader context. That's where another organization, London-based AccountAbility, enters the picture.

Last June, AccountAbility issued something called the AA1000S Assurance Standard, which outlines principles around verification and CSR auditing—and which the firm hopes will become the gold standard of CSR verification standards. AccountAbility has credibility because of its governing constituencies—businesses, nonprofits, accountancies, researchers and academics, and consultancies—and its endorsement of GRI's reporting guidelines will likely give a boost to acceptance of both. "What we do is entirely complementary to what GRI does," says AccountAbility COO Mike Peirce. "It's a marriage made in heaven." In future, then, expect to see more annual reports that cite GRI guidelines verified by accountants using AccountAbility standards.

But the existence of these codes and organizations is only a first step; there's still a long way to go. According to a recent OECD survey, only one in five companies with codes of conduct share compliance information with the public, and third-party auditing remains the exception rather than the rule.

—A.J.V.

All of these factors have led to increasing corporate acceptance of the importance of citizenship. Every three years, BearingPoint, the consultancy formerly known as KPMG Consulting, surveys global *Fortune* 250 companies on corporate-responsibility issues. The latest survey found that 45 percent of the 250 companies surveyed issued environmental, social, and/or sustainability reports in 2001, up from 35 percent in 1998, and the number of U.S. companies that issued such reports increased 14 percent over the same period. Today, too, two-thirds of the world's largest companies use their Websites to trumpet their social and environmental activities.

Which is not to say that all these corporations have become true believers. "[W]e have to acknowledge," writes Steve Hilton, a British CSR consultant, "that fear of exposure and the need for compliance are the most powerful forces galvanizing the majority of active corporate citizens."

No Good Deed Goes Unpunished

As necessary as corporate citizenship may be, it still faces challenges from both inside and outside the corner office. Perhaps the most disheartening of these hurdles is that the most prominent corporate citizens rarely receive rewards commensurate with their prominence. As Hilton and Giles Gibbons, co-authors of the pro-CSR *Good Business: Your World Needs You*, point out, "Curiously, the companies whose hearts are most visibly fixed to their pinstriped sleeves tend to be the ones that attract the most frequent and venomous attacks from anti-business critics." Is this because critics feel that devious agendas lie behind the enlightened policies? Noreena Hertz, a British critic of corporate citizenship, wonders whether Microsoft, by putting computers in schools today, will determine how children learn tomorrow.

Is it that corporations haven't gotten their stories across properly, or that they *have*—and are still being vilified? The experience of McDonald's in this arena is revealing. Last April, the fast-food chain published its first social-responsibility report, composed of 46 pages summarizing its efforts in four categories: community, environment, people, and marketplace. Those efforts have been rewarded in some courts of public opinion: In 2000 and 2001 *Financial Times*/PricewaterhouseCoopers surveys of media and NGOs, McDonald's placed 14th among the world's most respected companies for environmental performance.

At the same time, few corporations have been attacked as savagely as McDonald's for its "citizenship." It has been portrayed as an omnivorous monster that destroys local businesses and culture, promotes obesity, treats its employees badly, and despoils the environment. McDonald's goes to great lengths to answer these charges in its social-responsibility report—which was itself widely criticized—but, like Nike, it can't help looking defensive. It will take a great deal more than a report of its good works to diminish the Golden Arches as a symbol of "capitalist imperialism" in the eyes of antiglobalists or to stanch the vitriol on such Websites as Mcspotlight.

There's no question that the bar is set exceedingly high in the arena of corporate social involvement. Philip Morris Cos. spends more than $100 million a year, most conspicuously in a series of TV commercials, on measures to discourage under-age smoking—and still critics charge that the Philip Morris campaign is a cynical PR stunt that actually *encourages* kids to smoke. The company has been accused of having "a profound conflict of interest that cannot be overcome."

Another tobacco company, BAT, the world's second-largest, put some members of the social-responsibility establishment in an uncomfortable position when, last July, it became the industry's first company to publish a social-responsibility report. Few knew what to think upon reading the tobacco company's blunt rhetoric—"[T]here is no such thing as a 'safe' cigarette. . . . We openly state that, put simply, smoking is a cause of certain serious diseases"—and the 18 pages devoted to the risks of smoking. BAT even had its report audited by an independent verifier. All this wasn't nearly enough to satisfy antismoking groups, of course—they continue to view the company with deep suspicion. Would anyone have predicted otherwise?

When accused of being overly suspicious, critics point to one company that, over the last six years, won numerous awards for its environmental, human rights, anti-corruption, anti-bribery, and climate-change policies; a company prominent on "most admired" and "best companies to work for" lists; a company that issued a report on the good deeds that supported its claim to be a top corporate citizen. That company was Enron.

No one would argue that Enron is typical, yet its debacle has tainted other companies. It also raises a difficult question about CSR: What is the link between how a company is managed—corporate governance—and corporate citizenship? Steve Hilton, speaking from London, says that the link is not really understood in the United Kingdom: "People here have not made the connection between the corporate-governance, executive-compensation, and accounting-fraud issues in the United States and operational issues that come under the heading of corporate citizenship. I would argue they're all part of the same thing."

So would Transparency International's Frank Vogl, co-founder of the anti-corruption NGO. He believes that CSR has been undermined because it has been disconnected from corporate-conduct issues. "Foreign public trust in Corporate America has been diminished," he said, "and there is scant evidence that U.S. business leaders recognize the global impact of the U.S. scandals."

Vogl says that, for most countries in the world, corruption is much more of a social-responsibility issue than either the environment or labor rights. "What U.S. businesspeople see as a facilitating payment may be seen in developing countries as a bribe," he comments, "and I think that provides some insight into why the United States ranks behind 12 other countries on the Transparency International Bribe Payers Index. To me, corporate citizenship means you don't bribe foreign officials. That's the worst kind of hypocrisy."

Will They Be Good in Bad Times?

The specter of hypocrisy raises its head in another quarter as well: Do employees of companies claiming to be good corporate citizens see their employer's citizenship activities as a diversion or cover-up to charges of bad leadership and poor management practices? Certainly, if recent surveys are a guide, top management needs to restore its credibility with employees. In a recent Mercer Human Resource Consulting study, only a third of the 2,600 workers surveyed agreed with the statement, "I can trust management in my organization to always communicate honestly." And a Walker Information survey of employees found that only 49 percent believe their senior leaders to be "people of high personal integrity." If CSR is perceived by employees merely as puffery to make top management look good, it will not get under an organization's cultural skin.

"Businesses needn't apologize for making products that other Americans want to buy."

Even if there is a genuine management commitment, corporations have other obligations that may take precedence, begging the question: Will corporations be good citizens in bad times as well as good? The experience of Ford Motor Co. brings the question to earth. In August, Ford issued its third annual corporate-citizenship report. Previous reports had drawn plaudits from environmentalists, but this one, coming at a time when the automaker faced financial difficulties, was attacked by the same environmentalists for failing to set aggressive goals for reducing greenhouse-gas emissions or improving gas mileage. Sierra Club's executive director called it "a giant step in the wrong direction for Ford Motor Co., for American consumers, and for the environment."

Lingering tough economic conditions may impel other companies to take their own "giant steps" backward. An old business saw has it that when times get tough and cuts have to be made, certain budgets are at the top of the list for cutbacks—advertising for one, public relations for another. For companies in which corporate citizenship is seen as an extension of public relations, of "image building" or "reputation management," it may suffer this fate.

Which is as it should be, say some critics. As *The Wall Street Journal* lectured CEO William Ford on its editorial page: "We also hope Mr. Ford has learned from his mistake of ceding the moral and political high ground to environmentalists . . . .

Businesses needn't apologize for making products that other Americans want to buy. Their first obligation is to their shareholders and employees and that means above all making an honest profit."

Attacked from All Sides

While many skeptics criticize the ways in which corporate social responsibility is enacted, some take matters a step further by asking if the concept should exist at all. Who would object to the idea of a company doing good, of moving beyond the traditional and literal bottom line, to take a larger view of the reason for its existence? You may be surprised: There are many critics, and they come from various and sometimes unpredictable directions.

First is a group that says corporate social responsibility is flawed at its heart because it's doing the right thing for the wrong reason. The right thing, they believe, is doing the right thing because it is right, as a matter of principle—not because it advances the firm's business interests. The rejoinder, of course, is that if a larger social or environmental good is met, we should not quibble about motivation. As corporate-governance activist Robert A.G. Monks points out: "You can get backing from institutional investors only if you talk a commercial idiom."

Next is a group of dissimilar critics who believe that, in attempting to pursue goals of corporate citizenship, companies are doing things that are none of their business. Paradoxically, these critics come from both the right and the left.

The right feels that the business of business should be business: As Michael Prowse argues in the *Financial Times*, the role of the corporation "is to provide individuals with the means to be socially responsible. Rather than trying to play the role of social worker, senior executives should concentrate on their statutory obligations. We should not expect benevolence of them, but we should demand probity: the socially responsible chief executive is the one who turns a profit without lying, cheating, robbing or defrauding anyone."

The left, on the other hand, feels that corporations are usurping the powers of government, to the detriment of the citizenry and democracy itself. Noreena Hertz, the British academic and broadcaster who wrote of *The Silent Takeover: Global Capitalism and the Death of Democracy,* is not only dubious about business taking over responsibilities that she feels properly belong to government—she is skeptical about business' ability to handle them: "[M]anagers of multinationals operating in the third world are often overwhelmed by the social problems they encounter, and understandably find it difficult to know which causes to prioritize . . . . Their contributions can be squandered, or diverted through corruption."

And what happens, she asks, when a corporation decides to pull out, if government has allowed private industry to take over its role? Worse still, she worries about situations in which a socially responsible corporation could use its position "to exact a stream of IOUs and quid pro quos, to demand ever more favorable terms and concessions from host governments."

Then there is a group of critics who see corporate citizenship as a diversionary ploy to placate a public outraged at dubious corporate practices. They will concede that Enron, WorldCom, and Tyco are egregious exceptions, but are other companies exemplars of probity? Hardly. Can companies be considered good corporate citizens when they move their headquarters to Bermuda to avoid taxes (and enrich their CEOs in the process)? Can companies like General Electric, Monsanto, Merck, SmithKline Beecham, and Chiquita Brands International claim the moral high ground when they have cut employee benefits in connection with mergers and spinoffs? And what of such companies as Wyeth, Wal-Mart, McKesson, and Merrill Lynch? Can they, ask the critics, be considered high-minded citizens when the top executives accumulate pots of money in their deferred-compensation accounts? This may be why PR *eminence grise* John Budd says, "For at least the next 18 post-Enron months, I certainly would not counsel any CEO to magically appear publicly as an enlightened champion of social responsibility. The circumstances make it automatic that it would be perceived as spinning."

Last, there is a group of critics that says that simply doing more good than we're doing now is not enough, that we have to rethink the nature of the beast—capitalism itself. Steven Piersanti, president of Berrett-Koehler Publishers, is in the thick of this intellectual contretemps. Last fall, his firm published two books that took divergent views on the issue. The first, *Walking the Talk*, was written by Swiss industrialist Stephan Schmidheiny, along with two colleagues at the World Business Council for Sustainable Development, Chad Holliday of DuPont and Philip Watts of Royal Dutch/Shell. "It advances a reformist view that major changes are needed in our business world," says Piersanti, "but that these changes can best be achieved by reforms within our existing economic structures, institutions, and systems." The second book, *Alternatives to Economic Globalization: A Better World Is Possible*, presents "an activist view that existing economic structures are insufficient and that new structures, institutions, and systems are needed in the world."

It's likely that doubts about the nature and purpose of corporate citizenship will continue to be raised from all quarters. But with social-responsibility reporting and verification initiatives in place and likely government regulation down the road, there's reason to think that their voices will become more isolated.

—A.J.V.

Does the "Business Case" Really Have a Case?

But hold on: What about the so-called business case for corporate citizenship—that it contributes to making "an honest profit"? Unfortunately, it's difficult to quantify in cost-benefit terms what that contribution is. Not something to be concerned about, says Simon Zadek, CEO of AccountAbility, a London-based institute that has established CSR verification standards. (See "Bringing Standards Up to Code.") "It is a fact that the vast majority of day-to-day business decisions are taken without any explicit cost-benefit analysis," he says, pointing to employee training as an example of a corporate expenditure that is difficult to quantify in cost-benefit terms. What he doesn't mention is that, when business is suffering, training is usually among the expenditures to be cut back or eliminated.

Ultimately, Zadek concedes that, in strictly quantifiable terms, one cannot make a cost-benefit case for corporate citizenship. "Although the question 'Does corporate citizenship pay?' is technically right, it is misleading in practice," he says. "Rephrasing the core question as 'In what ways does corporate citizenship contribute to achieving the core business strategy?' is far preferable."

To some hardheaded corporate types, Zadek's reasoning may seem disingenuous, but even the hardheads can't be dismissive—at least publicly. Moreover, they would probably acknowledge that corporate citizenship, in concept and practice, has come too far to be ignored. In the future, it may well become what Steve Hilton calls a "hygiene factor," a condition of doing business. Hilton's firm, Good Business, consults with firms on citizenship issues. "I think business leaders are coming to realize CSR's potential to go beyond a compliance/risk-management issue into a genuine business tool," he says. "That's been the rhetoric all along, but the reality has been that it's been a slightly marginal issue. With few exceptions, it's been seen as an add-on, without being incorporated into core business decision-making."

This is Zadek's point when he argues the case for what he calls "third-generation corporate citizenship." The first generation is defined by cause-related marketing and short-term reputation management. The second occurs when social and environmental objectives become a core part of long-term business strategy; as an example, he points to automakers competing in the arena of emission controls. The third generation is based on collective action, where corporations join with competitors, NGOs, and government "to change the underlying rules of the game to ensure that business delivers adequate social and environmental results."

Changing the rules means, for one thing, a more level playing field. "In CSR," says AccountAbility COO Mike Peirce, "companies that are leaders might suffer a penalty if there's a big gap between themselves and laggards in the field, so they'd like everybody ticking along at at least a basic level." In other words, a socially responsible company does not want to be penalized financially for being socially responsible. Of course, a cynic might reply that if CSR indeed provides the competitive advantage that its proponents insist it does, then it is the laggards that should suffer the severest financial penalty.

Expect citizenship proponents to make corporate governance itself the issue.

To convince doubters, efforts are being made to schematically quantify corporate social responsibility. In a recent *Harvard Business Review* article titled "The Virtue Matrix: Calculating the Return on Corporate Responsibility," Roger L. Martin makes a point of treating corporate responsibility as a product or service like any other. According to Martin, who is dean of the University of Toronto's Rotman School of Management, his matrix can help companies sort out such questions as whether a citizenship initiative will erode a company's competitive position.

Even if Martin's formula seems overly clinical, it supports the trend toward closer analysis of what social responsibility means and what it brings to corporations practicing it. But analysis will take you only so far. "[I]t is impossible to prove the direction of the flow of causality," writes Chad Holliday, chairman and CEO of DuPont and co-author of *Walking the Talk: The Business Case for Sustainable Development*. "Does a company become profitable and thus enjoy the luxury of being able to worry about environmental and social issues or does the pursuit of sustainability make a company more profitable?"

But for large public companies, the question of whether it truly pays to be good will be asked less and less; for them, it will be *necessary* to be good, if only to avoid appearing Neanderthal. That means that corporate social responsibility, itself nothing less than a growth industry today, will become "normalized" into corporate cultures.

Yes, there will be an effort to level the playing field in CSR, but, further, expect citizenship proponents to attempt to raise the field to a higher level by making corporate governance itself the issue. "Unless we make basic structural changes," says Marjorie Kelly, the editor of *Business Ethics* magazine and a frequent critic of CSR, "it'll be nothing but window dressing. The corporate scandals have given a real-world demonstration that business without ethics collapses, and that has given us an extraordinary opportunity to change the way we do business."

A.J. VOGL is editor of *Across the Board*. He wrote "Worry About the Details" in the Sept/Oct issue.

Trust in the Marketplace

JOHN E. RICHARDSON AND LINNEA BERNARD McCORD

Traditionally, ethics is defined as a set of moral values or principles or a code of conduct.

. . . Ethics, as an expression of reality, is predicated upon the assumption that there are right and wrong motives, attitudes, traits of character, and actions that are exhibited in interpersonal relationships. Respectful social interaction is considered a norm by almost everyone.

. . . the overwhelming majority of people perceive others to be ethical when they observe what is considered to be their genuine kindness, consideration, politeness, empathy, and fairness in their interpersonal relationships. When these are absent, and unkindness, inconsideration, rudeness, hardness, and injustice are present, the people exhibiting such conduct are considered unethical. A genuine consideration of others is essential to an ethical life. (Chewning, pp. 175–176).

An essential concomitant of ethics is of trust. Webster's Dictionary defines trust as "assured reliance on the character, ability, strength or truth of someone or something." Businesses are built on a foundation of trust in our free-enterprise system. When there are violations of this trust between competitors, between employer and employees, or between businesses and consumers, our economic system ceases to run smoothly. From a moral viewpoint, ethical behavior should not exist because of economic pragmatism, governmental edict, or contemporary fashionability—it should exist because it is morally appropriate and right. From an economic point of view, ethical behavior should exist because it just makes good business sense to be ethical and operate in a manner that demonstrates trustworthiness.

Robert Bruce Shaw, in *Trust in the Balance*, makes some thoughtful observations about trust within an organization. Paraphrasing his observations and applying his ideas to the marketplace as a whole:

1. Trust requires consumers have confidence in organizational promises or claims made to them. This means that a consumer should be able to believe that a commitment made will be met.
2. Trust requires integrity and consistency in following a known set of values, beliefs, and practices.
3. Trust requires concern for the well-being of others. This does not mean that organizational needs are not given

appropriate emphasis—but it suggests the importance of understanding the impact of decisions and actions on others—i.e. consumers. (Shaw, pp. 39–40)

Companies can lose the trust of their customers by portraying their products in a deceptive or inaccurate manner. In one recent example, a Nike advertisement exhorted golfers to buy the same golf balls used by Tiger Woods. However, since Tiger Woods was using custom-made Nike golf balls not yet available to the general golfing public, the ad was, in fact, deceptive. In one of its ads, Volvo represented that Volvo cars could withstand a physical impact that, in fact, was not possible. Once a company is "caught" giving inaccurate information, even if done innocently, trust in that company is eroded.

Companies can also lose the trust of their customers when they fail to act promptly and notify their customers of problems that the company has discovered, especially where deaths may be involved. This occurred when Chrysler dragged its feet in replacing a safety latch on its Minivan (Geyelin, pp. A1, A10). More recently, Firestone and Ford had been publicly brought to task for failing to expeditiously notify American consumers of tire defects in SUVs even though the problem had occurred years earlier in other countries. In cases like these, trust might not just be eroded, it might be destroyed. It could take years of painstaking effort to rebuild trust under these circumstances, and some companies might not have the economic ability to withstand such a rebuilding process with their consumers.

A *20/20* and *New York Times* investigation on a recent *ABC 20/20* program, entitled "The Car Dealer's Secret" revealed a sad example of the violation of trust in the marketplace. The investigation divulged that many unsuspecting consumers have had hidden charges tacked on by some car dealers when purchasing a new car. According to consumer attorney Gary Klein, "It's a dirty little secret that the auto lending industry has not owned up to." (*ABC News 20/20*)

The scheme worked in the following manner. Car dealers would send a prospective buyer's application to a number of lenders, who would report to the car dealer what interest rate the lender would give to the buyer for his or her car loan. This interest rate is referred to as the "buy rate." Legally a car dealer is not required to tell the buyer what the "buy rate" is or how much the dealer is marking up the loan. If dealers did most of the loans at the buy rate, they only get a small fee. However, if they were able to convince the buyer to pay a higher rate, they made considerably more money. Lenders encouraged car dealers to charge the buyer a higher rate than the "buy rate" by agreeing to split the extra income with the dealer.

David Robertson, head of the Association of Finance and Insurance Professionals—a trade group representing finance managers—defended the practice, reflecting that it was akin to a retail markup on loans. "The dealership provides a valuable service on behalf of the customer in negotiating these loans," he said. "Because of that, the dealership should be compensated for that work." (*ABC News 20/20*)

Careful examination of the entire report, however, makes one seriously question this apologetic. Even if this practice is deemed to be legal, the critical issue is what happens to trust when the buyers discover that they have been charged an additional 1–3% of the loan without their knowledge? In some cases, consumers were led to believe that they were getting the dealer's bank rate, and in other cases, they were told that the dealer had shopped around at several banks to secure the best loan rate they could get for the buyer. While this practice may be questionable from a legal standpoint, it is clearly in ethical breach of trust with the consumer. Once discovered, the companies doing this will have the same credibility and trustworthiness problems as the other examples mentioned above.

The untrustworthiness problems of the car companies was compounded by the fact that the investigation appeared to reveal statistics showing that black customers were twice as likely as whites to have their rate marked up—and at a higher level. That evidence—included in thousands of pages of confidential documents which *20/20* and *The New York Times* obtained from a Tennessee court—revealed that some Nissan and GM dealers in Tennessee routinely marked up rates for blacks, forcing them to pay between $300 and $400 more than whites. (*ABC News 20/20*)

This is a tragic example for everyone who was affected by this markup and was the victim of this secret policy. Not only is trust destroyed, there is a huge economic cost to the general public. It is estimated that in the last four years or so, Texas car dealers have received approximately $9 billion of kickbacks from lenders, affecting 5.2 million consumers. (*ABC News 20/20*)

Let's compare these unfortunate examples of untrustworthy corporate behavior with the landmark example of Johnson & Johnson which ultimately increased its trustworthiness with consumers by the way it handled the Tylenol incident. After seven individuals, who had consumed Tylenol capsules contaminated by a third party died, Johnson & Johnson instituted a total product recall within a week costing an estimated $50 million after taxes. The company did this, not because it was responsible for causing the problem, but because it was the right thing to do. In addition, Johnson & Johnson spearheaded the development of more effective tamper-proof containers for their industry. Because of the company's swift response, consumers once again were able to trust in the Johnson & Johnson name. Although Johnson & Johnson suffered a decrease in market share at the time because of the scare, over the long term it has maintained its profitability in a highly competitive market.

Certainly part of this profit success is attributable to consumers believing that Johnson & Johnson is a trustworthy company. (Robin and Reidenbach)

The e-commerce arena presents another example of the importance of marketers building a mutually valuable relationship with customers through a trust-based collaboration process. Recent research with 50 e-businesses reflects that companies which create and nurture trust find customers return to their sites repeatedly. (Dayal . . . . p. 64)

In the e-commerce world, six components of trust were found to be critical in developing trusting, satisfied customers:

- State-of-art reliable security measures on one's site
- Merchant legitimacy (e.g., ally one's product or service with an established brand)
- Order fulfillment (i.e. placing orders and getting merchandise efficiently and with minimal hassles)
- Tone and ambiance—handling consumers' personal information with sensitivity and iron-clad confidentiality
- Customers feeling that they are in control of the buying process
- Consumer collaboration—e.g., having chat groups to let consumers query each other about their purchases and experiences (Dayal . . . , pp. 64–67)

Additionally, one author noted recently that in the e-commerce world we've moved beyond brands and trademarks to "trustmarks." This author defined a trustmark as a

. . . (D)istinctive name or symbol that emotionally binds a company with the desires and aspirations of its customers. It's an emotional connection—and it's much bigger and more powerful than the uses that we traditionally associate with a trademark. . . . (Webber, p. 214)

Certainly if this is the case, trust—being an emotional link—is of supreme importance for a company that wants to succeed in doing business on the Internet.

It's unfortunate that while a plethora of examples of violation of trust easily come to mind, a paucity of examples "pop up" as noteworthy paradigms of organizational courage and trust in their relationship with consumers.

In conclusion, some key areas for companies to scrutinize and practice with regard to decisions that may affect trustworthiness in the marketplace might include:

- Does a company practice the Golden Rule with its customers? As a company insider, knowing what you know about the product, how willing would you be to purchase it for yourself or for a family member?
- How proud would you be if your marketing practices were made public. . . . shared with your friends. . . . or family? (Blanchard and Peale, p. 27)
- Are bottom-line concerns the sole component of your organizational decision-making process? What about human rights, the ecological/environmental impact, and other areas of social responsibility?
- Can a firm which engages in unethical business practices with customers be trusted to deal with its

employees any differently? Unfortunately, frequently a willingness to violate standards of ethics is not an isolated phenomenon but permeates the culture. The result is erosion of integrity throughout a company. In such cases, trust is elusive at best. (Shaw, p. 75)

- Is your organization not only market driven, but also value-oriented? (Peters and Levering, Moskowitz, and Katz)
- Is there a strong commitment to a positive corporate culture and a clearly defined mission which is frequently and unambiguously voiced by upper-management?
- Does your organization exemplify trust by practicing a genuine relationship partnership with your customers— *before, during, and after* the initial purchase? (Strout, p. 69)

Companies which exemplify treating customers ethically are founded on a covenant of trust. There is a shared belief, confidence, and faith that the company and its people will be fair, reliable, and ethical in all its dealings. ***Total trust is the belief that a company and its people will never take opportunistic advantage of customer vulnerabilities***. (Hart and Johnson, pp. 11–13)

References

ABC News 20/20, "The Car Dealer's Secret," October 27, 2000.

Blanchard, Kenneth, and Norman Vincent Peale, *The Power of Ethical Management*, New York: William Morrow and Company, Inc., 1988.

Chewning, Richard C., *Business Ethics in a Changing Culture* (Reston, Virginia: Reston Publishing, 1984).

Dayal, Sandeep, Landesberg, Helen, and Michael Zeissner, "How to Build Trust Online," *Marketing Management*, Fall 1999, pp. 64–69.

Geyelin, Milo, "Why One Jury Dealt a Big Blow to Chrysler in Minivan-Latch Case," *Wall Street Journal*, November 19, 1997, pp. A1, A10.

Hart, Christopher W. and Michael D. Johnson, "Growing the Trust Relationship," *Marketing Management*, Spring 1999, pp. 9–19.

Hosmer, La Rue Tone, *The Ethics of Management*, second edition (Homewood, Illinois: Irwin, 1991).

Kaydo, Chad, "A Position of Power," *Sales & Marketing Management*, June 2000, pp. 104–106, 108ff.

Levering, Robert; Moskowitz, Milton; and Michael Katz, *The 100 Best Companies to Work for in America* (Reading, Mass.: Addison-Wesley, 1984).

Magnet, Myron, "Meet the New Revolutionaries," *Fortune*, February 24, 1992, pp. 94–101.

Muoio, Anna, "The Experienced Customer," *Net Company*, Fall 1999, pp. 025–027.

Peters, Thomas J. and Robert H. Waterman Jr., *In Search of Excellence* (New York: Harper & Row, 1982).

Richardson, John (ed.), *Annual Editions: Business Ethics 00/01* (Guilford, CT: McGraw-Hill/Dushkin, 2000).

_____, *Annual Editions: Marketing 00/01* (Guilford, CT: McGraw-Hill/Dushkin, 2000).

Robin, Donald P., and Erich Reidenbach, "Social Responsibility, Ethics, and Marketing Strategy: Closing the Gap Between Concept and Application," *Journal of Marketing*, Vol. 51 (January 1987), pp. 44–58.

Shaw, Robert Bruce, *Trust in the Balance*, (San Francisco: Jossey-Bass Publishers, 1997).

Strout, Erin, "Tough Customers," *Sales Marketing Management*, January 2000, pp. 63–69.

Webber, Alan M., "Trust in the Future," *Fast Company*, September 2000, pp. 209–212ff.

Dr. John E. Richardson is Professor of Marketing in the Graziadio School of Business and Management at Pepperdine University, Malibu, California.

Dr. Linnea Bernard McCord is Associate Professor of Business Law in the Graziadio School of Business and Management at Pepperdine University, Malibu, California.

Businesses Grow More Socially Conscious

Edward Iwata

Activists have argued for decades that companies, as good corporate citizens, are morally obligated to adopt socially responsible business practices. On their end, companies say they exist to sell products, make money and please shareholders—not to save the world.

But those clashing views may be finding common ground, say business experts on the movement known as "corporate social responsibility," or CSR.

There's growing evidence that companies are embracing CSR practices—whether it's reducing factory and transportation pollution, using natural materials for packaging or treating workers fairly—because they believe such strategies can be profitable and socially responsible.

"All of a sudden, corporate responsibility is an idea whose time has arrived," says Julie Fox Gorte, chief social investment strategist at the Calvert Group, which manages socially responsible mutual funds. "We're seeing more companies who think it's not just a philosophy, but good for business, too."

Study Shows Value

Christine Arena, a San Francisco business consultant and author of *The High-Purpose Company,* says more corporations are using CSR not for feel-good philanthropy or to polish their public image, but as long-term corporate strategy.

Arena and 10 MBA students at McGill University studied 75 U.S. corporations, including Wal-Mart, McDonald's, Volvo, JetBlue, outdoor retailer Patagonia, clothing designer Eileen Fisher and agricultural products company John Deere.

They found that many are visionary, risk-taking companies that Arena calls "the early adopters, the alphas of the modern business world." The companies are staking their business growth and future on environmental and social goals. For instance:

- **General Electric (GE).** CEO Jeffrey Immelt announced GE's "Ecoimagination" initiative two years ago, and the conglomerate hopes to double its revenue from environmentally clean technology to $20 billion by 2010. Among the products and services: fuel-efficient jet and train engines, wind turbine power, energy-saving fluorescent light bulbs and water purification projects.

- **Toyota (TM).** Critics scoffed when it launched the Prius hybrid car in the USA in 2000 and in Japan a decade ago. Today, the Prius is so popular that Toyota expects to sell millions of hybrid cars and SUVs worldwide by 2010 in the Prius, Highlander, Lexus and Camry models. Now, Ford Motor, Nissan, General Motors and others are going the hybrid route.

- **Wegmans Food Markets.** While many businesses suffer from poor staff morale, this $4 billion retailer boasts a worker-friendly culture and cost savings from low turnover of employees. Workers enjoy generous salaries and benefits, vacation time and training. Each year, 130,000 job hunters apply to Wegmans—ranked No.1 in *Fortune*'s "Best Large Companies to Work For" list in 2005.

"It's not a fleeting fad," Arena says. "These companies are investing money in a way that creates social, environmental and financial value. They can't afford to stop investing in this higher purpose."

But many companies still ignore CSR issues, she says. In her study, 14 of 75 failed the litmus test. They preached social values, but made fewer investments in CSR practices than "high-purpose" companies did.

Companies such as ExxonMobil (XOM), she says, face lawsuits and a public backlash when they fall short on environmental and social issues. A federal judge recently ruled that ExxonMobil must pay $2.5 billion in damages from the Exxon Valdez oil tanker spill in 1989.

Economists and executives have debated for decades whether CSR practices help the bottom line. The late economist Milton Friedman panned social values in the boardroom, saying the No.1 goal of businesses is to boost shareholder value. Leading scholars such as David Vogel, author of *The Market for Virtue,* believe the positive impact of CSR on businesses is overblown.

But CSR gained momentum in the 1980s, when the anti-apartheid movement forced firms to withdraw investments from South Africa, and in the 1990s, when garment and retail companies were blasted for their suppliers' sweatshop labor conditions. More companies realized they could not ignore the link between their businesses and social issues.

In the most sweeping research on the topic, the University of Redlands' Marc Orlitzky and the University of Iowa's Sara Rynes and Frank Schmidt looked at 52 studies—covering 34,000 companies worldwide—on corporate social responsibility over a 30-year period.

'A Virtuous Cycle'

Their 2004 study found that well-run, profitable businesses also boasted strong social and environmental records, and vise versa. Overwhelmingly, firms that rewarded employees with good work climates and higher pay and benefits ultimately saw stronger sales and stock prices, plus less employee turnover.

"It's a virtuous cycle," Rynes says. "As a company becomes more socially responsible, its reputation and financial performance go up, which causes them to become even more socially responsible."

Clearly, CSR isn't going away.

"Some still think CSR is a distraction," Orlitzky says. "But more business strategists now believe that social responsibility has economic value."

Hundreds of corporations churn out annual "CSR reports" that tout their social consciences and business practices. Investors poured $179 billion in 2005—up from only $12 billion a decade earlier—into socially responsible mutual funds, reports the Social Investment Forum. Businesses and environmental groups are even joining forces.

Last month, the U.S. Climate Action Partnership—a new alliance that includes GE, DuPont (DD), Alcoa (AA), Caterpillar (CAT), Duke Energy (DUK), Environmental Defense and the Natural Resources Defense Council—urged lawmakers and the White House to reduce greenhouse gas emissions and hasten technology research.

DuPont's Transition

Many CSR experts point to DuPont, the $27 billion chemical manufacturer in Wilmington, Del., as a company evolving successfully from the old smokestack industry era into the environmentally aware 21st century.

DuPont used to rely heavily on fossil fuels to make paint, plastics and polymers. But in the 1990s, DuPont—renowned for its R&D that created products such as the synthetic fiber nylon—decided to pour billions of dollars into safe, environmentally friendly products.

For instance, DuPont and British food refiner Tate & Lyle make Bio-PDO—a corn-based chemical used in cosmetics, detergents and material in carpeting and clothing—at a $100 million plant in Loudon, Tenn.

Since 1990, DuPont has cut greenhouse gas emissions by 72% and air carcinogen emissions by 92% at its facilities worldwide, says Dawn Rittenhouse, DuPont's director of sustainable development.

But DuPont, like other companies that claim to be socially responsible, still faces some issues.

DuPont faces lawsuits alleging that perfluorooctanoic acid (PFOA), a chemical compound used in the making of Teflon, poses public health risks and contaminates drinking water—charges denied by DuPont.

Two years ago, DuPont agreed to a $16 million settlement with the Environmental Protection Agency after it was accused of failing to report data on PFOA, a likely carcinogen. DuPont later volunteered to halt by 2015 all PFOA emissions from its plants.

Beyond the legal fights, DuPont keeps plowing new ground. The company vows to make $2 billion a year in revenue by 2015 from 1,000 products that save energy and reduce pollutants.

"What's good for business," Rittenhouse says, "must also be good for the environment and for people worldwide."

Office Romance

Are the rules changing?

JANET LEVER, GAIL ZELLMAN, AND STEPHEN J. HIRSCHFELD

There's a reason why many companies frown upon office romance. Several reasons, actually, all good ones: In the worst-case scenarios, accusations of favoritism or retaliation after breakups lead to wrenching lawsuits; in milder cases, flirtation and affairs breed damaging gossip, and romantic liaisons—whether leading to traumatic break-up or blissful marriage—can result in the loss of valued employees. Given a choice, no manager would prefer his staff to be distracted by varying degrees of sexual tension.

But managers don't have that choice. A set of policy guidelines posted on the company intranet won't stamp out workplace relationships. Sexual-harassment trainers advise employees to leave their sexuality at home, but people don't want to. Flirtation makes work more exciting; it justifies dressing up and affirms people's sex appeal in ways that most spouses no longer do. For single employees, work is the best—sometimes the only—place to meet romantic partners. For many workers, it's either the office or Match.com.

Managers especially may worry about the consequences, legal and otherwise, but flirtation is part of the work scene for most Americans. In the *Elle*/MSNBC.com Office Sex and Romance Survey, a 2002 online poll, two-thirds of the 31,207 respondents said that "there's a lot of flirting going on" in their current work environment. As one respondent said, "people are, by their nature, sexual beings and they feel happiest in an environment that allows them to express that sexuality." Married employees are as likely as single ones to flirt back if they think it's all in fun. Another respondent added, "Everyone knows who is willing to flirt and who isn't, and those lines are hardly ever crossed."

And for better or worse, the well-publicized sexual-harassment cases of recent years have not deterred verbal, and nonverbal, sex play. Said another respondent, "sidelong glances and lustful grins are an added incentive to be at my desk each day."

Executives, and their HR teams, must face the fact that workplace romances are not only here to stay but on the rise, and do a better job of managing them to minimize negative consequences. Roughly half of workers have already had at least one office romance, and all trends point in the same direction: More men and women will seek dates and mates at work because the declining gender segregation of our labor force, informal socializing, and casual dress codes have blurred the distinction between work and the dating scene. Add the trend toward later marriage (median ages are way beyond the school years: 25 for women and 27 for men) and the continued high rate of extramarital affairs and divorce, and making such a prediction is easy.

In fact, studies suggest that work is already the number-one meeting ground where people find their spouses. One office-sex survey respondent offered an explanation that was reiterated by many others, "Work is the best place to meet a life partner. You can get to know one another on a casual basis, observe each other under stress, thereby having a pretty good idea of a person's character before starting to date."

Co-workers aren't just hooking up off duty. Every survey that poses a question about sexual activity on work premises finds some respondents admitting to succumbing to temptation—or just taking a risk for the thrill of it. One respondent described having sex on the desk in his cubicle at 1 A.M.: "I said, 'We're crazy. We're going to die if anyone sees us,' but we kept on going and that made it incredible."

And surveys also reveal many instances of workers finding colleagues in flagrante delicto. Survey firm Roper-Starch reports that almost one in ten respondents to a recent poll admits to "making love at work" themselves, while one in eight respondents say they've surprised others who were "making love at work." The more comprehensive *Elle*/MSNBC.com survey learned that nearly as many

Can Sex Surveys Be Trusted?

The short answer: In anonymous sex surveys, most people tell the truth on most questions. There's not much incentive to lie. The longer answer: The more embarrassing or stigmatizing the behavior is—especially a sex act—the more people underreport it. On the subject of workplace romance, that means that respondents who were single at the time of their office dalliance are reliable reporters, but statistics on extramarital affairs, or on cross-ranks relationships where there are no-fraternization rules or norms, are likely to be too low. Read them as "*at least* XX percent of Americans cheated on a spouse with a coworker and *at least* XX percent of bosses slept with a subordinate."

Surprisingly, although many readers take online surveys less seriously than national telephone polls, recent studies suggest that when asked about very personal sexual acts or attitudes, respondents are more likely to be truthful on Web surveys than on the phone because they trust in the anonymity of computers. Although telephone polls are still seen as the gold standard in surveying, they have a big drawback when the subject is sex: Most respondents are phoned in their homes in the evening, within earshot of spouses and kids, so many lie about fooling around—or even flirting—at work. To further tarnish the "gold," all the screening devices such as answering machines, caller ID, and privacy managers (not to mention the people missed because they've given up their land lines altogether) have caused response rates (the proportion of people selected randomly who actually get polled) to plummet to 30 percent or lower, compared to rates of 60 percent just twenty years ago.

Causing another source of bias in both telephone polls and online surveys are the people who "opt out" because they are uncomfortable with the topic—instead of lying, they just choose not to participate. These people don't affect the honesty of reporting by those who take the survey, but their self-exclusion makes the survey less representative of all those who could have responded. Web surveys—most being based on volunteers—have the opposite problem: Those who "opt in" will overrepresent those most interested in the topic. In the case of workplace romance, that means that people who've had office affairs—whether they had good or disastrous experiences—are more likely to take the time to answer such a survey, leading to overestimates of the proportion of workers involved. Given the opposing biases of online surveys and telephone polls, calculating an average can produce reasonable ranges.

Finally, huge samples from surveys on popular sites like MSNBC.com offer researchers a few other advantages: As the number of "wired" Americans grows, participants from different backgrounds allow researchers to analyze important subpopulations that are barely represented in conventional polling. Perhaps the most significant advantage is that people can have the option to use their own words—as the narratives used in this article illustrate—to explain complex situations or consequences rather than forcing them to select from A, B, C, or D.

—J.L.

respondents had sex play with a co-worker *during* work as *after* hours (about half of these people said oral sex and/or intercourse was involved). The *Elle*/MSNBC.com survey was the only one to ask about consequences: Of those 7 percent of respondents who were caught, 87 percent said that the only repercussion was embarrassment. One man wrote in that his boss apologized for disturbing him!

Getting Burned—or Not

Other than the risk of getting caught in the act, what are the real repercussions of office romance? Seven in ten respondents to a Roper-Starch poll endorsed the statement, "Dating a co-worker is like playing with fire." Most HR managers and executives surveyed by the Society for Human Resource Management (SHRM) agreed that "workplace romances are dangerous" for organizations, too. But the fact that beliefs are widespread doesn't necessarily make them true. A Roper-Starch poll found that only one in twelve people who dated someone from work reported any kind of "unpleasant breakup." Managers similarly report few dire consequences. Of the nearly fifteen thousand supervisors and managers who answered the *Elle*/MSNBC.com survey, nine out of ten said that they never, or almost never, witness workplace romances that become so problematic that someone from HR has to get involved.

Managers, just like the rank-and-file, have exaggerated notions of the risks because the worst-case scenarios—like the flagrant favoritism at Enron or Boeing's firing of CEO Harry Stonecipher when his affair with a subordinate embarrassed the company—are the ones that get media attention. Fictional accounts, as in the films *Disclosure* and *Fatal Attraction*, dramatize the risks to career, marriage, and physical safety, but they don't seem to inhibit office romance. Certainly these mass-mediated impressions are mitigated by the happy feelings generated when co-worker friends dance at the wedding of two nice colleagues who met on the job.

When Romance Ends up in Court

A manager-employee affair is unwise, no doubt—but sexual harassment? Could be. Last July, the California Supreme Court ruled that an employer can be liable for sexual harassment where a supervisor shows "widespread favoritism" toward an employee with whom he is having a consensual sexual affair. *Miller v. Department of Corrections* will immediately affect the one in eight Americans who work in California, along with any employers that have headquarters or branches in the state. And since most other states tend to follow California in the employee-rights arena, the ruling may end up having greater national implications.

In this case, a high-level manager was having consensual sexual relationships with several female direct reports. The manager made no effort to keep the affairs private; in fact, the women publicly discussed the nature of their relationships and, at times, boasted about them. There were several "incidents of public fondling," and, often, the women who were having the affairs publicly "squabbled" over their boss. Two female employees who were not having affairs with their boss sued, claiming that his relationship with the other women created a sexually hostile work environment for them, although he had not propositioned them. They claimed that the boss' girlfriends got unwarranted promotions and other benefits, and that his girlfriends frequently retaliated against other women, believing that their boss had no power to control them.

The employer argued that the plaintiffs had not been sexually harassed because they were never solicited for sexual favors, but the California Supreme Court rejected that argument, ruling that any employee can be victimized by sexual harassment even if she was never sexually propositioned by his or her supervisor. It held unanimously that, under the state law, "widespread" sexual favoritism in a workplace can create a "hostile work environment" because it implicitly conveys a "demeaning message . . . to female employees that they are viewed by management as 'sexual playthings' or that the way required for women to get ahead in the workplace is by engaging in sexual conduct with their supervisors or the management."

Some may feel relieved that the court limited its holding to cases of "widespread" sexual favoritism. It specifically noted that ordinarily there would be no liability in the case of "an isolated instance of favoritism on the part of a supervisor toward a female employee with whom the supervisor is conducting a consensual sexual affair."

In light of this decision, employers should be looking to update their harassment policies in several ways. First, an employer must decide if it wants to have an outright ban on supervisor-subordinate consensual relationships. If a policy of non-fraternization between boss and employee is not going to be implemented, then the employer must at least have a policy informing workers that it frowns upon these relationships and encourages or even requires employees to disclose these relationships to upper management. Finally, these policies should encourage employees who believe they have been negatively impacted by these relationships to raise the issue with an appropriate member of management.

—S.H.

Of course, some awful personal and organizational consequences do occur on occasion. Among the *Elle*/MSNBC.com respondents who had had a romance with a co-worker, 12 percent said that at least one of them got transferred or left the company. Some workers leave the company after messy endings, as one woman wrote: "I dated a co-worker because I was lonely, but when I moved on, he made my life hell, moping about, crying, and whining. I left the state and never made that mistake again." One man lamented the loss of one of his supervisors after an involvement with a colleague: "He left a void, difficult to fill due to his expertise in a specialized field."

A management trainee was sent to Florida for a four-day class, and one of his female colleagues called in sick that same week. Their suspicious boss went to the airport to meet the man's plane and saw both of his workers walking off it. When they returned to work Monday, both were fired.

Many Casanovas in management stay on the job but, when they are indiscreet, lose the respect of their staff. "The general manager was known for having affairs at work," said one employee, "one clueless bimbo couldn't figure out why the rest of us resented her—as if their moans and groans could not be heard through the walls of his office." Morale nosedives when bosses engage in flagrant favoritism. One supervisor complained, "Several VPs had affairs and promoted their girlfriends, giving them positions of authority and high salaries. It was the culture of the place and it was HELL."

Women are both beneficiaries and victims of sex-charged workplaces. One in three women, compared to one in five men, say they play up their sexuality at work, but others intentionally play it down. Some women admit to benefiting from their sexuality, like the one who had a relationship with her supervisor's boss: "He gave me some great opportunities and lots of invaluable career advice." One woman proudly stated, "Sex

Who Can Date Whom?

In the abstract, Americans overwhelmingly agree that even the boss has the right to look for love at work—whether among peers or subordinates. Yet there's a consensus that dating up or down the reporting line is a bad idea. A Roper-Starch poll found that 72 percent of respondents agreed with the statement "never date your boss"; 70 percent agreed, "never date someone who reports to you."

So would employees accept limited restrictions on their freedom of association? In short, yes. The *Elle*/MNBC.com survey found that six in ten employees who work for an employer that prohibits sexual relationships between supervisors and subordinates favored that policy over having no regulation; for comparison, only two in ten employees who worked where there were no regulations on office romance supported having any restrictions. In other words, once reasonable prohibitions are imposed, they come to be appreciated.

Even so, in our preferred policy, there are no prohibitions about dating up and down the chain, which reconciles people's belief that even the boss has the right to search for love (and employees have a right to try to "marry up") with their fears that their co-workers' personal ties could have unfair consequences for them or the group's morale. Under a disclosure policy, a supervisor dating a subordinate would have to let her boss know about a breakup, too, so the manager can pay close attention to future performance reviews and promotion or demotion situations to ensure objectivity.

—J.L.

and office politics go hand-in-hand, and I play the game pretty well. I have no regrets that my relationships with co-workers have opened doors for me—the modern workplace is very competitive."

But women who exploit their sexuality reap resentment from male and female colleagues alike. One man in sales complained, "Female salespeople have told me that they have no problems being flirty to close a deal. Women can't have it both ways, but in my experience that is reality." A female co-worker said, "I can't stand it when some women dress like they're at a nightclub." Another added, "Your personality should come out first, not your boobs."

Women are both beneficiaries and victims of sex-charged workplaces.

But plenty of women expressed resentment, too, that they were subject to rumors that they were hired or promoted only because some supervisor found them sexy. Attractive women executives were outraged by archaic stereotypes that they were sleeping with their bosses. As one pleaded, "Please do not pre-judge us by how we look. Plenty of us prefer to use our brains rather than our bodies to advance ourselves." But the stereotypes definitely persist: Four in ten respondents to the *Elle*/MSNBC.com survey said that women who were promoted quickly were invariably subject to gossip that they had slept their way to the top, while four in ten of those respondents believed these rumors to be true.

Another common problem with sexuality in the workplace is the diversion of energy and waste of company time and resources that it often involves. One woman admitted having daily cybersex with a co-worker for six months, followed by sneaking off to stairwells for quick kissing and touching. A man at a technology firm said that flirtations there were mostly electronic: "Me and four female co-workers would go to the private chat room and lay out the fantasies we wanted to live out on the weekend."

Still, in most cases, office romance doesn't present an immediate crisis for manager or company. But it's always a potential factor—just because you may not have had to deal with problems stemming from sexual issues in the office yet doesn't mean that won't happen someday soon. We are using workers' own words to emphasize the point that the workplace is increasingly full of conflicts waiting to blossom into problems, and that managers clearly aren't taking this growing phenomenon seriously enough—if they were, they would put in place explicit policies that reduce the potential for conflicts of interest and the morale problems that can result from consensual sexual relationships. The percentage of workplace romances that go really bad may be small, but they can create mighty big problems for the company; indeed, a California Supreme Court decision last July may expand the number of companies vulnerable to harassment suits. Yet only 12 percent of companies surveyed by the AMA have any written guidelines on employee dating; SHRM surveys show similarly low figures.

The lack of corporate policy reflects a widespread belief that organizations can simply sidestep this sensitive topic because if consensual relationships go sour, they're covered by existing policies that prohibit sexual harassment and retaliation. That reasoning ignores all the employee-relations problems that can grow out of consenting unions that *don't* end. As alluded to above, fallout issues can include personnel leaving or needing to transfer

What a Policy Looks Like

An example of a corporate disclosure policy that limits its scope to supervisory relationships:

The Company is committed to fostering a professional work environment where all employees are treated fairly and impartially by their managers. Intimate personal relationships between supervisors and subordinates may result in workplace problems, such as a lack of objectivity in supervising and evaluating employees, the perception of favoritism by other employees (whether justified or not), and the potential for sexual harassment claims if a relationship ends. Therefore, supervisors are strongly discouraged from dating, engaging in amorous relationships with, or participating in sexual relations with employees who report to them, either directly or indirectly. Any supervisor who engages in such a relationship must immediately disclose the existence of that relationship to his or her immediate supervisor or Vice President of Human Resources. Upon receiving that information, the Company will make a decision as to whether it will continue to permit a direct reporting relationship or whether one or both of the employees in question must be transferred or required to seek employment elsewhere.

Questions about the application of this policy should be directed to the Human Resources Department.

due to either nepotism restrictions or a couple's desire to separate home from work life. When a couple is allowed or chooses to stay in the same department or division, managers may need to shift responsibility for job assignments, evaluations, and promotion to avert the appearance of favoritism or conflict of interest.

Avoiding a policy creates its own problems. When dating policies are implied rather than explicit, employees and managers are uncertain about the repercussions of workplace romances. Leaving it to managers to decide what to do on a case-by-case basis can lead to claims of discrimination and inconsistent treatment. Managers need training to deal with these issues in a practical and consistent fashion, and few get that training. Besides, even when employers look the other way, co-workers may not, and their reactions to office scandal can be quite damaging.

So What's the Best Policy?

Many companies strive to create a climate that discourages workplace romances because of fear of complications; others celebrate their "M&M's" (met and married). Innovative companies—especially high-tech firms—recognize that their inadvertent function as dating services can actually be a plus, boosting morale and helping the company attract and retain a young workforce asked to put in long hours and travel frequently.

And young people affirm that workplace romances can be worth any risks: Two-thirds of respondents under age 35 in the Roper-Starch poll said that working with attractive persons of the opposite sex adds excitement to their jobs, and one-third of all respondents indicated that meeting potential dates at work is important, endorsing the statement, "[I] never have a chance to meet anyone I don't work with." Studies consistently find that about one in four workplace liaisons results in marriage. And companies' mating opportunities don't appeal just to the young—one labor analyst has pointed out that one in three American workers age 55 and over is currently single.

We recommend taking a step that many people at every level of the organization will find uncomfortable to contemplate: developing a broad "personal relationship policy" that includes but goes beyond sexual relationships and mandates disclosure of close personal relationships as defined in the policy. Even though sexual involvement is perceived as posing the greatest threat to objectivity, close after-hours friendships are important to note as well: Research supports our suspicion that "old boy" buddies—and now "old girls," too—get more job perks than "lovers." That's why a policy should address potential conflicts with marital, extended-family, and close-friendship relationships as well as romantic ones.

Here's how the process actually works: The company develops and distributes guidelines on when a relationship must be disclosed—that is, when there's a potential conflict of interest or compromising situation. Each employee decides whether she has a conflict that requires disclosure and, if so, goes to her supervisor or to HR and has a closed-door discussion. The boss and HR talk afterward and decide whether, given the organizational structure, they are comfortable with the relationships. If yes, then the employee is warned about keeping the relationship separate from work, and the supervisor can be on alert to keep an eye on the situation.

Will disclosing relationships be awkward? Probably, especially for those who have romantic relationships to explain. But the process, if handled properly, doesn't have to be embarrassing for anyone involved, and there are real payoffs on both managerial and organizational levels. We know of or have worked with several Silicon Valley clients that currently have either a written disclosure policy or a stated but unwritten practice, and the companies that have implemented policies report that they work quite effectively—a

A Different Take on Office Romance

Lisa Mainiero, professor of management at Fairfield University's Dolan School of Business, offers thoughts on developments in corporate America since her 1989 book *Office Romance: Love, Power, and Sex in the Workplace*.

—Matthew Budman

Since you wrote *Office Romance*, have you seen changes in how companies deal with workplace relationships?

Definitely. At the time I wrote the book, some companies actually felt compelled to fire one of the two parties—and usually it was the lower-level person, who usually was a woman. Now firms are more comfortable with romance in their auspices across the board—unless a conflict of interest is presented, such as when it is a case of a direct-report relationship.

Are executives more concerned about workplace relationships since recent high-profile cases such as that of Harry Stonecipher at Boeing?

Yes. I think the Boeing case really showed the executive ranks that they serve as role models for the entire corporation, and that their personal behavior is tightly observed and evaluated. Especially in the case of Boeing, which is one of the few firms I have seen that has an articulate, well-developed code of ethics that addresses this issue.

Should companies make romance an HR priority?

Office romance is inevitable. People are meeting and dating in the workplace as a natural course of events. It is a serious issue if the romance occurs across hierarchical lines, such as between a boss and a direct report. But if the romance occurs between two peers who work in different departments, then it really is not a serious issue that will affect motivation and workplace productivity at all.

Of course, when there's a breakup, things can get messy very quickly. In most cases, the breakup is uneventful because the employees work for different departments. But in other cases, you may have a direct-report relationship where harassment is taking place. Any situation of harassment requires immediate attention from HR.

How strongly, or often, are workplaces affected by morale problems stemming from perceived favoritism and conflicts of interest?

The issue of concern is that sex can be traded for power. If the relationship occurs between a boss and a direct report, or between a subordinate and a higher-level officer, almost always employee morale is affected because favoritism is suspected. HR issues are more about perception than facts. In some cases, the perceptions become the facts, or at least are treated as facts, even though they may not necessarily be the facts of the case. Employees assume favoritism even if there isn't any. If it is a peer relationship, however, employee morale is usually not affected. This is because employees have a fair sense that confidential information is not being traded that might adversely affect them, that the romance is taking place on a level playing field. In fact, I found cases where co-workers were cheering for the romance.

Should companies be encouraging—or even mandating—employees to disclose their close workplace relationships?

This is not reasonable. Believe me, I had numerous stories of cloak-and-dagger activities—people switching cars at stoplights, coming and going at odd hours to ensure that their romance stayed secret. But I also had numerous stories of employees who suspected that a romance was going on who went to their boss about it. If the romance is a problem, employees will tell. That is the point when management should take action, because employees are basically saying that there is a morale problem caused by unfair actions and sharing of information. It would be great if management would create an atmosphere of trust and confidentiality, though. That will only happen if the rules are clear and that people are not punished—fired—for falling in love at work. In many large firms, it is a simple matter to transfer one of the parties, and then the problems go away.

If not disclosure, what policies should companies have on office romance?

Develop a corporate policy that clearly states that personal relationships between direct reports are not condoned, and that personal relationships that represent a conflict of interest will be investigated. But people don't need to be fired, either—there needs to be a middle ground. Also develop a policy of professionalism so that it is clear that personal behavior stays at home and work is work. But otherwise let love reign free—peer relationships and relationships between employees in different divisions are largely harmless until a conflict of interest takes place.

few clients have been able to transfer valuable employees to avoid conflicts, thereby both keeping them on staff and allowing their relationships to continue. Even some huge corporations have moved toward the practice—General Motors has operated under a policy that includes the "basics of disclosure" for several years.

A disclosure policy gives the company the explicit prerogative to decide whether an employee's ties may adversely affect the performance of her responsibilities. The manager can then determine whether it's realistic to keep the individuals working closely together or whether, organizationally, it makes more sense to move them apart—or, if that's not feasible, invite one to look for a job elsewhere.

Is it realistic to *mandate* that everyone disclose his potentially compromising relationships, including employees engaging in extramarital affairs and gay and lesbian employees who may not feel safe enough to reveal their sexual orientation? We recognize that disclosure policies are more problematic for those employees, even those in a municipality, state, or company with anti-discrimination policies. No one wants to jeopardize his working situation even if he's on sound legal footing. But these types of relationships may have even more ramifications than benign, conventional ones, and managers shouldn't be left in the dark. The crucial step is to establish and nurture a nonjudgmental climate—employees must be guaranteed that their disclosures will be revealed only to the few with a need to know, who will hold them in strict confidence.

Given that a personal-relationship policy will surely be seen as intrusive—and given that there's usually no immediate crisis demanding its being put in place—it is important to voice support from top management and explain clearly why one is necessary. Employees are being asked, after all, to tell their supervisors about their sex lives, their infidelities, and their sexual orientation. This is a lot to ask. But the boss doesn't need to know (and probably doesn't want to know) nitty-gritty details—just enough to provide opportunity for discussion about potential conflicts of interest. And employees aren't expected to disclose a single date or two, or to keep a running account of flirtations—only once an intimate relationship has developed.

In our experience working with corporate clients, when managers are informed of relationships—or even illicit affairs—they *do* keep the information confidential, because in training they learn that failing to do so will get them in trouble. As part of that training program, supervisors are given an incentive to disclose their own affairs too; if not, they will be held personally responsible and subject to discipline or termination if problems arise as a result. (It's worth noting that even when an employee decides *not* to take the risk of disclosing a relationship, the company gains some legal protection by having such a policy—it demonstrates that the company takes the issue seriously and is trying to prevent problems.)

This part of the training is essential for the company's protection: One in four supervisors and managers who answered the *Elle*/MSNBC.com survey admitted having had a sexual relationship with a direct report.

Some employees recognize the virtue of disclosure policies right away. As one worker said, "Requiring disclosure of all intra-office romances keeps things under control. It becomes harder for someone to claim he or she was pressured into having the relationship when there are no secrets. It is also harder to pressure someone when they know the relationship will be revealed. At work, secrecy is bad; openness is good."

Others, understandably, are more skittish—in fact, one of the biggest concerns about these policies is that they will alienate employees. In two consecutive national polls commissioned by the Employment Law Alliance, 62 to 66 percent of Americans agreed with the statement, "Employees feel that romantic relationships at work are personal and private and should not be regulated by employers." That's why it is absolutely essential that the personal-relationship policy be seen as fair and necessary, and that managers and HR be held to the highest standards of conduct.

The Workplace vs. the Real World

We've mentioned that a big concern with disclosure policies is the obligation they impose to consistently enforce them. An organization is at risk whenever it doesn't treat everyone's personal relationships in the same way—whether it's singles dating versus an extramarital affair, or equal-status co-workers versus cross-rank couples (even involving the CEO). Having a policy *minimizes* this risk by creating guidelines rather than leaving decisions up to individual managers. Organizations are also vulnerable to charges of sexual discrimination when they consistently dismiss the female partner—most often the one with lower rank or seniority—because the male is harder to replace. A disclosure policy represents an opportunity to remind managers that the organization must be sensitive to such issues.

A personal-relationship policy is a good place to remind employees that public displays of affection—especially those that could be viewed by co-workers—are unprofessional and subject to disciplinary action. And reminders about improper use of company e-mail and voice mail belong in the policy covering consensual sexual relationships as well as in the one on sexual harassment. Data indicate that what a sender intends as playful and flirtatious, a recipient may see as sexual, insulting, or intimidating. Such a policy can be a good place to underscore differences between dating at work versus elsewhere. Two examples: People who are not interested in a co-worker's sexual attention need to say so clearly, whereas in the "real world," one can just keep saying "I'm busy"; and in the "real world," the rebuffed can hang around and beg for "another chance," while at work once someone communicates that sexual attention is no longer wanted, it must cease. Finally, such a policy can remind employees that they always have the right to decline their colleagues' invitations for informal socializing off-duty.

To deserve their employees' trust, companies must promulgate strict confidentiality policies, enforce them rigorously, and publicly punish any violations. And companies must also raise the awareness of managers and supervisors about their personal risks and responsibilities. Most of them naïvely believe that their own con-sensual relationships will not create a problem because they would never actually retaliate or engage in favoritism. But they should not confuse what they believe to be true with what gets decided in a courtroom; ultimately, a manager may be leaving it up to twelve jurors to decide what occurred.

JANET LEVER is professor of sociology at California State University at Los Angeles and author of the *Elle*/MSNBC.com Office Sex and Romance Survey; **GAIL ZELLMAN** is a senior research psychologist at the RAND Corp. in Santa Monica, Calif.; and **STEPHEN J. HIRSCHFELD** is CEO of the international Employment Law Alliance and a partner in the San Francisco law firm of Curiale Dellaverson Hirschfeld Kraemer & Sloan.

Scams Unmasked!

Identity thieves have more tricks than ever—and so should you. Here are the best and latest ways to keep crooks from stealing your name and your money (adapted from Scam-Proof Your Life).

SID KIRCHHEIMER

Spreading the word on how to sidestep scams is my business. And sometimes I get to practice what I preach.

I had just finished speaking with one fraud victim—a retired salesperson from Georgia bilked out of $4,500 in a bogus work-at-home scheme—when my telephone rang.

"Hello," said a pleasant voice. "I'm calling from your mortgage company. And I see from our records that you may qualify for a lower loan rate."

Interestingly, she did not mention the name of the company that gets my monthly mortgage check. Even more telling was the fact that I had refinanced just two months earlier—and mortgage interest rates had climbed since then.

"Really?" I replied, glancing at the caller ID gizmo on my desk. "Tell me more." The incoming call was marked private. It was about 8:00 in the evening, a time when most mortgage-loan officers are home digesting dinner.

"Well, sir," she said, "based on your excellent credit history, I think we can save you hundreds of dollars a month with our much more attractive rate."

"Is that right?" I encouraged her. "What's the rate?"

"Before I can answer," she replied, "I just need to verify some information—your Social Security number and bank account numbers—to make sure they match our records and that you really qualify for this great mortgage rate."

Hmm. "Do you know my name?" I asked her, since she hadn't used it yet.

She gave the one listed in the phone book—which is not *Kirchheimer.* To spot telemarketers, who continue to phone my home despite my enrollment in the National Do Not Call Registry, I use a pseudonym as my white pages listing (having an unlisted number costs extra).

"Seriously," I said, "do you expect me to fall for this?"

She gave a harsh little laugh. "You'd be amazed how many people do," she sneered. And then she hung up.

Actually, I wouldn't be amazed—and neither should you. Last year almost 9 million Americans were robbed of private financial information, and half didn't know how the damage was done—

their credit cards maxed out, bank accounts cleaned out, or credit ratings sunk after criminals took out loans in their names.

Yes, the national epidemic of identity theft is still with us, courtesy of telephone and email scams, card "skimming" at cash machines and merchants, wayward checks, stolen wallets, and wholesale downloading of company data.

The biggest source of U.S. consumer fraud, identity theft takes an enormous toll. Criminals posing as other people last year ripped off a record $56.6 billion in cash, goods, and services. While two thirds of victims had no out-of-pocket expense (because banks and credit card companies seldom ask victims to cover any charges), for about 3 million folks the average cost of repairing their credit was nearly $1,200. And for all victims the average time to set the record straight was 40 hours.

Fortunately, the growth of ID theft seems to be slowing. After cases reported to the Federal Trade Commission (FTC) nearly tripled from 2001 through 2004, last year's increase was just 3 percent. And the biggest annual survey on the subject, by the Better Business Bureau and Javelin Strategy & Research, showed the number of victims declined slightly for a second consecutive year.

But that doesn't mean you can let down your guard. On the contrary, with consumers getting wise to the ways of identity thieves and altering habits to thwart them, you can bet the scamsters will do their best to sabotage your basic protective measures. Which is why, in addition to the time-tested actions everyone should take, I recommend an additional layer of safety that even the wiliest crook will find tough to crack.

Your Documents
Good Move: Lighten the Wallet

The most frequent source of information for ID thieves is you. According to the Javelin survey, among victims who knew how their numbers were pilfered, 30 percent of frauds began with a lost or stolen wallet, checkbook, or credit card. So rule number one is "Leave home without it." Don't carry a crib sheet with PIN codes for your plastic; don't carry your Social Security card. And that check you tote everywhere "just in case"? It's a needless risk. One credit card will pull you through most emergencies—and is easy to cancel in case of theft.

Better Move: Lock 'Em Up

Here's a statistic that may surprise you: one in seven cases of ID theft traced to a source turns up a family member or other trusted associate the victim shouldn't have trusted. So it's no use leaving things home if they're vulnerable there, too. Your checkbook, cards, and any important papers (such as mortgage, insurance, and investment records) should be under lock and key wherever they are. A locking metal file cabinet or desk drawer may be the answer.

Your Credit
Good Move: Monitor All Accounts

Though some banks alert you to unusual activity on a credit card, it's more likely you'll detect a crime before your bank does. In 2005, Javelin found, frauds first noticed by victims were uncovered a month sooner than those financial institutions fingered. Besides regularly checking credit card and bank statements, it's good to scan your credit history for inquiries on existing accounts and applications for new loans. You can get one free credit history annually from each of the three major bureaus (Experian, Equifax, and TransUnion) at www.annualcreditreport.com. By rotating your requests, you can receive a report every four months.

For a monthly fee you can also get credit-monitoring services to notify you of activity. These services mushroomed in recent years as identity theft reached critical mass, but some take a week or longer to alert you. Sift through the competition until you find one with daily alerts via email.

Better Move: Freeze Access

Recent laws in eight states let you freeze access to your credit file to keep anyone—legit or not—from reviewing your standing or opening loans in your name. A burgeoning trend, freeze laws have been under consideration in at least 18 other states. For consumers who don't plan to apply for new credit anytime soon, it's a mighty shield, and convenient, too. The rest of us can benefit with just a few extra steps.

Freezes that used to be applied by credit bureaus only after ID thieves struck are available free by law to any citizen in Colorado (starting in July) and New Jersey. Consumers in California, Connecticut, Louisiana, Maine, Nevada, and North Carolina can stop credit tampering cold for a small fee—generally up to $10. And for another $5 or $10 the same eight states allow a credit thaw when you need a new loan. Freezes are also available by law to ID-theft victims in Illinois, Texas, Vermont, and Washington.

Your Trash
Good Move: Shred the Evidence

Rather than merely folding, spindling, or mutilating your unwanted mail, feed anything bearing sensitive information into a crosscut (or "confetti") shredder. This makes it virtually impossible for garbage divers to read your data or use credit card "convenience checks" and new offers. While assiduous tearing by hand can do the job, $75 or less will get you a decent shredder. Heavier-duty models run to $200.

To make sure mail isn't diverted before it reaches the shredder, get your letters delivered to a secure location. A street-side mailbox doesn't make the grade. Police say these boxes are favored targets of ID thieves looking for checks to steal. A box by your door is a safety improvement; a mail slot into the house is better still. For even more security, consider renting a box at the local post office.

Better Move: Opt Out of Offers

Spend less time sorting and shredding by opting out of solicitations for new credit cards, mortgages, or other loans. To eliminate future trash at its source, call the credit bureaus' dedicated line at 888-567-8688 from your home telephone or register at www.optoutprescreen.com.

If you call, an automated voice-response system will request your name, telephone number, and Social Security number; don't worry, the credit bureau has it already as part of your credit history. You can opt out for five years or forever. (And if you haven't done so already, by all means register your phone numbers with the National Do Not Call Registry maintained by the FTC at 888-382-1222 or www.donotcall.gov. Unless they're from charities, political groups, surveys, or companies with which you have ties, telemarketers are barred from calling registered numbers. So you'll know any call you do get is suspect.)

Your Checks
Good Move: Frustrate Forgers

All it takes to empty your bank account, says fraud fighter Frank W. Abagnale (the former con artist portrayed by Leonardo DiCaprio in the 2002 movie *Catch Me If You Can*) is a signed check and a pan of acetone, the active ingredient in nail polish remover.

Here's the scam: a crook tapes over your signature front and back, then soaks the check in acetone to wash away everything but the printer's ink and your John Hancock. Dried and carefully peeled, it's—presto!—a blank check signed by you. And thanks to "bounce protection" from banks, the scamster can even overdraw your account.

Abagnale's cure? He tested major pen brands as part of his second career advising banks and law enforcement on how to fight check fraud and found only Uni-ball gel pens resist washing; now the pens carry his endorsement.

Better Move: Use a Blanker Check

Even tamperproof checks offer thieves valuable tidbits—various account numbers—if you obligingly add them at the payee's behest. "A check can be handled by dozens of people from the payee's company, its bank, your bank, and various vendors who process checks," Abagnale notes.

The solution: skip the numbers or just write the last few. "If you return that payment stub—and you always should—there's no reason to write your account number," he says. Crooks can use the information to acquire cell phones and open utility accounts at other addresses, helping them establish an entire separate identity with your name.

Your printed checks can also say less. When you order a new batch, have just your initials and last name printed, and keep phone numbers off them altogether. Order checks from your bank, not from independent vendors, and seek out security features such as paper that acetone stains.

Your Monthly Bills
Good Move: Mail Safe

As you've probably gathered by now, there's a lot not to like about checks. Mari J. Frank, a California attorney who became an identity-theft expert after being victimized herself, suggests you stop writing checks altogether. Even if you don't, drop bill payments at a post office or U.S. Postal Service mailbox. That's safer than just putting the flag up on your own box or leaving letters in an open mail bin at your workplace.

Better Move: Bank Online

Here's another, possibly stronger, incentive for reducing your dependence on checks: they're on their way out. More than a third of U.S. households with bank accounts bank online, and because paperless transactions are cheaper, expect banks to do everything in their power to launch your accounts into cyberspace, too. The benefits aren't just the savings on postage, the ease, and the convenience. Financial services are adding more security—and protections from liability for customers in the case of fraud—as electronic payments of all kinds become more common.

Your Computer
Good Move: Scrub That Software

Some measures against online ID thieves are high tech and some are common sense. All are best applied early and often. Every home computer should have security software that updates regularly; every user needs to resist the bait from con artists "phishing" for suckers via email.

The unseen danger comes from "spyware," which sneaks onto your computer to track your actions online. One kind, known as adware, merely gauges your interests to help websites predict what advertising might grab your attention. A more sinister sort of spyware monitors your every keystroke and reports back to a waiting attacker.

How does spyware infiltrate your computer? By hiding inside a downloaded program. It can even worm its way in from an email you open or Web link you click on.

"You should think twice about installing freebie software, no matter how enticing it appears," says Doug Tygar, a professor of computer science at the University of California, Berkeley, "and scan your computer once a week or more with a good anti-spyware program."

Tygar recommends Ad-Aware, itself a free download—but one you can trust. In an impromptu test I conducted, Ad-Aware quarantined more than ten intruders that had escaped the notice of a brand-name $50 anti-spyware program.

To avoid helping crooks invade your computer, remember that messages from strangers always pose a risk—and that strangers sometimes pose as friends. Real banks never send emails asking for your account information. Nor will an Internet service provider. Rather than click on a Web link within email, type the address yourself or link to it from a search engine. Secure sites display the padlock icon in the frame surrounding the Web page, not within it, and have addresses preceded by *https*—the *s* stands for "secure."

Better Move: Evade and Escape

The most popular Web browser is Microsoft's Internet Explorer, which comes installed on most personal computers along with Microsoft's Windows operating system. Small wonder, then, that most viruses and spyware are geared to infiltrate it. One way of ducking the scamsters, Tygar suggests, is using other browsers such as Firefox or Opera. (Download these for free at www.getfirefox.com and www.opera.com.)

Another maneuver that leaves thieves in the lurch is to get a second (and sometimes third) free email account from MSN's Hotmail, Yahoo!'s Mail, or Google's Gmail so you can segregate your online shopping from banking and private correspondence. And don't use your name or a familiar word as part of any address. Scramble some letters and numbers instead. These measures will make it a lot harder for phishers to find you by chance and lure you to scam websites.

Your Pass Codes
Good Move: Guard the Cards

About 9 percent of traceable ID thefts in 2004 occurred during transactions offline, the cyberspace term for being out and about. Perhaps you sent a credit card away with your waiter, who skimmed its numbers in a magnetic reader, noted the security code on the back, and duplicated the plastic later. Or maybe the skimmer was installed over the card slot of a cash machine. Or a perp behind you in line peeked at your card—that's known as shoulder surfing.

Though I can tell you to never let a credit card out of your sight, paranoia has its own costs to your quality of life. While it's good to be alert to unnecessary risks, let your liability be your guide. Credit (though not debit) card issuers must by law pick up any fraud tab over $50; monitoring your monthly bill will limit any damage.

At cash machines the basic defense is physical—obstruct the view. When possible, go inside the bank branch to use the automated tellers—or the human ones. To reduce the hazard posed by a pirated cash card, call your bank and request a per-day limit on ATM withdrawals from your accounts.

Better Move: Try Disguises

Two can play at switching identities. While you can't slough off your Social Security number, you can and should obscure other facts, because using your real birth date as a PIN code, or reciting your mother's maiden name to every bank, invites trouble. Thieves can ferret out public records online, notes ID-theft expert Mari Frank. Instead, she says, "fabricate a maiden name and pick a bogus birthday—ones you can easily remember, of course."

The same goes for your listing in the telephone directory (it can be changed with a quick call to your phone carrier). Just as dropping your name from email addresses helps you fly below thieves' radar, a listing under a name other than your own allows you to spot junk mail and telemarketing calls in a snap—as I did with the "mortgage lender" who had my name wrong when she phoned.

Sometimes a good offense really is the best defense.

Reprinted from *AARP The Magazine,* May/June 2006, pp. 79–82, 118. Copyright © 2006 by Sid Kirchheimer. Reprinted by permission of American Association for Retired Persons (AARP) and Sid Kirchheimer. www.aarpmagazine.org 1-888-687-2227.

Click Fraud
The Dark Side of Online Advertising

BRIAN GROW AND BEN ELGIN

Martin Fleischmann put his faith in online advertising. He used it to build his Atlanta company, MostChoice.com, which offers consumers rate quotes and other information on insurance and mortgages. Last year he paid Yahoo! Inc. and Google Inc. a total of $2 million in advertising fees. The 40-year-old entrepreneur believed the celebrated promise of Internet marketing: You pay only when prospective customers click on your ads.

Now, Fleischmann's faith has been shaken. Over the past three years, he has noticed a growing number of puzzling clicks coming from such places as Botswana, Mongolia, and Syria. This seemed strange, since MostChoice steers customers to insurance and mortgage brokers only in the U.S. Fleischmann, who has an economics degree from Yale University and an MBA from Wharton, has used specially designed software to discover that the MostChoice ads being clicked from distant shores had appeared not on pages of Google or Yahoo but on curious Web sites with names like insurance1472.com and insurance060.com. He smelled a swindle, and he calculates it has cost his business more than $100,000 since 2003.

Fleischmann is a victim of click fraud: a dizzying collection of scams and deceptions that inflate advertising bills for thousands of companies of all sizes. The spreading scourge poses the single biggest threat to the Internet's advertising gold mine and is the most nettlesome question facing Google and Yahoo, whose digital empires depend on all that gold.

The growing ranks of businesspeople worried about click fraud typically have no complaint about versions of their ads that appear on actual Google or Yahoo Web pages, often next to search results. The trouble arises when the Internet giants boost their profits by recycling ads to millions of other sites, ranging from the familiar, such as cnn.com, to dummy Web addresses like insurance1472.com, which display lists of ads and little if anything else. When somebody clicks on these recycled ads, marketers such as MostChoice get billed, sometimes even if the clicks appear to come from Mongolia. Google or Yahoo then share the revenue with a daisy chain of Web site hosts and operators. A penny or so even trickles down to the lowly clickers. That means Google and Yahoo at times passively profit from click fraud and, in theory, have an incentive to tolerate it. So do

> # Rogues Glossary
>
> The murky world of Web advertising has its own jargon
>
> ## Click Fraud
>
> Clicking on Internet advertising solely to generate illegitimate revenue for the Web site carrying the ads; those doing the clicking typically also get paid.
>
> ## Parked Web Site
>
> A site typically with little or no content except for lists of Internet ads, often supplied by Google or Yahoo; many of them are the source of false clicks.
>
> ## Paid-to-Read
>
> A PTR site pays members to look at other Web sites and offers from marketers; often used to generate fake clicks on parked Web sites.
>
> ## Clickbot
>
> Software that can be used to produce automatic clicks on ads; some versions employed in click fraud can mask the origin and timing of clicks.
>
> ## Botnet
>
> A collection of computers infected with software that allows them to be operated remotely; networks of thousands of machines can be used in click fraud.

smaller search engines and marketing networks that similarly recycle ads.

Slipping Confidence

Google and Yahoo say they filter out most questionable clicks and either don't charge for them or reimburse advertisers that have been wrongly billed. Determined to prevent a backlash, the Internet ad titans say the extent of click chicanery has been exaggerated, and they stress that they combat the problem vigorously. "We think click fraud is a serious but manageable issue," says John Slade, Yahoo's senior director for global product management. "Google strives to detect every invalid click that passes through its system," says Shuman Ghosemajumder, the search engine's manager for trust and safety. "It's absolutely in our best interest for advertisers to have confidence in this industry."

That confidence may be slipping. A *BusinessWeek* investigation has revealed a thriving click-fraud underground populated by swarms of small-time players, making detection difficult. "Paid to read" rings with hundreds or thousands of members each, all of them pressing PC mice over and over in living rooms and dens around the world. In some cases, "clickbot" software generates page hits automatically and anonymously. Participants from Kentucky to China speak of making from $25 to several thousand dollars a month apiece, cash they wouldn't receive if Google and Yahoo were as successful at blocking fraud as they claim.

"It's not that much different from someone coming up and taking money out of your wallet," says David Struck. He and his wife, Renee, both 35, say they dabbled in click fraud last year, making more than $5,000 in four months. Employing a common scheme, the McGregor (Minn.) couple set up dummy Web sites filled with nothing but recycled Google and Yahoo advertisements. Then they paid others small amounts to visit the sites, where it was understood they would click away on the ads, says David Struck. It was "way too easy," he adds. Gradually, he says, he and his wife began to realize they were cheating unwitting advertisers, so they stopped. "Whatever Google and Yahoo are doing [to stop fraud], it's not having much of an effect," he says.

Spending on Internet ads is growing faster than any other sector of the advertising industry and is expected to surge from $12.5 billion last year to $29 billion in 2010 in the U.S. alone, according to researcher eMarketer Inc. About half of these dollars are going into deals requiring advertisers to pay by the click. Most other Internet ads are priced according to "impressions," or how many people view them. Yahoo executives warned on Sept. 19 that weak ad spending by auto and financial-services companies would hurt its third-quarter revenue. Share prices of Yahoo and Google tumbled on the news.

Google and Yahoo are grabbing billions of dollars once collected by traditional print and broadcast outlets, based partly on the assumption that clicks are a reliable, quantifiable measure of consumer interest that the older media simply can't match. But the huge influx of cash for online ads has attracted armies of con artists whose activities are eroding that crucial assumption and could eat into the optimistic expectations for online advertising. (Advertisers generally don't grumble about fraudulent clicks coming from the Web sites of traditional media outlets. But there are growing concerns about these media sites exaggerating how many visitors they have—the online version of inflating circulation.)

The success of Google and Yahoo is based partly on the idea that clicks are reliable

Most academics and consultants who study online advertising estimate that 10% to 15% of ad clicks are fake, representing roughly $1 billion in annual billings. Usually the search engines divide these proceeds with several players: First, there are intermediaries known as "domain parking" companies, to which the search engines redistribute their ads. Domain parkers host "parked" Web sites, many of which are those dummy sites containing only ads. Cheats who own parked sites obtain search-engine ads from the domain parkers and arrange for the ads to be clicked on, triggering bills to advertisers. In all, $300 million to $500 million a year could be flowing to the click-fraud industry.

Law enforcement has only lately started focusing on the threat. A cybercrime unit led by the FBI and U.S. Postal Inspection Service just last month assigned two analysts to examine whether federal laws are being violated. The FBI acted after noticing suspected cybercriminals discussing click fraud in chat rooms. The staff of the Senate Judiciary Committee has launched its own informal probe.

Many advertisers, meanwhile, are starting to get antsy. Google and Yahoo have each settled a class action filed by marketers. In late September a coalition of such major brands as InterActive Corp.'s Expedia.com travel site and mortgage broker LendingTree is planning to go public with its mounting unease over click fraud, *BusinessWeek* has learned. The companies intend to form a group to share information and pressure Google and Yahoo to be more forthcoming. "You can't blame the advertisers for being suspicious," says Robert Pettee, search marketing manager for LendingTree, based in Charlotte, N.C. "If it's your money that's going out the door, you need to be asking questions." He says that up to 15% of the clicks on his company's ads are bogus.

In June, researcher Outsell Inc. released a blind survey of 407 advertisers, 37% of which said they had reduced or were planning to reduce their pay-per-click budgets because of fraud concerns. "The click fraud and bad sites are driving people away," says Fleischmann. He's trimming his online ad budget by 15% this year.

Google and Yahoo insist there's no reason to fret. They say they use sophisticated algorithms and intelligence from advertisers to identify the vast majority of fake clicks. But the big search engines won't disclose the specifics of their methods, saying illicit clickers would exploit the information.

Some people who have worked in the industry say that as long as Google and Yahoo distribute ads to nearly anyone with a rudimentary Web site, fraud will continue. "Advertisers should be concerned," says a former Yahoo manager who requested anonymity. "A well-executed click-fraud attack is nearly impossible, if not impossible, to detect."

Although 5 feet 6 and 135 pounds, Marty Fleischmann is no one to push around. He barked orders at much bigger oarsmen while serving as coxswain on the varsity crew team at Yale in the mid-1980s. His shyness deficit surfaced again when he later played the role of Jerry Seinfeld in the student follies at Wharton. Married and the father of three children, he tends to pepper his conversation with jargon about incentives and efficiencies.

Follow the Money

Click fraud schemes vary and often involve a complicated chain of relationships. Here's one way the process can work:

1. XYZ Widgets signs up with Google or Yahoo to advertise on the Internet, agreeing to pay the search engine every time somebody clicks on an XYZ ad.
2. Google or Yahoo displays the ad on its own site but also recycles it to millions of affiliates, including "domain parking" companies.
3. Domain-parking outfits feed the Google or Yahoo ad to thousands of "parked" Web sites, some of which are nothing more than lists of ads.
4. A fraud artist who owns a parked site circulates it to "paid to read" (PTR) groups, whose members receive small payments to visit sites and click on ads.
5. When a PTR member clicks on the XYZ ad, the company is billed. Yahoo or Google shares the proceeds with the domain parker, the fraudster, and the clickers.

Korean Clones

Fleischmann's daily immersion in click statistics fuels his indignation. How, he wants to know, did he receive traffic this summer from PCs in South Korea which are clicking on insurance1472.com and insurance060.com? The only content on these identical sites—and five other clones with similar names—are lists of Yahoo ads, which occasionally have included MostChoice promotions. Fleischmann's spreadsheets revealed, not surprisingly, that all of the suspected Korean clickers left his site in a matter of seconds, and none became customers. The two individuals registered as owning the mysterious insurance sites are based in South Korea. They didn't respond to requests for comment, and most of the sites disappeared in late summer, after MostChoice challenged Yahoo about them.

"If this was costing [Yahoo] money instead of making it," they would have stopped it

---

Fleischmann, like most other advertisers, has agreed to let Google and Yahoo recycle his ads on affiliated sites. The search engines describe these affiliates in glowing terms. A Google "help" page entitled "Where will my ads appear?" mentions such brand names as AOL.com and the Web site of *The New York Times*. Left unmentioned are the parked Web sites filled exclusively with ads and sometimes associated with click-fraud rings.

Google and Yahoo defend their practice of recycling advertising to domain-parking firms and then on to parked sites, saying that the lists of ads on the sites help point Internet surfers toward relevant information. Google notes that it allows advertisers to identify sites on which they don't want their ads to run.

But this Google feature doesn't apply to many parked sites, and Yahoo doesn't offer the option at all. In any event, excluding individual sites is difficult for marketers that don't do the sort of time-consuming research MostChoice does. Whether they know it or not, many other companies are afflicted in similar ways. At *BusinessWeek's* request, Click Forensics Inc., an online auditing firm in San Antonio, analyzed the records of its 170 financial-services clients and found that from March through July of this year, 13 companies had received clicks from Web sites identified as dubious by MostChoice.

Yahoo declined to comment on insurance1472, -060, and other suspect sites in its ad network. The Sunnyvale (Calif.) search giant stressed that in many cases it doesn't deal directly with parked sites; instead, it distributes its ads by means of domain-parking firms.

BusinessWeek's independent analysis of the MostChoice records turned up additional indications of click fraud. Over the past six months, the company received 139 visitors through an advertisement on the parked site healthinsurancebids.com, which offers only ads supplied by Yahoo. Most of these visitors were located in Bulgaria, the Czech Republic, Egypt, and

Before he and partner Michael Levy co-founded their financial-information company in 1999, Fleischmann worked in Atlanta at the management consulting firm A.T. Kearney Inc., advising major corporations in the shipping and pharmaceutical industries. One lesson he says he learned is that big companies are loath to cut off any steady source of revenue. Google and Yahoo are no different, he argues.

That cynicism several years ago contributed to MostChoice's assigning an in-house programmer to design a system for analyzing every click on a company ad: the Web page where the ad appeared, the clicker's country, the length of the clicker's visit to MostChoice's site, and whether the visitor became a customer. Few companies go to such lengths, let alone companies with only 30 employees and revenue last year of just $6.4 million.

To Fleischmann, the validity of his clicks, for which he pays up to $8 apiece, has become an obsession. Every day he pores over fresh spreadsheets of click analysis. "I told Yahoo years ago," he says, "'If this was costing you money instead of making you money, you would have stopped this.'"

Google, he says, does a better job than Yahoo of screening for fraud. But neither adequately protects marketers, he argues. Until March, 2005, Google, based in Mountain View, Calif., charged advertisers twice for "double clicks," meaning those occasions when a user unnecessarily clicks twice in quick succession on an ad. Confirming this, Google's Ghosemajumder says that before the company made the change, it felt it had to focus "on issues of malicious behavior," though now it identifies double clicks and bills for only one.

Taking the Search Engines to Court

Under pressure from advertisers, Google Inc. and Yahoo! Inc are adjusting the way they deal with click fraud. Several lawsuits filed on behalf of hundreds of advertisers have helped fuel the modest changes.

In June, Yahoo agreed to settle a class action filed in federal court in Los Angeles on behalf of advertisers alleging they had been billed for fake clicks. Without admitting wrongdoing, yahoo said it would grant refunds for bad clicks since January, 2004, that advertisers bring to its attention. The potential cost to Yahoo isn't clear. The company also agreed to appoint an in-house advocate to represent advertisers. The search engine said it would periodically invite marketers to inspect its now-secret fraud-detection systems. Separate from the settlement, Yahoo says that next year it will give marketers more control over where their ads appear.

Google reached its own settlement with unhappy advertisers in July in state court in Texarkana, Ark., where a judge approved a pact valued at $90 million. The agreement provides $30 million in cash for lawyers but only advertising credits for class members. Dissatisfied, a group of advertisers is seeking to challenge the settlement in appellate court. "The rot is so pervasive," says Clarence E. Briggs, III, a leader of the breakaway group. Briggs, a former Army ranger, says his company, Advanced Internet Technologies in Fayetteville, N.C., has detected $90,000 of bad clicks on its Google ads.

Google, which denied any liability, has since announced it will pull back its cloak of secrecy and show individual advertisers the proportion of their clicks it has deemed invalid and for which they weren't billed.

—Ben Elgin and Brian Grow

Evolution of a Scam

The purpose of click fraud has changed in recent years

Version 1.0

Companies clicked on a rival's Internet advertisements, running up its ad bills and squeezing the competition. The ads in question typically appeared on Google, Yahoo and other search engine sites.

Version 2.0

Today click fraud is much more likely to occur on small Web sites that carry ads recycled from Yahoo and Google. Fraudsters arrange for fake clicks on the ads and split the resulting revenue with the search engines.

Ukraine. Their average stay on MostChoice.com was only six seconds, and none of them became a customer.

Healthinsurancebids.com offers a revealing entry point into the click-fraud realm. It is one of several parked sites registered to Roland Kiss of Budapest. Kiss also owns BestPTRsite.com. "PTR" refers to "paid to read." In theory, paid-to-read sites recruit members who agree to read marketing e-mails and Web sites tailored to their interests. PTR site operators pay members for each e-mail and Web site they read, usually a penny or less.

In reality, many PTR sites are click-fraud rings, some with hundreds or thousands of participants paid to click on ads. BestPTRsite says it has 977 members. On Aug. 23 its administrator sent an e-mail to members containing a list of parked sites filled with ads. One of these sites, mortgagebg.com, which is also registered to Kiss, has been a source of apparently bogus clicks on MostChoice. The e-mail instructed members to click on different links every day, a common means to avoid detection. Members were also told to cut and paste text from the Web pages they click as proof of their activity. "If you send us back always the same link you will get banned and not paid! So take care and visit everyday a new link," the e-mail said.

Reached by telephone, Kiss says that his registration name is false and declines to reveal the real one. He says he's the 23-year-old son of computer technicians and has studied finance. He owns about 20 paid-to-read sites, he says, as well as 200 parked sites stuffed with Google and Yahoo advertisements. But he says he will take down healthinsurancebids.com to avoid discovery. He claims to take in $70,000 in ad revenue a month, but says that only 10% of that comes from PTRs. The rest, he says, reflects legitimate clicks by real Web surfers. He refrains from more PTR activity, he claims, because "it's no good for advertisers, no good for Google, no good for Yahoo." It's not unusual for people who are involved in PTR activity to profess that they restrict their behavior in some way for the good of advertisers and the big search engines.

After joining several PTR groups, *BusinessWeek* reporters received a torrent of e-mail showcasing hundreds of parked sites filled with Google and Yahoo ads. The groups urged participants to click aggressively on ads. "People don't click because they're interested in the subject," says Pam Parrish, a medical editor in Indianapolis who has participated in PTR sites. "They're clicking on ads to get paid."

Parrish, 52, says that when she started three years ago, PTR sites drew clickers like herself: potential customers looking to pick up a few spare dollars. At one point, she says she belonged to as many as 50 such sites but earned only about $200 all told. More recently, she says, most PTR sites have dropped the pretense of caring whether members are interested in the sites they visit. Parrish and others active on PTR sites say click fraud became more blatant as Google and Yahoo made their ads more widely available to parked sites.

Google and Yahoo say they filter out most PTR activity. "We manage that very well," says Google's Ghosemajumder. "It hasn't been an issue across our network, but it's something we take very seriously." Yahoo adds that PTR sites carrying its ads are in "very serious violation" of its standard distribution

Advertisers in China Are Getting Burned, Too

China has a reputation in the U.S. as a haven for click-fraud artists. Now, Chinese advertisers say they, too, have fallen victim to the proliferating racket.

In August, Chinese advertisers carrying placards even staged a small demonstration in front of the Beijing office of Baidu.com. China's top search engine. Leading the protest was Dr. Liu Wenhua, director of the Beijing Zhongbei Cancer Medical Research Center. Liu claims that his center, which advertises its services online, has suffered from fraudulent clicks on its ads on a Baidu-affiliated music and entertainment site. Baidu has offered a refund, Liu says, but he turned it down, preferring to take Baidu to court. "I'm not satisfied," the doctor says.

Zhang Xinwei, a partner with the Beijing Hetong Law Office, represents Liu and four other advertisers that also have sued Baidu, alleging fraud. "The problem is very serious," says Zhang. Another plaintiff, Land of Maples Tourism & Culture Exchange, a Beijing travel agency specializing in trips to Canada, has hired a different lawyer. Steven Donne, who runs the agency, says he became suspicious of a batch of 600 clicks this summer because they all came from one source. But Donne feared he wouldn't be able to prove click fraud, so his suit focuses on a claim that Baidu manipulates search results to punish certain advertisers. The legal cases are all in a preliminary stage.

Baidu officials declined to comment but provided a statement denying any impropriety. "Baidu places the highest priority on preventing fraudulent clicks," it said. "We have set up numerous measures both through automated technology and manual efforts to prevent fraudulent clicks and the effectiveness of which [has] been verified by [an] independent third party. . . . We are, however, continuing to invest aggressively in safeguarding measures which will help ensure that our customers and users continue to have the best possible experience."

Despite such assurances, advertisers say concern is spreading. Executives at Analysys International, an info tech researcher in Beijing, noted earlier this year that clicks on its ads on Baidu soared without any uptick in business. In April alone, Analysys burned through one-third of its modest yearly online marketing budget of $3,800. "It was like crazy," says CEO Edward Yu.

This spring, Analysys conducted a survey of 2,000 online advertiser in China and found that one-third believe they have been click-fraud victims. Yu continues to patronize. Google's Chinese affiliate, but he has stopped buying advertising from Baidu and Yahoo China, which is owned by Alibaba.com. Porter Erisman, a spokesman for Alibaba, said in an e-mail that "click fraud is a serious but manageable issue," adding that less than 0.01% of his company's customers have complained.

—Bruce Einhom

agreement. Yahoo says it scans its network for PTR activity, but declines to describe its methods.

PTR impresarios often don't fit the profile of an illicit kingpin. Michele Ballard runs a 2,200-member network called the-Owl-Post.com from her home in the small town of Hartford, Ky. On disability since a 1996 car accident, Ballard, 36, lives with her ailing mother and her cat, Sassy. She says she works day and night running Owl-Post, a five-year-old group named after the postal system in the Harry Potter novels. Sometimes, Ballard says she takes a break at lunchtime to tend her vegetable garden or help her elderly neighbors with theirs.

She sends her members a daily e-mail containing links to parked Web pages, many of them filled with Google ads. Her e-mails, decorated with smiley faces, suggest to members: "If you could just give a click on something on each page." She owns some of the parked pages, so she gets a share of the revenue when ads on them are clicked. She claims her take amounts to only about $60 a month, noting that if she made more than $85, the government would reduce her $601 monthly disability check.

In August, Google cut off a domain parking firm that hosted some of Ballard's sites. Showing her resilience, she moved the sites to other domain parkers, although none of those currently distributes Google ads. "Google would prefer you not to send out ads on paid e-mails, because they get too much crappy traffic," she says in a phone interview. She realizes that advertisers would get angry "if they knew we were just sitting here, clicking and not interested" in their wares. But, she adds, "They haven't figured that out yet."

Despite these views, Ballard says she doesn't think she's doing anything improper, let alone illegal. While investigations of some Internet criminals have revealed evidence of click fraud, the activity itself hasn't been the subject of prosecution. Ballard says Owl-Post is "like a huge family" whose members sometimes help out colleagues in financial distress. She says the network includes people who have low incomes and are desperate to earn cash to pay their bills. "A lot of people would be hurt if [the PTR business] crashed," she says.

Google's Ghosemajumder says any operation inviting people to click on ads is encouraging fraud, but he expresses skepticism about the overall scale of PTR activity: "People have a great tendency to exaggerate when they say they can attack Google's service."

Networks of human clickers aren't the only source of fake Web traffic. Scores of automated clicking programs, known as clickbots, are available to be downloaded from the Internet and claim to provide protection against detection. "The primary use is to cheat advertising companies," says Anatoly Smelkov, creator of Clicking Agent, a clickbot he says he has sold to some 5,000 customers worldwide.

The brazen 32-year-old Russian software developer lives in the city of Novosibirsk in western Siberia and says he received a physics degree from the state university there. A fan of the British physicist and author Stephen W. Hawking, Smelkov says Clicking Agent is a sideline that generates about $10,000 a year for him; he also writes software for video sharing and other purposes.

"A lot of people would be hurt [if the paid-to-read business] crashed," says one organizer

Clickbots are popular among online cheats because they disguise a PC's unique numerical identification, or IP address, and can space clicks minutes apart to make them less conspicuous. Smelkov shrugs off his role in facilitating deception. He points out that the first four letters of the name of his company, Lote-Soft Co., stand for "living on the edge." Teasing, he asks: "You aren't going to send the FBI to me, are you?"

Past Media Scandals

Allegations that some publishers and TV companies deceive advertisers go back many decades. Now the problem has moved online:

Newspapers and Magazines

Outrage over circulation fraud, employed to boost ad rates, led to the 1914 creation of the Audit Bureau of Circulations. But that didn't stop some publishers from faking the numbers. In 2004 a scandal tainted Tribune's *Newsday* and its Spanish-language *Hoy*, Belo's *Dallas Morning News*, and Sun-Times Media's *Chicago Sun-Times*.

Television

Broadcasters set ad rates using surveys of how many people are tuned in during four "sweeps" periods a year. Advertisers complain that some networks and local stations use contests and other stunts to attract extra attention during sweeps. The American Association of Advertising Agencies says this practice "has been going on for decades."

Internet

Click fraud, generating bogus mouse clicks on an online ad, isn't the only way advertisers can get ripped off on the Internet. Some ads are priced according to "impressions," the number of Web surfers who see it, regardless of whether they click. Now there is concern that some media companies commit impression fraud by overstating the number of visitors to their sites.

Google and Yahoo say they can identify automated click fraud and discount advertisers' bills accordingly. Jianhui Shi, a Smelkov customer who goes by the name Johnny, says that for this very reason he steers away from Google and Yahoo ads. An unemployed resident of the booming southern Chinese city of Shenzhen, Jianhui says he has used Clicking Agent to click all sorts of ads on sites he controls, making about $20,000 a year from this activity. While he doesn't click on Google and Yahoo ads, he says that more skilled Chinese programmers modify Clicking Agent to outwit the American search engines. "Many in China use this tool to make money," he wrote in an e-mail to *BusinessWeek*.

Back at the bare-bones MostChoice offices in north Atlanta, Marty Fleischmann continues to demand recompense. He says he has received refunds from Google and Yahoo totaling only about $35,000 out of the $100,000 he feels he is owed. In one exchange, MostChoice e-mailed Google to point out 316 clicks it received in June from ZapMeta.com, a little-known search site. MostChoice paid an average of $4.56 a click, or roughly $1,500 for the batch. Only one converted into a customer. Google initially responded that "after a thorough manual review" some bad clicks were filtered out before MostChoice was charged. Refund request: denied.

But as clicks from ZapMeta kept arriving, Fleischmann demanded in an Aug. 7 e-mail to Google: "You should be trusting us and doing something about [ZapMeta] as a partner, instead of finding more ways to refute our data or requests." (*BusinessWeek*'s e-mail to ZapMeta's site and its registered owner, Kevin H. Nguyen, elicited no response.)

Finally, on Aug. 8, Google admitted that clicks from ZapMeta "seem to be coming through sophisticated means." A Google employee who identified himself only as "Jason" added in an e-mail: "We are working with our engineers to prevent these clicks from continuing." MostChoice received a $2,527.93 refund that included reimbursement for suspect clicks from an additional site as well.

Google says it has refunded MostChoice for all invalid clicks and won't charge for any additional ZapMeta clicks until the situation is resolved. But Google also says it doesn't believe ZapMeta has done anything improper. As of late September, ZapMeta continued to carry ads that had been recycled from Google, although not MostChoice ads.

Randall S. Hansen, a professor of marketing at Stetson University in Deland, Fla., sees a larger lesson in tales of this sort. "We are just beginning to see more and more mainstream advertisers make the Internet a bigger part of their ad budget, and move dollars from print and TV," says Hansen, who has held marketing jobs at *The New Yorker* and *People* magazines. "But if we can't fix this click-fraud problem, then it is going to scare away the further development of the Internet as an advertising medium. If there is an undercurrent of fraud, then why should a large advertiser be losing $1 million, or maybe not know how much it is losing?"

With Moira Herbst

Global Diversity: The Next Frontier

Peter Ortiz

Corporate America faces a challenging enough task understanding the increasingly diverse United States, but to remain competitive, companies must address what happens on a larger playing field.

Embracing diversity globally requires an appreciation of distinctive societal, governmental and cultural values, including a lack of metrics that U.S. diversity leaders rely upon as benchmarking tools.

For example, while racial and ethnic demographics serve Rohini Anand as valuable measures for evaluating work-force diversity at Sodexho in the United States, the senior vice president and chief diversity officer doesn't always have that type of ready information in other countries.

"In France . . . you can't identity people by ethnicity or race," says Anand, whose company, Sodexho, is No. 14 on The 2006 DiversityInc Top 50 Companies for Diversity list. "All you can do is collect gender information, so it becomes extremely challenging if you don't know what the numbers and percentages are in your work force to establish any target."

So how does Sodexho handle this challenge? Inclusively. Anand relies on the viewpoints of a 12-person global task force from South America, Australia, Asia and Europe. The group meets virtually once a month to discuss the company's action plan and to share and report on best practices as well as understand the cultural nuances that define diversity in their respective societies.

Sodexho, which has operations in more than 70 countries, started its diversity initiative in North America four years ago when Anand came on board and found a champion in then-Sodexho CEO of North America, Michel Landel. Now as CEO of Sodexho Alliance, Landel advocates for diversity on a global scale. About 10 percent to 15 percent of managers' total bonuses are linked to diversity objectives for recruiting, retention and promotion of women and people of color in the United States, she says.

"That's his commitment, his passion, his realization of the need for cultural competence, and the success of our business is what really took it to [another] level," she says. "He has taken the same tenor and tone to the global arena as well where he is making it very much a part of his legacy and his strategy." With the global initiative 1.5 years old, Sodexho is beginning to address the diversity challenges in France. "One of the first things we're doing is to develop some training programs for our managers,

particularly around recruiting to make sure that there is unbiased recruiting as well as to allow managers the opportunity to recognize talent," Anand says.

The Greater Global Challenge

Deeply embedded customs and values in countries can make it difficult for U.S. corporations to carry out even the most basic equality measures. In South Korea, for example, there still is a cultural expectation that women stay home and take care of their children, leading many companies, both South Korean and foreign, to ignore investment in training women, says Michalle E. Mor Barak, a professor at the University of Southern California's School of Social Work and Marshall School of Business.

"It's not just that you are not utilizing half of the potential work force to its fullest, but you're also not addressing the expectations of your potential [women] customers," Mor Barak says. "To some extent you need diversity to address the varying expectations of your potential customers. Different viewpoints can greatly enrich the company's vision."

Mor Barak, who has published articles on global work force diversity and inclusion, including a book, *Managing Diversity: Toward a Globally Inclusive Workplace,* says many U.S. companies don't know how to address diversity issues in other countries. This results in a disparity between diversity initiatives at home and abroad. A good first step is working with people who are familiar with the foreign and U.S. culture.

"You create a bridge between the two and come up with initiatives that will promote diversity while being respectful of the local culture," Mor Barak says.

In France, the principle behind not identifying residents by race and ethnicity is meant to promote equality by identifying every French citizen, regardless of skin color or ethnicity, as French. A potential drawback is a lack of data companies can use to learn about diversity in French society, but this shouldn't limit a proactive company from learning about its own work-force diversity. Mor Barak suggests distributing surveys that ask employees how they identify themselves and how included they feel in the organization.

"On the advantage side, any accommodation for diversity in the long run benefits the organizational mission because it introduces a variety of ideas and thinking that can help the company be more creative and cater to different groups of customers," she says.

American Express' global team is divided into a U.S. and international council and was created in 2003. The international council consists of four regions: Europe-Middle East-Africa; Latin America and Caribbean; Japan, Asia-Pacific, Australia; and Canada. American Express is No. 30 on The 2006 DiversityInc Top 50 Companies for Diversity list.

Henry Hernandez, vice president and chief diversity officer, says the company has "to be sensitive to the fact that we may have to differentiate between what might be able to be done or approached from a U.S. perspective versus international." Where American Express may be similar to other corporations that are proactive on diversity initiatives in the United States, the financial-services giant must be cognizant on a global scale as well. Nearly half of the company's more than 66,000 employees live outside the United States.

"It really does have to span across the globe," Hernandez says.

The company must remain sensitive to the knowledge, awarness, skill sets and competencies that will differ from region to region.

Different Historic Perspectives

The United States has had a head start in corporate diversity that can be traced back to the Civil Rights Movement and the fight for equality and rights.

"It wasn't even referred to then as diversity, but when you think of the evolution, it's been a long one, whereas outside the United States, it may not have even been addressed that way," Hernandez says.

Bernard Anderson, an assistant secretary in the U.S. Department of Labor under former President Clinton, points out that progressive diversity initiatives by U.S. corporations are rooted in the Civil Rights Movement. Only when the U.S. government made employment discrimination illegal and created opportunities through the Civil Rights Act of 1964 and Affirmative Action did opportunities start to really filter down through corporate America.

"Before 1964, it was perfectly legal to deny employment to minority groups and women without explaining why," Anderson says.

Anderson, who today is a professor of management at the Wharton School of Business at the University of Pennsylvania, says that during Clinton's term, critics unfairly linked affirmative action with taking away opportunities for white men. This led many corporations to instead adapt the term "diversity," which gave broader meaning.

"Affirmative action for the most part is limited to employment, and diversity goes beyond employment . . . Diversity deals with work and family life and a lot of things that affirmative action never touched," Anderson says. "Diversity is now the mechanism that, in addition to broadening opportunities to groups previously excluded, also helps the firms be more financially successful."

Anderson notes—and DiversityInc Top 50 research supports—that more than 80 percent of U.S. corporations don't have diversity initiatives, but most of those that do are Fortune 500 companies. At the same time, Anderson, a self-described "voracious" critic of U.S. corporations, says "there is not a country in this world" that offers the same opportunities for people of color and women as the United States. But Anderson is doubtful that many large corporations that also operate globally can ensure their proactive diversity practices are followed outside the United States.

"What they do overseas will depend entirely upon national policies of countries they are operating in regarding equal-employment opportunities," he says.

With the exception of a few countries, including South Africa and some Scandinavian countries, most foreign governments have not mandated laws that create a solid foundation for diversity initiatives to thrive. U.S. corporations with strong diversity programs that give them a competitive advantage at home may not see the same results overseas.

Anderson also advised the Rev. Leon Sullivan on the Sullivan Principles he developed in 1977. These principles pushed for companies operating in South Africa under apartheid to honor human rights and equal opportunity in their businesses. While a number of U.S. companies signed on during apartheid, Sullivan could not find any Western European company that would do the same, Anderson says.

That lack of comprehension of the value of diversity remains. In France today, he notes it is difficult for women to gain employment in certain occupations, such as construction and manufacturing.

"Unless the cultural and moralistic values of that country support equal employment . . . an American company attempting to operate diversity programs overseas might operate at a competitive disadvantage in that market," Anderson says.

The Global Success Stories

Global diversity at HSBC is embodied in its description as the "The World's Local Bank," encompassing 284,000 employees in 76 countries and territories. These employees also serve more than 125 million customers. HSBC's U.S. operation is No. 13 on The 2006 DiversityInc Top 50 Companies for Diversity list.

In 2005, the London-based financial-services organization counted one-third of its pretax profits from North America, another third from Europe and two-thirds from the Asia Pacific region, according to Michael Shearer, senior manager, global diversity. On a global level, diversity is not just about "visible difference such as gender, ethnicity, disability or age," Shearer says. "It is also about different perspectives on working and leadership style, problem solving, managing relationships, creativity and business growth. Put simply, we see this as [an] important and growing focus because, by drawing on local knowledge and different perspectives of colleagues around the world, [it] enables us [to] serve our customers better."

In Australia, Sodexho partners with organizations in developing strategies to better recruit and retain employees from the indigenous aboriginal population. But learning best practices goes both ways and any leading role the United States plays should not be interpreted as a "here we are to show you how it's done" attitude, Anand says.

"In Scandinavian countries, as far as gender was concerned, there were some big surprises around policies for me," she says. "Women get 12 months of maternity leave and men have to use one month of that leave."

Failure of fathers to use that one month results in forfeiture of the entire 12-months' leave, Anand says. In Norway, a law requires that at least one woman sit on corporate boards, she says.

"Many countries are much better than the United States in terms of work/life balance issues, and that has been a big learning [experience] for me," Anand says.

Companies in countries that fail to address shortcomings in best practices could hurt their operations as they increasingly find themselves competing for talent globally. As its global task force continues to exchange diversity practices, Sodexho hopes to draw talent worldwide.

"It's going to be another differentiator for us," Anand says. "It will position us to manage our work force better and position us to take advantage of emerging markets."

American Express utilizes a training module for managers, Valuing Diversity and Practicing Inclusion, to maintain a consistency with its world operations. But inherent in that consistency is the understanding that adjustments may be made to adapt to local cultures. The company piloted the training module in Latin America in 2004.

"We actually identify facilitators who are sensitive to and knowledgeable about those particular markets," Hernandez says. "We always allow them a period of time to be able to adapt, modify and customize some materials so that it resonates well with employees."

While many of the managers worldwide speak English, the company also finds that managers from outside the United States are more engaged during the training when it is done in their native languages. One training example, titled Alejandro's Dilemma, educates managers about missed opportunities during a virtual telephone conference call. An employee may come from a culture where it is impolite to interrupt and be reluctant to offer ideas during the conference call.

"You have to be cognizant of the fact that someone who is at a meeting might be sitting quietly and has an incredible amount to contribute but isn't given the opportunity, or when the call is over, might not know the way to express themselves," Hernandez says.

The company has diversity goals linked to compensation for vice presidents and higher.

The objective is "to equip our leaders with being able to address cultural differences and being able to manage across borders," Hernandez says. Another program, Cultures at Work, combines classroom learning and an online tool, "cultural navigator," for managers.

Through its Group Diversity Management Committee, HSBC shares best-practice approaches from different regions by using an employee-diversity intranet system. The company also offers in-depth cultural training that includes intensive language training for employees sent to other countries and 400 permanently expatriated, globally mobile international managers.

"We can see two benefits to cross-cultural competence," Shearer says. "It helps us understand the diversity—and needs—of customer markets . . . [and] it helps employees to think differently and openly, to see beyond established parameters."

Trouble in Toyland

Lawmakers, Wal-Mart vow action amid recalls; Lead-tainted products and other hazards spur plans for hearings and better oversight.

ABIGAIL GOLDMAN

Amid a fresh spate of toy recalls, members of Congress said Thursday that they would hold hearings about product safety and Wal-Mart Stores Inc. vowed to increase testing and oversight of the playthings it sold.

But neither of those actions will guarantee a trouble-free toy aisle any time soon, according to activists who contend that legislation is needed to mandate stricter standards.

"The government agencies and the quality control operations in the companies that are supposed to prevent these problems are not working," said Jean Halloran, a food and product safety expert for Consumers Union, the publisher of Consumer Reports. "You need to start from the point of view that to a large degree, you're on your own. You are the one who has to protect yourself and your family."

In Washington, a House subcommittee requested information from 19 companies responsible for recent recalls of more than 9 million lead-tainted children's products imported from China.

The subcommittee on commerce, trade and consumer protection also said it would hold a hearing on the issue next month.

"I am outraged that in 2007 lead-tainted products continue to endanger the health of our children," said Rep. Bobby L. Rush (D-Ill.). "Children put everything into their mouths—if they swallow trinkets made with high quantities of lead, it can kill them."

Meanwhile Wal-Mart—the nation's largest retailer and No. 1 toy seller—said it would ask toy manufacturers to resubmit safety test results for toys already on shelves or on their way to Wal-Mart or Sam's Club stores.

Wal-Mart said it was increasing its third-party testing, adding an average of 200 more toy safety tests a day.

The retailer, which said it would share its test results with the toy industry and other retailers, identified a priority list of about 5,000 toys that are targeted at children younger than 3 and which are made with either paint or magnets—two hazards identified in recent recalls, company executives said.

The retailer also said it was in discussions with manufacturers and an industry trade group about a children's product seal of approval, which would certify that a product passed independent safety tests. In addition to toy problems, the retailer this year recalled children bibs because the vinyl material on them could contain lead.

"We have heard from customers that they are still concerned," said Laura Phillips, Wal-Mart's merchandise manager for toys. "We are trying to play a role here to alleviate their concerns and reassure them about the safety of the products that they are going to be buying."

Some consumer activists, however, were unimpressed.

"These are things they should have been doing already— the manufacturers, the distributors and the retailers," said Edmund Mierzwinski, who handles toy safety issues for U.S. Public Interest Research Group. "The toy manufacturers and the department stores have worried too much about price and not enough about quality. So they're responsible for this mess."

Halloran, of Consumers Union, said the best advice her group and others have are common-sense ways to protect children. A list of ways to prevent lead poisoning, on the ConsumerReports.org blog, includes such steps as checking toys against the government's recall list.

The group also recommends discarding toys with chipped paint, deteriorated plastic or other worn parts. The group suggests avoiding all toy jewelry for young children, because those playthings are often imported and have in the past been associated with lead charms or paint—a serious problem because small children often suck on the metal decorations they wear.

Consumers Union also suggests that all toddlers be tested for lead exposure by their pediatricians.

More important, Halloran said, the government needs to take more responsibility for ensuring product safety. The group supports proposed legislation that would require third-party safety certification for children's products and expand the authority and funding of the agency that ensures product safety.

The toy industry's biggest trade group said its members had a good system of safety standards and compliance and that the group was working toward a "uniform safety program."

A safety seal is another possibility, said an executive with the Toy Industry Assn., whose members make up about 80% of the $22 billion in annual domestic toy sales.

"The first step for us is enhancing the system and making sure the system works," said Joan Lawrence, the group's vice president of standards and regulatory affairs. "I don't know if hearings are necessary because we have long been in conversations with individual members and we plan to continue those conversations."

Although officials with the federal agency that oversees toy safety stress that they have recalled fewer toys this year than in 2006, a series of high-profile toy problems has heightened consumer attention, particularly with lead contamination of children's products.

Earlier this week, four toy companies recalled more than 340,000 Chinese-made toys with popular characters such as Curious George and SpongeBob SquarePants because of potential contamination from lead.

Those recalls followed a series of Chinese-made toy recalls from the nation's biggest toy maker, El Segundo-based Mattel Inc., which early this month warned about possible lead paint problems on 1.5 million Fisher-Price infant and preschool toys then, two weeks later, recalled more than 400,000 die-cast vehicles for the same reason.

And in June, toy maker RC2 Corp. recalled 1.5 million Thomas & Friends wooden train toys, also imported from China, because of possible lead paint.

Japan's Diversity Problem

Women are 41% of work force but command few top posts; 'a waste,' says Carlos Ghosn.

GINNY PARKER WOODS

U.S. computer giant Hewlett-Packard Co. knows first-hand the challenge of promoting women to management positions in Japan.

Throughout the company's global operations, women hold some 20% of managerial posts. In the U.S., that figure is over 25%. But in Japan, women occupy fewer than 4% of H-P's management jobs—so low, in fact, that "we had to do something," says Akiko Kawai, an H-P manager in charge of a new company program to promote Japanese women.

To motivate female employees, Ms. Kawai organized a support group that encourages women to discuss topics like communication skills, time management and balancing work and family life. As a mentoring effort, H-P has also paired up-and-coming women with high-ranking managers—most of whom by definition are men. One male mentor, Masaru Someya, a marketing director, says of the woman he worked with: "She was very highly skilled, but she didn't realize how good she was."

That professional women lack confidence is just one of the reasons why Japan—the world's second-largest economy and home to large, global companies like Toyota Motor Corp. and Sony Corp.—lags far behind other nations when it comes to promoting women in the workplace.

The dearth of Japanese women in managerial roles even goes well beyond the challenge of balancing work and home life—an issue that confronts female corporate ladder-climbers around the globe. In Japan, professional women face a set of socially complex issues—from overt sexism to deep-seated attitudes about the division of labor—problems that are not easily reversed.

Japanese women historically have played a subservient role in society, with advancements coming later than for their counterparts in Europe and the U.S. Women here, for instance, didn't gain voting rights until after World War II—and even then only because the law was written into a U.S.-drafted constitution. The country still prohibits women from remarrying for six months after a divorce to ensure that she is not pregnant with her ex-husband's child.

In the 1960s, many women, whose own mothers worked on the farm or at family-owned businesses, deemed it a privilege to focus on the home while their husbands worked long hours in fast-growing companies to keep the nation's economy humming. As the feminist movement in the U.S. emboldened women world-wide to fight for equality, parallel steps for Japanese women focused outside the workplace, with women largely accepting the gender separation of professional roles. Even today, many women in their thirties—prime career years—choose to bow out of office life altogether to raise children.

The result: Even as more women graduate from university and make up 41% of the work force, including part-timers, the legacy still continues. Men still tend to be hesitant to employ women as managers, assuming women can't handle the responsibility. And women themselves, not seeing many role models, are reluctant to rise to the challenge, thinking they're not cut out to manage.

In a speech last year to students at Japan Women's University, Carlos Ghosn, chief executive of Nissan Motor Co., told the audience that Japanese companies need to increase women's ranks to ensure future profitability and encouraged his listeners to believe in themselves. "The fact that women in Japan lack confidence makes it a very few number of women who take management responsibility," Mr. Ghosn said. "This is a waste, and we are feeling it and intend to make it better." Nissan plans to fill 5% of its management posts with women over the next few years from a current 1.6%.

Women in managerial positions concede that the burden of change is high. "Doing support-type work is somehow psychologically easier," says Motoko Honma, a 44-year-old H-P marketing specialist. Women in Japan, she believes, tend to see management work as a risk to their personal lives and are dogged by the old-fashioned notion that aggressive behavior is unattractive.

"Men tend to have a very fixed idea of what women are like," says Hitomi Mori, who is in charge of a program to boost the women's ranks at electronics maker Sharp Corp., where currently 21 of 3,412 managers are female. Meanwhile, many women "draw the line on themselves," she adds.

Japan's government—responding to mounting international criticism about the paucity of women's career opportunities—has made moves to improve the situation. In 1986, the country passed a law barring sex discrimination in the workplace. But real progress has been limited. In 1985, only 1% of division chiefs at Japanese companies of 100 employees or more were women. By 2004, that figure had crept up to just 2.7%.

The Japanese government says it wants to boost the ranks of women workers, partly to help solve demographic problems brought on by an aging population. Already, the work force is shrinking as fewer young Japanese enter the professional pipeline. Worker ranks will diminish further starting in 2007, when the first baby boomers retire. Keeping more women on a career track, especially after they have children, could help arrest that trend.

These days, firms from banks to auto makers are rushing to launch new programs to train and retain female managers. Sharp, which wants to triple the ranks of women managers by the fiscal year ending March 2008, created a special division last year for that purpose.

Women in Japan face sexism and deeply held attitudes about the division of labor.

A few months ago, the company began a program for several dozen women with management potential, with plans to give them a three-year career development plan. The company also profiled female employees in an internal magazine—complete with quotes from male employees praising the female managers they work with. "She reacts quickly and gets the work done effectively," one manager says about a female marketing supervisor. "She's a leader who pulls the team along."

In Japan, Western companies like H-P have typically been more active in adopting policies to encourage women managers. Under a mentoring program that officially began in 2004, the company aims to raise its levels by 1% each year by promoting more Japanese women to management posts.

So far, there have been challenges, including the appearance of tokenism. When one Japanese woman was made a manager and encouraged to be a role model, she promptly quit. "She misunderstood and thought that she'd gotten there just because she was a woman," Ms. Kawai says. "This became stressful to her."

A few big firms, like tech company Sanyo Electric Co., have recently appointed women as CEOs. But these are still exceptions. And many critics believe that Sanyo's recent appointment of former journalist Tomoyo Nonaka as CEO was an attempt by the company to impress the public, since she has no management or manufacturing experience. "She's more or less a figurehead," says Mariko Fujiwara, director of the Hakuhodo Institute of Life & Living, a Tokyo think tank that keeps tabs on consumer sentiment and trends.

In a discussion with journalists earlier this year, Ms. Nonaka addressed such detractors: "I know that people think my role is just decorative," she said. "My mission, however, is very important."

Along her own career path, H-P's Ms. Kawai suffered from insecurities. A few years after entering the company in 1974, a boss told her that management was really a man's job. She got discouraged and decided to quit to become a teacher. She changed her mind after a chance encounter with another male manager who encouraged her to stay on.

To keep other women from becoming similarly discouraged, last year she took female employees to an international women's summit in South Korea. Female chief executives and government ministers from other countries chatted with them about their struggles to advance their careers. The Japanese women were surprised at how "regular" these powerful women seemed, Ms. Kawai says. "The women realized that rising to the top is not an impossible dream, but something they can actually do themselves."

Erin White, Jathon Sapsford and Miho Inada contributed to this article.

How Barbie Is Making Business a Little Better

Corporations such as Mattel, Nike and Home Depot are using their clout to improve working conditions around the world.

EDWARD IWATA

The sewing factory in Tepeji del Rio, Mexico, made cute Barbie costumes under a Mattel license, but its workplace allegedly was horrendous.

According to a complaint filed last fall with the U.S. Labor Department by a Mexican union, the Rubie's de Mexico factory: employed underage workers, forced employees to work overtime and take pregnancy tests, and subjected workers to chemical smells that caused vomiting and fainting. A Mattel inspection of the plant found violations of Mattel's global-manufacturing codes of conduct. One violation was workers could not choose which union to join, contrary to Mattel's "right to free association" policy, says Mattel and Stephen Coats, head of the U.S./Labor Education in the Americas Project, a labor rights group.

Mattel says it recently severed ties with Rubie's after it missed a Jan. 31 deadline to fix that violation. Attorneys for Rubie's de Mexico, a contractor for Mattel licensee Rubie's Costume in New York, deny the allegations in the labor complaint, calling Rubie's "a responsible corporate citizen . . . that hopes to work with Mattel again."

Since launching its codes in 1997, Mattel has cut off several dozen suppliers and licensees whose factories fell short of Mattel's standards—a model for codes adopted recently by the International Council of Toy Industries.

"We call it zero tolerance," says Mattel Senior Vice President Jim Walter. "If we find evidence of systematic violations, we're not going to do business with you."

> **"We call it zero tolerance. If we find evidence of systematic violations, we're not going to do business with you."**
> **—Jim Walter, Mattel senior vice president**

Mattel is one of many U.S. corporations taking social responsibilities more seriously in foreign markets, from the rain forests of Asia to civil-war-torn Africa. As Yahoo, Google and other Internet giants face harsh criticism for their business practices in China, more companies realize it's smart business to be good corporate citizens in the exploding global economy.

Companies have come a long way since the 1980s, when public outrage against apartheid forced many to withdraw their investments in South Africa, and the 1990s, when apparel and footwear companies were attacked for sweatshop labor conditions in suppliers' plants.

In earlier decades, businesses viewed such issues—known as corporate social responsibility, or CSR—as annoyances. Corporations closed ranks when attacked by labor and human rights activists and environmentalists.

Now CSR practices play a key role in business strategy. Companies are closely monitoring their supply chains. They're teaming with activists and government officials to tackle problems. Manufacturers such as General Electric and Ford Motor are investing billions of dollars in energy-saving products and plants.

"Ten years ago, only a handful of companies looked seriously at this," says Bennett Freeman, a former State Department official who is managing director at the Burson-Marsteller public relations firm. "Now, every major company has to act on the issue. It's a business imperative."

Harsh Realities

The global economy is forcing U.S. multinationals to deal with harsher social and political realities, from civil violence in Nigeria to the dictatorship in China. Activists continue to pressure companies to conduct business with a conscience.

Which statement best describes the role that large corporations should play in society?

High investor returns balanced with contributions to public good

84%

16%

Provide highest returns to investors

Which statement best describes the overall contribution that large corporations make to the public good?

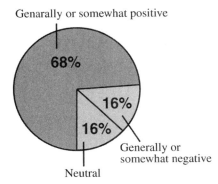

Generally or somewhat positive

68%

16%

16%

Generally or somewhat negative

Neutral

Figure 1 Businesses accept social responsibility. Business executives around the world say that corporations need to be responsive to shareholders and contribute to the public good. These are the questions asked and their responses.

Companies also fear bad publicity and legal woes, such as lawsuits filed by labor lawyers against Coca-Cola, Exxon-Mobil and other companies, accusing them of complicity in human rights abuses abroad.

Not all executives, though, think that corporate social responsibility is a business priority. Companies can do little when faced with civil wars and authoritarian regimes, and it's near-impossible to police the many thousands of contractors in worldwide supply chains.

But corporations clearly are moving on the issue by adopting:

Codes of conduct. About 2,000 companies have joined the United Nations Global Compact, which urges businesses to embrace labor, human rights and environmental practices, from banning child and forced labor to using environmentally sound technologies.

Hundreds of company and voluntary industry codes also have sprung up in apparel and toy manufacturing, electronics, jewelry, the coal, nuclear and chemical industries and other sectors.

Critics say companies have little incentive to obey the codes. Manufacturers, for instance, didn't lessen pollution until they faced stiffer environmental laws and criminal prosecution.

"Most companies are getting a free pass with these codes of conduct," says Terry Collingsworth, an attorney at the International Labor Rights Fund.

But supporters say the codes—such as the electronic industry's backed by Intel and other high-tech titans—give U.S. companies standard manufacturing and workplace rules amid conflicting international laws.

"They're a good first step," says Aron Cramer, president of Business for Social Responsibility, a non-profit group of corporations. "Now an army of people around the world are reviewing factories and improving work conditions."

Home Depot polices itself. Since the late-1990s, the company—which sells 8,000 wood products—has stopped buying from suppliers who get wood from endangered trees and rain forests.

The company spends more than $400 million a year on so-called certified wood approved by industry environmental standards, says Home Depot Vice President Ron Jarvis.

Social goals that boost business. In 2004, business professors Frank Schmidt and Sara Rynes at the University of Iowa looked at 52 studies on corporate social responsibility over 30 years. They found that well-run, profitable businesses also boasted solid social and environmental records.

"Socially aware companies add value to their products and services," says CEO Jeffrey Hollender of Seventh Generation, a natural home-products firm.

Companies are setting benchmarks for performance on social issues. Like Seventh Generation, Mattel and Cisco Systems, they're putting out "corporate responsibility" reports similar to annual financial reports.

Hoping to spark local economies in countries where they do business, Cisco and other firms are investing heavily in education and job training in Africa, Asia, Latin America and the Middle East.

Over the past decade, Cisco has poured $250 million into computer-network training programs with 220,000 graduates in developing nations, says Tae Yoo, a Cisco vice president.

FedEx, working with non-profit Environmental Defense and industrial manufacturer Eaton, is betting good environmental practices will pay off.

Two years ago, the delivery company launched a pilot project using 20 hybrid electric trucks in New York, Sacramento,

Accepting Responsibility

Business executives around the world say that corporations need to be responsive to shareholders and contribute to the public good. Responses to the following questions:

- Which statement best describes the role that large corporations should play in society?
- High investor returns balanced with contributions to public good 84%
- Provide highest returns to investors 16%

Which statement best describes the overall contribution that large corporations make to the public good?

- Generally or somewhat positive 68%
- Generally or somewhat negative 16%
- Neutral 16%

Sources: McKinsey Quarterly survey of 4,238 global business executives in 116 nations conducted in December 2005.

Washington and Tampa. The goal: to slash smog-causing emissions by 75% and get 50% more travel on the same amount of diesel fuel.

If all goes well, FedEx will use hybrid trucks to replace aging vehicles in its fleet of 30,000 delivery trucks in the USA and Canada, says FedEx environmental head Mitch Jackson.

"Companies come into this with a lot of cynicism," says Gwen Ruta at Environmental Defense. "Once they study the issues, they see it's a huge business benefit and the right thing to do."

Critics such as David Vogel, a University of California, Berkeley, business professor and author of *The Market for Virtue,* says corporate social responsibility is overrated. Investors don't care, and consumers won't pay higher prices for environmentally safe goods.

"Companies will make the world a better place as long as it doesn't cost too much," he says. "That's the limit of corporate responsibility."

Better monitoring. A decade ago, U.S. companies had few people to inspect thousands of manufacturing sites. Their superficial audits "didn't get at the root causes of problems," says Auret van Heerden, executive director of the non-profit Fair Labor Association.

Today, Van Heerden says, more corporations are strengthening their monitoring and teaching suppliers how to better run their plants and manage workers.

The Fair Labor Association estimates that 30 or 40 companies—including Reebok, Patagonia, Liz Clairborne and Phillips-Van Heusen—now have rigorous, first-class audit programs.

Mattel sends inspection teams to some of its 300 suppliers' sites in China, Indonesia and other countries. Armed with a 50-page checklist, they eyeball safety conditions, interview workers and ensure employees are treated well.

The audits—by Mattel and Prakash Sethi, a business professor at Baruch College and founder of the International Center for Corporate Accountability—praise some plants but warn others to shape up or lose Mattel's business.

"It's not empty rhetoric," Sethi says. "Vendors have a financial incentive to comply with Mattel's codes."

Nike also is a seasoned veteran of audits. In the 1990s, the company was a favorite target of activists because of foreign sweatshops run by its suppliers.

Now Nike inspects many of its 1,000 suppliers' factories worldwide. It grades them from A to D and warns poorly run sites to improve or get dropped, says Nike Vice President Dusty Kidd.

"Beyond the policing," Kidd says, "factories need to manage their work and manage it well."

That's no easy task—especially in countries with authoritarian regimes. Look at the problem facing Yahoo, Google, Microsoft and Cisco Systems, which were blasted last month by Congress and human rights groups for their Internet and sales practices in China.

Critics accuse the companies of compromising their values so the Chinese authorities will let them operate in the huge market. Despite the growing number of U.S. companies there, labor conditions and violence against workers have worsened, charges Sharon Hom, executive director of Human Rights in China. "Their presence alone will not lead to improvements," Hom says.

A Fundamental Purpose

The Internet companies disagree.

"We take our ethical and moral issues super-seriously," says Andrew McLaughlin, senior policy counsel at Google. "As an information company, freedom of speech and expression are fundamental to our purpose."

Google protects the confidentiality of users from the Chinese government and also tells users when a search result on google.cn.com, the company's Chinese website, is being censored.

The Internet companies also are consulting with human rights groups, U.S. government officials and scholars to draw up business guidelines for China.

Companies are doing the right thing by staying in China, says Edward Ahnert, a business professor at Southern

Methodist University and former president of the ExxonMobil Foundation. "Engaging the Chinese is better than shunning them," he says.

Reebok, for instance, is trying to improve the lot of Chinese workers. The company runs democratic-style elections in seven factories, with employees enthusiastically joining committees that work with management.

Reebok Vice President Doug Cahn says the company has shown "that workers' voices could be heard in China." The long-run goal: more worker-management collaboration in all of Reebok's 160 supplier factories in China.

As the China debate heats up, it's clear that companies' social responsibilities will loom larger everywhere as international trade grows.

"We're drafting rules of the road in the new global economy," says Michael Posner, executive director of Human Rights First. "We've made progress, but there's still a long way to go."

UNIT 4

Ethics and Social Responsibility in the Marketplace

Unit Selections

Key Points to Consider

- What responsibility does an organization have to reveal product defects to consumers?

- Given the competitiveness of the business arena, is it possible for marketing personnel to behave ethically and both survive and prosper? Explain. Give suggestions that could be incorporated into the marketing strategy for firms that want to be both ethical and successful.

- Name some organizations that make you feel genuinely valued as a customer. What are the characteristics of these organizations that distinguish them from their competitors? Explain.

- Which area of marketing strategy is most subject to public scrutiny in regard to ethics—product, pricing, place, or promotion? Why? Give some examples of unethical techniques or strategies involving each of these four areas.

Student Web Site

www.mhcls.com/online

Internet References

Further information regarding these Web sites may be found in this book's preface or online.

Business for Social Responsibility (BSR)
http://www.bsr.org/
Total Quality Management Sites
http://www.nku.edu/~lindsay/qualhttp.html
U.S. Navy
http://www.navy.mil

From a consumer viewpoint, the marketplace is the "proof of the pudding" or the place where the "rubber meets the road" for business ethics. In other words, what the company has promulgated about the virtues of its product or service has little meaning if the company's actual marketing practices and its treatment of the consumer contradict its claims.

At its core, marketing has a very noble and moral purpose: to satisfy human needs and wants and to help people through the exchange process. Marketing involves the coordination of the variables of product, price, place, and promotion to effectively and efficiently address the needs of consumers. Unfortunately, at times the unethical marketing practices of some firms have cast a shadow of suspicion over marketing in general. Since marketing is the aspect of business that is most visible to the public, it has perhaps taken a disproportionate share of the criticism directed toward the free-enterprise system.

This unit takes a careful look at the strategic process and practice of incorporating ethics into the marketplace. The first subsection, *Marketing Strategy and Ethics,* contains articles describing how marketing strategy and ethics can be integrated in the marketplace. The first article wrestles with the question: "Is Marketing Ethics an Oxymoron?" The last four articles in this subsection reveal the use of direct-to-consumer (DTC) advertising of prescription drugs, the significant impact of technology on marketing and ethics, why marketing should be a key leader in corporate citizenship, and how word-of-mouth marketers are getting mixed reviews by the public.

In the next subsection, *Ethical Practices in the Marketplace,* the first two articles delineate the importance of having an organizational culture that encourages and supports sound ethical behavior and socially responsible business practices. The last article in this subsection describes how the proliferation of swag may have undercut the integrity of the press.

Is Marketing Ethics an Oxymoron?

PHILIP KOTLER

Every profession and business has to wrestle with ethical questions. The recent wave of business scandals over inaccurate reporting of sales and profits and excessive pay and privileges for top executives has brought questions of business ethics to the fore. And lawyers have been continuously accused of "ambulance chasing," jury manipulation, and inflated fees, leaving the plaintiffs with much less than called for in the judgment. Physicians have been known to recommend certain drugs as more effective while receiving support from pharmaceutical companies.

Marketers are not immune from facing a whole set of ethical issues. For evidence, look to Howard Bowen's classic questions from his 1953 book, *Social Responsibilities of the Businessman:*

"Should he conduct selling in ways that intrude on the privacy of people, for example, by door-to-door selling? Should he use methods involving ballyhoo, chances, prizes, hawking, and other tactics which are at least of doubtful good taste? Should he employ 'high pressure' tactics in persuading people to buy? Should he try to hasten the obsolescence of goods by bringing out an endless succession of new models and new styles? Should he appeal to and attempt to strengthen the motives of materialism, invidious consumption, and keeping up with the Joneses?" (Also see Smith, N. Craig and Elizabeth Cooper-Martin (1997), "Ethics and Target Marketing: The Role of Product Harm and Consumer Vulnerability," *Journal of Marketing,* July, 1–20.)

The issues raised are complicated. Drawing a clear line between normal marketing practice and unethical behavior isn't easy. Yet it's important for marketing scholars and those interested in public policy to raise questions about practices that they may normally endorse but which may not coincide with the public interest.

We will examine the central axiom of marketing: Companies that satisfy their target customers will perform better than those that don't. Companies that satisfy customers can expect repeat business; those that don't will get only one-time sales. Steady profits come from holding onto customers, satisfying them, and selling them more goods and services.

This axiom is the essence of the well-known marketing concept. It reduces to the formula "Give the customer what he wants." This sounds reasonable on the surface. But notice that it carries an implied corollary: "Don't judge what the customer wants."

Marketers have been, or should be, a little uneasy about this corollary. It raises two public interest concerns: (1) What if the customer wants something that isn't good for him or her? (2) What if the product or service, while good for the customer, isn't good for society or other groups?

When it comes to the first question, what are some products that some customers desire that might not be good for them? These would be products that can potentially harm their health, safety, or well-being. Tobacco and hard drugs such as cocaine, LSD, or ecstasy immediately come to mind.

As for the second question, examples of products or services that some customers desire that may not be in the public's best interest include using asbestos as a building material or using lead paint indiscriminately. Other products and services where debates continue to rage as to whether they are in the public's interest include the right to own guns and other weapons, the right to have an abortion, the right to distribute hate literature, and the right to buy large gas guzzling and polluting automobiles.

EXECUTIVE briefing

Marketers should be proud of their field. They have encouraged and promoted the development of many products and services that have benefited people worldwide. But this is all the more reason that they should carefully and thoughtfully consider where they stand on the ethical issues confronting them today and into the future. Marketers are able to take a stand and must make the effort to do so in order to help resolve these issues.

We now turn to three questions of interest to marketers, businesses, and the public:

1. Given that expanding consumption is at the core of most businesses, what are the interests and behaviors of companies that make these products?
2. To what extent do these companies care about reducing the negative side effects of these products?
3. What steps can be taken to reduce the consumption of products that have questionable effects and is limited intervention warranted?

Expanding Consumption

Most companies will strive to enlarge their market as much as possible. A tobacco company, if unchecked, will try to get everyone who comes of age to start smoking cigarettes. Given that cigarettes are addictive, this promises the cigarette company "customers for life." Each new customer will create a 50-year profit stream for the cigarette company if the consumer continues to favor the same brand—and live long enough. Suppose a new smoker starts at the age of 13, smokes for 50 years, and dies at 63 from lung cancer. If he spends $500 a year on cigarettes, he will spend $25,000 over his lifetime. If the company's profit rate is 20%, that new customer is worth $5,000 to the company (undiscounted). It is hard to imagine a company that doesn't want to attract a customer who contributes $5,000 to its profits.

The same story describes the hard drug industry, whose products are addictive and even more expensive. The difference is that cigarette companies can operate legally but hard drug companies must operate illegally.

Other products, such as hamburgers, candy, soft drinks, and beer, are less harmful when consumed in moderation, but are addictive for some people. We hear a person saying she has a "sweet tooth." One person drinks three Coca-Colas a day, and another drinks five beers a day. Still another consumer is found who eats most of his meals at McDonald's. These are the "heavy users." Each company treasures the heavy users who account for a high proportion of the company's profits.

All said, every company has a natural drive to expand consumption of its products, leaving any negative consequences to be the result of the "free choice" of consumers. A high-level official working for Coca-Cola in Sweden said that her aim is to get people to start drinking Coca-Cola for breakfast (instead of orange juice). And McDonald's encourages customers to choose a larger hamburger, a larger order of French fries, and a larger cola drink. And these companies have some of the best marketers in the world working for them.

Reducing Side Effects

It would not be a natural act on the part of these companies to try to reduce or restrain consumption of their products. What company wants to reduce its profits? Usually some form of public pressure must bear on these companies before they will act.

The government has passed laws banning tobacco companies from advertising and glamorizing smoking on TV. But Philip Morris' Marlboro brand still will put out posters showing its mythical cowboy. And Marlboro will make sure that its name is mentioned in sports stadiums, art exhibits, and in labels for other products.

Tobacco companies today are treading carefully not to openly try to create smokers out of young people. They have stopped distributing free cigarettes to young people in the United States as they move their operations increasingly into China.

Beer companies have adopted a socially responsible attitude by telling people not to over-drink or drive during or after drinking. They cooperate with efforts to prevent underage people from buying beer. They are trying to behave in a socially responsible manner. They also know that, at the margin, the sales loss resulting from their "cooperation" is very slight.

McDonald's has struggled to find a way to reduce the ill effects (obesity, heart disease) of too much consumption of their products. It tried to offer a reduced-fat hamburger only to find consumers rejecting it. It has offered salads, but they weren't of good quality when originally introduced and they failed. Now it's making a second and better attempt.

Limited Intervention

Do public interest groups or the government have the right to intervene in the free choices of individuals? This question has been endlessly debated. On one side are people who resent any intervention in their choices of products and services. In the extreme, they go by such names as libertarians, vigilantes, and "freedom lovers." They have a legitimate concern about government power and its potential abuse. Some of their views include:

- The marketer's job is to "sell more stuff." It isn't the marketer's job to save the world or make society a better place.
- The marketer's job is to produce profits for the shareholders in any legally sanctioned way.
- A high-minded socially conscious person should not be in marketing. A company shouldn't hire such a person.

On the other side are people concerned with the personal and societal costs of "unregulated consumption." They are considered do-gooders and will document that Coca-Cola delivers six teaspoons of sugar in every bottle or can. They will cite statistics on the heavy health costs of obesity, heart disease, and liver damage that are caused by failing to reduce the consumption of some of these products. These costs fall on everyone through higher medical costs and taxes. Thus, those who don't consume questionable products are still harmed through the unenlightened behavior of others.

Ultimately, the problem is one of conflict among different ethical systems. Consider the following five:

Ethical egoism. Your only obligation is to take care of yourself (Protagoras and Ayn Rand).
Government requirements. The law represents the minimal moral standards of a society (Thomas Hobbes and John Locke).
Personal virtues. Be honest, good, and caring (Plato and Aristotle).
Utilitarianism. Create the greatest good for the greatest number (Jeremy Bentham and John Stuart Mill).
Universal rules. "Act only on that maxim through which you can at the same time will that it should become a universal law" (Immanuel Kant's categorical imperative).

Clearly, people embrace different ethical viewpoints, making marketing ethics and other business issues more complex to resolve.

Let's consider the last two ethical systems insofar as they imply that some interventions are warranted. Aside from the weak gestures of companies toward self-regulation and appearing concerned, there are a range of measures that can be taken by those wishing to push their view of the public interest. They include the following six approaches:

1. Encouraging these companies to make products safer. Many companies have responded to public concern or social pressure to make their products safer. Tobacco companies developed filters that would reduce the chance of contracting emphysema or lung cancer. If a leaf without nicotine could give smokers the same satisfaction, they would be happy to replace the tobacco leaf. Some tobacco companies have even offered information or aids to help smokers limit their appetite for tobacco or curb it entirely.

> **Every company has a natural drive to expand consumption of its products, leaving any negative consequences to be the result of the "free choice" of consumers.**

Food and soft drink companies have reformulated many of their products to be "light," "nonfat," or "low in calories." Some beer companies have introduced non-alcoholic beer. These companies still offer their standard products but provide concerned consumers with alternatives that present less risk to their weight or health.

Auto companies have reluctantly incorporated devices designed to reduce pollution output into their automobiles. Some are even producing cars with hybrid fuel systems to further reduce harmful emissions to the air. But the auto companies still insist on putting out larger automobiles (such as Hummers) because the "public demands them."

What can we suggest to Coca-Cola and other soft drink competitors that are already offering "light" versions of their drinks? First, they should focus more on developing the bottled water side of their businesses because bottled water is healthier than sugared soft drinks. Further, they should be encouraged to add nutrients and vitamins in standard drinks so these drinks can at least deliver more health benefits, especially to those in undeveloped countries who are deprived of these nutrients and vitamins. (Coca-Cola has some brands doing this now.)

What can we suggest to McDonald's and its fast food competitors? The basic suggestion is to offer more variety in its menu. McDonald's seems to forget that, while parents bring their children to McDonald's, they themselves usually prefer to eat healthier food, not to mention want their children eating healthier foods. How about a first-class salad bar? How about moving more into the healthy sandwich business? Today more Americans are buying their meals at Subway and other sandwich shops where they feel they are getting healthier and tastier food for their dollar.

There seems to be a correlation between the amount of charity given by companies in some categories and the category's degree of "sin." Thus, McDonald's knows that over-consumption of its products can be harmful, but the company is very charitable. A cynic would say that McDonald's wants to build a bank of public goodwill to diffuse potential public criticism.

2. Banning or restricting the sale or use of the product or service. A community or nation will ban certain products where there is strong public support. Hard drugs are banned, although there is some debate about whether the ban should include marijuana and lighter hard drugs. There are even advocates who oppose banning hard drugs, believing that the cost of policing and criminality far exceed the cost of a moderate increase that might take place in hard drug usage. Many people today believe that the "war on drugs" can never be won and is creating more serious consequences than simply dropping the ban or helping drug addicts, as Holland and Switzerland have done.

Some products carry restrictions on their purchase or use. This is particularly true of drugs that require a doctor's prescription and certain poisons that can't be purchased without authorization. Persons buying guns must be free of a criminal record and register their gun ownership. And certain types of guns, such as machine guns, are banned or restricted.

3. Banning or limiting advertising or promotion of the product. Even when a product isn't banned or its purchase restricted, laws may be passed to prevent producers from advertising or promoting the product. Gun, alcohol, and tobacco manufacturers can't advertise on TV, although they can advertise in print media such as magazines and newspapers. They can also inform and possibly promote their products online.

Manufacturers get around this by mentioning their brand name in every possible venue: sports stadiums, music concerts, and feature articles. They don't want to be forgotten in the face of a ban on promoting their products overtly.

4. Increasing "sin" taxes to discourage consumption. One reasonable alternative to banning a product or its promotion is to place a "sin" tax on its consumption. Thus, smokers pay hefty government taxes for cigarettes. This is supposed to have three effects when done right. First, the higher price should discourage consumption. Second, the tax revenue could be used to finance the social costs to health and safety caused by the consumption of the product. Third, some of the tax revenue could be used to counter-advertise the use of the product or support public education against its use. The last effect was enacted by California when it taxed tobacco companies and used the money to "unsell" tobacco smoking.

5. Public education campaigns. In the 1960s, Sweden developed a social policy to use public education to raise a nation of non-smokers and non-drinkers. Children from the first grade up were educated to understand the ill effects of tobacco and alcohol. Other countries are doing this on a less systematic and intensive basis. U.S. public schools devote parts of occasional courses to educate students against certain temptations with mixed success. Girls, not boys, in the United States seem to be more prone to taking up smoking. The reason often given by girls is that smoking curbs their appetite for food and consequently helps them avoid becoming overweight, a problem they consider more serious than lung cancer taking place 40 years later.

Sex education has become a controversial issue, when it comes to public education campaigns. The ultra-conservative camp wants to encourage total abstinence until marriage. The more liberal camp believes that students should be taught the risks of early sex and have the necessary knowledge to protect themselves. The effectiveness of both types of sex education is under debate.

6. Social marketing campaigns. These campaigns describe a wide variety of efforts to communicate the ill effects of certain behaviors that can harm the person, other persons, or society as a whole. These campaigns use techniques of public education, advertising and promotion, incentives, and channel development to make it as easy and attractive as possible for people to change their behavior for the better. (See Kotler, Philip, Eduardo Roberto, and Nancy Lee (2002), *Social Marketing: Improving the Quality of Life,* 2nd ed. London: Sage Publications.) Social marketing uses the tools of commercial marketing—segmentation, targeting, and positioning, and the four Ps (product, price, place, and promotion)—to achieve voluntary compliance with publicly endorsed goals. Some social marketing campaigns, such as family planning and anti-littering, have achieved moderate to high success. Other campaigns including anti-smoking, anti-drugs ("say no to drugs"), and seat belt promotion have worked well when supplemented with legal action.

Social Responsibility and Profits

Each year *Business Ethics* magazine publishes the 100 best American companies out of 1,000 evaluated. The publication examines the degree to which the companies serve seven stakeholder groups: shareholders, communities, minorities and women, employees, environment, non-U.S. stakeholders, and customers. Information is gathered on lawsuits, regulatory problems, pollution emissions, charitable contributions, staff diversity counts, union relations, employee benefits, and awards. Companies are removed from the list if there are significant scandals or improprieties. The research is done by Kinder, Lydenberg, Domini (KLD), an independent rating service. (For more details see the Spring 2003 issue of *Business Ethics.*)

The 20 best-rated companies in 2003 were (in order): General Mills, Cummins Engine, Intel, Procter & Gamble, IBM, Hewlett-Packard, Avon Products, Green Mountain Coffee, John Nuveen Co., St. Paul Companies, AT&T, Fannie Mae, Bank of America, Motorola, Herman Miller, Expedia, Autodesk, Cisco Systems, Wild Oats Markets, and Deluxe.

The earmarks of a socially responsible company include:

- Living out a deep set of company values that drive company purpose, goals, strategies, and tactics
- Treating customers with fairness, openness, and quick response to inquiries and complaints
- Treating employees, suppliers, and distributors fairly
- Caring about the environmental impact of its activities and supply chain
- Behaving in a consistently ethical fashion

The intriguing question is whether socially responsible companies are more profitable. Unfortunately, different research studies have come up with different results. The correlations between financial performance (FP) and social performance (SP) are sometimes positive, sometimes negative, and sometimes neutral, depending on the study. Even when FP and SP are positively related, which causes which? The most probable finding is that high FP firms invest slack resources in SP and then discover the SP leads to better FP, in a virtuous circle. (See Waddock, Sandra A. and Samuel B. Graves (1997), "The Corporate Social Performance-Financial Performance Link," *Strategic Management Journal,* 18 (4), 303–319.)

Marketers' Responsibilities

As professional marketers, we are hired by some of the aforementioned companies to use our marketing toolkit to help them sell more of their products and services. Through our research, we can discover which consumer groups are the most susceptible to increasing their consumption. We can use the research to assemble the best 30-second TV commercials, print ads, and sales incentives to persuade them that these products will deliver great satisfaction. And we can create price discounts to tempt them to consume even more of the product than would normally be healthy or safe to consume.

But, as professional marketers, we should have the same ambivalence as nuclear scientists who help build nuclear bombs or pilots who spray DDT over crops from the airplane. Some of us, in fact, are independent enough to tell these clients that we will not work for them to find ways to sell more of what hurts people. We can tell them that we're willing to use our marketing toolkit to help them build new businesses around substitute products that are much healthier and safer.

But, even if these companies moved toward these healthier and safer products, they'll probably continue to push their current "cash cows." At that point, marketers will have to decide whether to work for these companies, help them reshape their offerings, avoid these companies altogether, or even work to oppose these company offerings.

Remember Marketing's Contributions

Nothing said here should detract from the major contributions that marketing has made to raise the material standards of living around the world. One doesn't want to go back to the kitchen where the housewife cooked five hours a day, washed dishes by hand, put fresh ice in the ice box, and washed and dried clothes in the open air. We value refrigerators, electric stoves, dishwashers, washing machines, and dryers. We value the invention and diffusion of the radio, the television set, the computer, the Internet, the cellular phone, the automobile, the movies, and even frozen food. Marketing has played a major role in their instigation and diffusion. Granted, any of these are capable of abuse (bad movies or TV shows), but they promise and deliver much that is good and valued in modern life.

Marketers have a right to be proud of their field. They search for unmet needs, encourage the development of products and services addressing these needs, manage communications to inform people of these products and services, arrange for easy accessibility and availability, and price the goods in a way that represents superior value delivered vis-à-vis competitors' offerings. This is the true work of marketing.

PHILIP KOTLER is S.C. Johnson and Son Distinguished Professor of International Marketing, Kellogg School of Management, Northwestern University. He may be reached at pkotler@nwu.edu.

Author's Note—The author wishes to thank Professor Evert Gummesson of the School of Business, Stockholm University, for earlier discussion of these issues.

Truth in Advertising

Rx Drug Ads Come of Age

Carol Rados

You may have seen the advertisement: A melodrama of crime and corruption, conflict and emotion, centering on indoor hit men like dust and dander, and outdoor hit men such as pollen and ragweed, all threatening to offend a young and very beautiful woman's nose. The 45-second broadcast ad covers everything from talking to your doctor to the possible side effects that people can expect. Then the narrator mentions "Flonase."

> **According to the U.S. General Accounting Office . . . pharmaceutical manufacturers spent $2.7 billion on DTC advertising in 2001 alone.**

Entertaining though it may be, the Food and Drug Administration says this promotional piece about nasal allergy relief also has all the elements of a well-crafted, easy-to-understand prescription drug advertisement directed at consumers, and it meets agency requirements for these ads.

Direct-to-consumer (DTC) advertising of prescription drugs in its varied forms—TV, radio, magazines, newspapers—is widely used throughout the United States. DTC advertising is a category of promotional information about specific drug treatments provided directly to consumers by or on behalf of drug companies. According to the U.S. General Accounting Office—the investigational arm of Congress—pharmaceutical manufacturers spent $2.7 billion on DTC advertising in 2001 alone.

The Controversy

Whether it's a 1940s, detective-style film noir of unusual allergy suspects or a middle-aged man throwing a football through a tire swing announcing that he's "back in the game," the DTC approach to advertising prescription drugs has been controversial. Some say that DTC promotion provides useful information to consumers that results in better health outcomes. Others argue that it encourages overuse of prescription drugs and use of

the most costly treatments, instead of less expensive treatments that would be just as satisfactory.

There seems to be little doubt that DTC advertising can help advance the public health by encouraging more people to talk with health care professionals about health problems, particularly undertreated conditions such as high blood pressure and high cholesterol.

DTC advertising also can help remove the stigma that accompanies; diseases that in the past were rarely openly discussed, such as erectile dysfunction or depression. DTC ads also can remind patients to get their prescriptions refilled and help them adhere to their medication regimens.

On the other hand, ads that are false or misleading do not advance—and may even threaten—the public health. While the FDA encourage DTC advertisements that contain accurate information, the agency also has the job of making sure that consumers are not misled or deceived by advertisements that violate the law.

"The goal here is getting truthful, non-misleading information to consumers about safe and effective therapeutic products so they can be partners in their own health care" says Peter Pitts, the FDA's associate commissioner for external relations. "Better-informed consumers are empowered to choose and use the products we regulate to improve their health."

How Ads Affect Consumers

The FDA surveyed both patients and physicians about their attitudes and experiences with DTC advertising between 1999 and 2002. The agency summarized the findings of these surveys in January 2003 in the report, *Assessment of Physician and Patient Attitudes Toward Direct-to-Consumer Promotion of Prescription Drugs.*

DTC advertising appears to influence certain types of behavior. For example, the FDA surveys found that among patients who visited doctors and asked about a prescription drug by brand name because of an ad they saw, 88 percent actually had the condition the drug treats. This is important, Pitts says, because physician visits that result in earlier detection of a disease, combined with appropriate treatment, could mean that more people

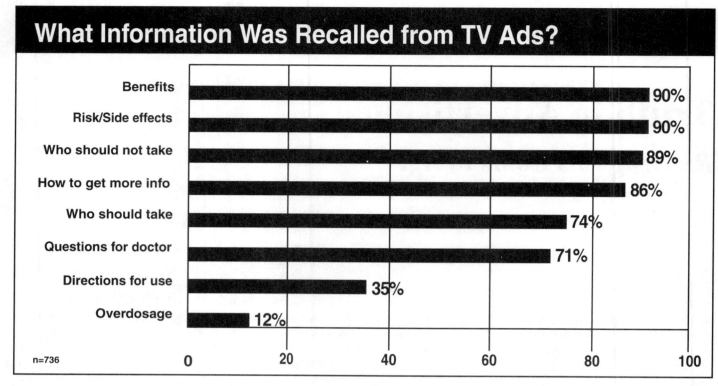

Figure 1 In three FDA surveys conducted in 1999 and 2002, patients reported recalling this information from TV ads.

will live longer, healthier, more productive lives without the risk of future costly medical interventions.

With the number of ailments Patricia A. Sigler lives with—diabetes, fibromyalgia, high blood pressure, high cholesterol, nerve damage, and a heart defect called mitral valve prolapse—the 64-year-old small business owner in Jefferson, Md., says that she's always on the lookout for medicines that might improve her quality of life, and that she pays attention to DTC ads for prescription drugs.

Some Doctors Don't Agree

Michael S. Wilkes, M.D., vice dean of the medical school at the University of California, Davis, says that two reasons he doesn't like DTC advertising are that patients may withhold information from their doctors or try to treat themselves. Aiming prescription drug ads at consumers can affect the "dynamics of the patient-provider relationship," and ultimately, the patient's quality of care, Wilkes says. DTC advertising can motivate consumers to seek more information about a product or disease, but physicians need to help patients evaluate health-related information they obtain from DTC advertising, he says.

"DTC advertising may cultivate the belief among the public that there is a pill for every ill and contribute to the medicalization of trivial ailments, leading to an even more overmedicated society," Wilkes says. "Patients need to trust that I've got their best interest in mind."

Others who favor DTC ads say that consumer-directed information can be an important educational tool in a time when

more patients want to be involved in their own health care. Carol Salzman, M.D., Ph.D., an internist in Chevy Chase, Md., emphasizes, however, that physicians still need to remain in control of prescribing medications.

"Doctors shouldn't feel threatened by their patients asking for a medicine by name," she says, "but at the same time, patients shouldn't come in expecting that a drug will be dispensed just because they asked for it."

Salzman says she finds it time-consuming "trying to talk people out of something they have their hearts set on." Wilkes agrees. Discussions motivated by ads that focus on specific drugs or trivial complaints, he says, could take time away from subjects such as a patient's symptoms, the range of available treatments, and specific details about a patient's illness.

Education or Promotion?

At least one patient advocacy group is concerned about what it says are the downsides of advertising prescription drugs directly to consumers, claiming that DTC ads often masquerade as educational tools, but provide more promotion than education. The ads, they say, provide little access to unbiased information.

"People need to be careful with ads that it isn't just hype that they're going to feel better, with no objectivity of the downsides," says Linda Golodner, president of the National Consumers League in Washington, D.C. Although all DTC advertisements must disclose risk information, she says what is typically communicated is a brand name, a reason to use the product, and an impression of the product. Golodner wants all

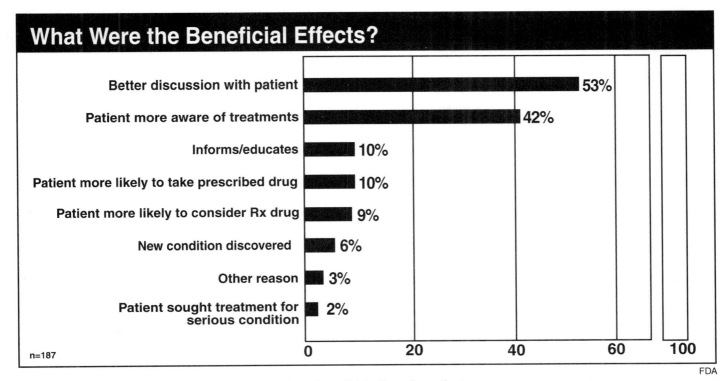

Figure 2 Physicians reported that DTC ads had these beneficial effects for patients.

offices within the FDA that have a responsibility for any aspect of DTC advertising to work together. "There's a lot of the same information out there, so why not bring it all together so that consumers can understand it better?"

Truth in Advertising

The FDA has regulated the advertising of prescription drugs since 1962, under the Federal Food, Drug, and Cosmetic Act and related regulations. The regulations establish detailed requirements for ad content. Most other advertising, including that of over-the-counter drugs, is regulated by the Federal Trade Commission under a different set of rules.

The FDA's Division of Drug Marketing, Advertising, and Communications (DDMAC) oversees two types of promotion for prescription drugs: promotional labeling and advertising. Advertising includes commercial messages broadcast on television or radio, communicated over the telephone, or printed in magazines and newspapers. Prescription drug ads must contain information in a "brief summary" relating to both risks and benefits. Recognizing the time constraints of broadcast ads, FDA regulations provide that a broadcast advertisement may include, instead of a brief summary information relating to the major risks. The ad must also make "adequate provision" for distributing the FDA-approved labeling in connection with the broadcast ad. This refers to the concept of providing ways for consumers to find more complete information about the drug.

Most ads fulfill this requirement by including a toll-free telephone number, a Web site address, or a link to a concurrently running print ad. They also encourage consumers to talk to their health care providers. Both print and broadcast ads directed at consumers may only make claims that are supported by scientific evidence.

DDMAC oversight helps ensure that pharmaceutical companies accurately communicate the benefits and risks of an advertised drug. The regulations require that advertising for prescription drugs must disclose certain information about the product's uses and risks.

In addition, advertisements cannot be false or misleading and cannot omit material facts. FDA regulations also call for "fair balance" in product claim ad. This means that the risks and benefits must be presented with comparable scope, depth, and detail, and that information relating to the product's effectiveness must be fairly balanced by risk information.

The FDA does not generally require prior approval of DTC ads, although companies are required to submit their ads to the FDA at the time they begin running. The agency, therefore, routinely examines these commercials and published DTC ads after they become available to the public. FDA, however, also is happy to review proposed ads if a drug company makes a request.

"We look at a lot of DTC ads before they run," says Kathryn J. Aikin, Ph.D., a social scientist in DDMAC. "Manufacturers typically want to be sure they're getting started on the right foot."

The Trouble with Ads

Of the three types of DTC advertisements, the first and most common—product-claim ads—mention a drug's name and the condition it is intended to treat, and describe the risks and

DTC Ads at a Glance

Product-claim ads:

- mention a drug by name
- make representations about the drug, such as its safety and effectiveness
- must have fair balance of information about effectiveness and risks
- are required to disclose risks in a "brief summary" of benefits and risks (for print ads)
- are required to give a "major statement" of risks and "adequate provision" for finding out more, such as a toll-free number (for broadcast ads).

Reminder ads:

- provide the name of the medication
- may provide other minimal information, such as cost and dosage form
- do not make a representation about the drug, such as the drug's use, effectiveness, or safety
- are not required to provide risk information.

Help-seeking ads:

- educate consumers about a disease or medical condition
- let people know that treatments exist for a medical condition
- don't name a specific drug
- are not required to provide risk information.

benefits associated with taking the drug. Some manufacturers have decided not to present this much information and instead, have made use of two other kinds of ads. "Reminder" ads give only the name of the product, but not what it is used for, and "help-seeking" ads contain information about a disease, but do not mention a specific drug. These help-seeking—or disease-awareness—ads can be extremely informative and, because they name no drug, they are not regulated by the FDA. Examples of help-seeking ads are those that mention high cholesterol or diabetes, and then direct you to ask your doctor about treatments. Reminder ads call attention to a drug's name, but say nothing about the condition it is used to treat, its effectiveness, or safety information. A reminder ad is not required to include risk information.

There has been a great deal of discussion about the brief summary that accompanies DTC print ads. The typical brief summary is not brief and uses technical language. This is because it reprints all of the risk information from the physician labeling. People have complained that the brief summary cannot be understood by consumers. Aikin says, "Patients do not typically read the brief summary in DTC print ads unless

they're interested in the product." Even then, she says, much information is likely glanced at, rather than fully read.

Public input and the FDA's own experiences with DTC promotion prompted the agency to publish two new draft guidances in February 2004: one on the brief summary, and one on help-seeking ads. These guidances are designed to encourage more informative, understandable ads.

Advertising Guidance

The draft guidance on the brief summary encourages companies to use consumer-friendly language and formats to convey prescription drug risk information—through a "less is more" approach. This approach focuses on the most serious and the most common risks of a drug, rather than listing every risk from the physician labeling. "Even though the information currently in the brief summary is complete, accurate, and in compliance," says Pitts, "it does not mean that patients are deriving the maximum benefit from it."

Sometimes marketers combine help-seeking ads with perceptually similar reminder ads in a way that causes the audience to perceive the two pieces as one advertisement. Appearing individually, these ads are exempted by regulation from the risk disclosure requirement. Combined, however, both ads can, in some cases, make a product-claim advertisement that requires risk disclosure.

The agency's recent draft guidance on help-seeking ads explains that help-seeking and reminder ads must appear distinct to avoid coming under the regulations for a product-claim ad. The draft guidance also address's the separation needed between the two types of ads—in space for print ads, and in time for TV ads.

Those in Violation

For companies that don't follow the rules, DDMAC's possible actions include two types of letters—"untitled" and "warning." These letters address advertisements that make misleading claims about a drug's effectiveness—violations such as overstating the effectiveness of the drug, suggesting a broader range of indicated uses than the drug has been approved for, and lack of risk information. In both types of letters, DDMAC asks that the advertisement be withdrawn.

Warning letters, which are sent to companies that have violated the law repeatedly or that have committed serious regulatory violations in their advertising, typically request corrective advertisements to assure that the audience that received the original false or misleading information also receives truthful and accurate information.

Untitled letters are usually, but not always, sent to companies for first-time offenses or for less serious violations.

For example, the 60-second DTC broadcast television ad featuring "Digger," the well-known animated dermatophyte microorganism touting Lamisil (terbinafine), a treatment for nail fungus, was initially found to be false or misleading. The FDA sent an untitled letter to the makers of Lamisil for overstating the drug's effectiveness, minimizing its risk information, and making an unsubstantiated superiority claim. As a result, the manufacturer, Novartis Pharmaceuticals Corp., stopped running that ad.

DDMAC recently sent a warning letter to Bristol-Myers Squibb Co. about false or misleading promotional materials for Pravachol (pravastatin sodium), a drug approved to lower cholesterol in people with high cholesterol, to help prevent heart attacks in people with high cholesterol or heart disease, and to help prevent stroke in people with heart disease. One of the company's ads misleadingly suggested that the drug had been proven to help prevent stroke in all people worried about having a stroke, regardless of whether or not they had heart disease.

Another ad, directed at diabetes patients, misleadingly suggested that Pravachol had been proven to help prevent heart attacks and stroke in people with diabetes. Following the warning letter, the company created a corrective ad campaign acknowledging that Pravachol had not been approved for these indications.

Assessing DTC advertising is an on-going process for the FDA. As more research surfaces, the agency will continue to evaluate DTC drug promotion and will take additional measures as appropriate to protect the public health.

From *FDA Consumer,* July/August 2004, pp. 21–24, 26–27. Published 2004 by U.S. Food and Drug Administration. www.fda.gov

Marketing, Consumers and Technology
Perspectives for Enhancing Ethical Transactions

The advance of technology has influenced marketing in a number of ways that have ethical implications. Growth in use of the Internet and e-commerce has placed electronic "cookies," spyware, spam, RFIDs, and data mining at the forefront of the ethical debate. Some marketers have minimized the significance of these trends. This overview paper examines these issues and introduces the two articles that follow. It is hoped that these entries will further the important "marketing and technology" ethical debate.

GENE R. LACZNIAK AND PATRICK E. MURPHY

Any casual survey of the twenty-first-century marketplace reveals an economic landscape of robust e-commerce and numerous emergent forms of technologically assisted marketing. An observer of this scene might assert for good reason that marketers are increasingly leveraging their new technology to erode the consumers' right to autonomy (Kelly and Rowland 2000). A number of these current technology aided practices are problematic in terms of their potential invasiveness (Marshall 1999), their violations of consumer privacy rights (Hemphill 2002) or simply their added disadvantage to consumers (Gordon 2002).

Consider just the following illustrations:

- **E-Commerce Cookies and Spyware.** When consumers log on to a website to seek purchase information or to conduct an online transaction, a "cookie" might be placed on their personal computers, allowing sellers to track movements on that and perhaps other Internet sites visited (Linn 2004). When consumers download software, part of the usage agreement (which often consumers fail to read due to its intentional length and complexity) sometimes includes the acceptance of shadow software that records site surfs and targets pop-up ads at these users. In these ways, marketers gather considerable information about how consumers traverse the web and in what specific sequence their purchase decision unfolds. A recent development regarding cookies is that more companies are only using first party cookies (put on by the site visited) and resisting third party cookies (placed by an outside company) to increase consumer trust (Kesmodel 2005).

- **Spam.** One of the least satisfying dimensions of the growing e-commerce environment is spam—unsolicited email that typically attempts to sell products and services to Internet users. The most irritating forms of such spam include advertisements for easy (high cost) financing, gambling sites, pornographic material and diet supplements. Worse, sometimes as consumers open spam message attachments to ascertain their nature, instructions are introduced to the computer "page jacking" users to a seller's website and possibly "mouse trapping" them so that efforts to electronically escape from that site dump them to a related site or a revised form of the original solicitation. Worse still, buyers receive faux messages from purportedly known business partners (a practice known as "phishing") asking the receiver to verify personal information that if rendered will aid identity theft (Borzo 2004). It is estimated that approximately 50 percent of all emails received can be categorized as spam (Swartz 2004). The Controlling the Assault of Non-Solicited Pornography and Marketing Act of 2003 (CAN-SPAM) went into effect in January 2004 and required companies to conspicuously label their commercial e-mails and provide clear methods to opt out of future ads (Chang 2004). Despite this legislation, consumer frustration with spam, along with lost personal and organizational productivity, has grown to alarming proportions (Davidson 2004; Friel 2005).

- **RFIDs.** Another technology on the ascendance involves RFIDs or radio frequency identification tags. Diffusion of this technology could also engender significant consumer privacy concerns and raise ethical questions (Covert 2004; Peslak 2005). RFIDs are millimeter-wide microchips (about the size of a match head) that can contain a substantial amount of data about the product in which it is imbedded. The microchip has the capacity to send out that information via wireless signal to a radio scanner. This is the same technology currently used for some drive-by toll booth passes as well as for quick gasoline purchases via electronic "key chain fob" rather than credit card swipe. Currently, RFIDs are used mainly for internal inventory tracking and control. For example, Wal-Mart uses this technology in its distribution centers and is requiring that it be incorporated by all its suppliers in the next couple of years (Feder 2003). Wal-Mart is getting some "push back" on this demand from suppliers primarily due to cost considerations (Hays 2004). And Pfizer is utilizing RFIDs to guarantee that certain of its drug products (e.g., Viagra) have not been counterfeited (Appleby 2004). However, as RFID technology becomes more widely applied and refined, it could potentially provide marketing researchers with the capability to "enter" a consumer's home or garage and, given the proper scanner-receivers, identify the nature, amount, and source of many of the products contained therein (Hajewski 2003).

- **Data Mining.** Market researchers are also accumulating, via computerized files, an increasing amount of information about their customers. Given the compiling capabilities of database software, much of the information is aggregated from disparate buying situations. Made easier by widespread consumer acceptance of preferred buyer cards and credit purchasing, such information is combined using personal identifiers such as phone number, household address, driver's license registration or even social security number (Loveman 2003). Then using "data mining" techniques—sophisticated multi-variable statistical models that can extract scattered information from large consumer data pools—marketers are able to construct individual consumer profiles for millions of shoppers (Berson et al. 2000; Murphy, et al. 2005). Disturbingly, these profiles are then copied and sold to other marketers who use it to predict likely purchase prospects for their goods and services. As a result, a growing and permanent record exists of what individual consumers buy, where they bought it, the price paid and the incentives that motivated the transaction. Amazingly, some marketers use this information to try to drive away consumers who they project will not be particularly profitable (McWilliams 2004).

Taking all of this into account, it is understandable that many consumers are troubled by certain technology aided marketing practices that might be construed as prying, irritating and exploitive. In fact, a 2003 Harris interactive poll of over one thousand U.S. adults found that 69 percent of respondents agreed that consumers have lost all control over how their personal information is collected and used (Loyle 2003). Some social observers have gone so far as to opine that privacy rights will be to the twenty-first century what civil rights and women's equality were to the twentieth.

It was with such concerns in mind that in the summer of 2003 the *Business Ethics Quarterly* issued a call for papers addressing ethical issues stemming from the technology and marketing nexus. While privacy questions are the most obvious

issue, erosion of other consumer rights such as *access* (e.g., the so-called digital divide), *property* (e.g., electronic copyrights), *security* (e.g., protection of sensitive consumer data by sellers), and *redress* (e.g., the ability to verify personal records) are increasingly being challenged by marketing approaches that rely heavily on the latest technologies. The ultimate economic and social ramifications of emergent marketing technology are uncertain, but it seems clear that many new ethical questions win arise. Thus, academic scholars were invited to provide their research based or analytic perspectives on any important dimension of such issues.

Marketers' Defense of Ethical Criticism

A perusal of the business and popular press suggests that marketing practitioners have already been mounting a defense to the perceived ethical criticisms of their new technologies. To illustrate this point, a few of the more common marketing apologetics are noted below.

- **Marketing practitioners assert that when the effects of a marketing technology or its application become socially troubling, the existing regulatory framework responds by outlawing or suppressing the most annoying and harmful transgressions.** They point to the 2003 institution of the federally administered *national no call* list that restricts telemarketers from contacting consumers that are signatories (Davidson 2003). If households listed on this roll are called (certain exceptions apply), telemarketers are subject to an $11,000 fine per violation. It is estimated that this legislation, in conjunction with existing state programs, will eliminate up to 90 percent of all telemarketing calls. Marketers also highlight the thirty-three states that have laws regulating spam (Mangalindan 2003) as well as the federal 2004 "Can Spam" Act, which mandates that e-sellers cannot hide behind false addresses, thus making their identities more traceable. Consumer groups, however, characterize the Act's provisions as ineffective because among other things it does nothing to control the flow of spam from non-domestic e-sellers (Davidson 2004). Finally, marketers underscore the Children's Online Privacy Protection Act of 2002 as a model example of how well the current oversight system works (Lans-Retsky 2004). Known as COPPA, this legislation safeguards a particularly vulnerable group, children, from most forms of online marketing research. For example, COPPA makes it a violation for any marketer to knowingly gather online personal information from children younger than thirteen years of age without specific parental consent. Already two major companies, Mrs. Fields Cookies and Hershey's (candy) Direct have incurred significant fines for COPPA violations (Loyle 2003). To date, COPPA is the only anti-privacy statute that has been passed in the United States.

- **Marketers contend that the problems attributed to new selling technologies are overstated, not really novel and represent only slightly different forms of old practices that are already well tolerated by consumers.** They observe that junk mail has long clogged household mailboxes; some consumers dislike it, others look forward to it. Marketers question how spam is any different than junk mail and recommend that consumers simply use the delete button more liberally (Goldman 2003). Furthermore, justifying their opinions with national survey data, marketers suggest there is great variability among consumers in their tolerance for direct selling (Milne and Rohm 2000). Marketers also argue that concerns about the privacy dimensions of RFID tagged products are widely overblown (Ody 2004). Yet in Texas, this technology is being used to track the movement of hundreds of young school children in order to provide a record that they entered or exited school buses and as an early warning sign of possible kidnapping (Richtel 2004).

- **Marketers emphasize that some aspects of the much discussed consumer privacy debate may be exaggerated because many consumers are willing to give away personal information quite readily.** For instance, the majority of consumers volunteer detailed demographic information on product warranty forms although only the most basic information (name and address) is required to activate the coverage for most products. Consumer acceptance of preferred shopper cards, used in exchange for various discounts and rewards at the sponsoring retailer, has never been stronger as buyers sign up in droves surely knowing that their every purchase is tracked in detail. And digital cable TV, tethered to interactive capability, is steadily increasing its subscriber base with customers presumably knowing that their viewing selections can be logged and classified. In short, many marketers believe that it is difficult to defend or even establish a scrupulous buyers' right to privacy when so many consumers signal by their actions that they simply don't mind sharing their personal information with vendors or at least are willing to hand it over in exchange for minimal perks. Business philosophers have observed as much (De George 1999). As one privacy director remarked in response to privacy statutes: "Forget laws and standards—you need to send the right message to the right person at the right time" (Lager 2005: 35).

Emerging Issues in Marketing and Technology

Of course, blanket defenses for widely varying applications of marketing technology are not particularly useful. As is necessary when significant new technologies impact the economy, numerous questions arise, some of an ethical nature, that need to be systematically investigated. With this special issue on marketing and technology. *Business Ethics Quarterly* hopes to advance the conversation about some of these questions in an analytic and reasoned fashion. The articles contained in this issue build on some already existing foundational work. A partial list of such writing includes Caudill and Murphy 2000, Donaldson 2001, and Peace et al. 2002, as well as Kracher and Corritore 2004. This last paper makes a particularly significant point about e-commerce, suggesting that it requires not so much a new ethics but a dedicated evaluation of the new manifestations of economic exchange from various traditional ethical frameworks. Kracher and Corritore also make a particularly strong case for the centrality of *trust* as a solution to many of the emerging problems of the electronic marketplace. Such advocacy adds to the themes previously expressed by Grabner-Kraeuter (2002), Hemphill (2002) and Koehn (2003).

The first paper in this special issue addresses "Privacy Rights on the Internet: Self Regulation or Government Regulation?" Norman E. Bowie and Karim Jamal (2006) review an earlier empirical study (Jamal, Maier, and Sunder 2003) and combine it with information gathered in the U.K. to examine whether high traffic websites are honoring their promises to consumers regarding privacy. This is a critical ethical and economic question because privacy concerns have been shown to be a major factor in depressing the growth rate of Internet shopping (Tedeschi 2000). Moreover, the extent of keeping privacy promises by Internet sellers will help determine whether the U.S. government needs to supplement current industry self regulation, presently implemented through various "assurance seals" and privacy policies that specify the subsequent usage of any buyer information that has been gathered. Some consumer advocates have called for European style restrictions prohibiting any secondary use of information provided by consumers (Scheibal and Gladstone 2000). The authors use Kantian reasoning to establish the centrality of a consumer's right to privacy. However, based on the significantly high compliance rates by U.S. sellers in apparently honoring buyer privacy (as demonstrated by their empirical test), government mandated regulation of privacy policies are *not* recommended at this time. Bowie and Jamal observe, however, that an explicit "opt-in" provision for any further usage of consumer information, beyond the original transaction, is the approach most aligned with the basic right of consumer autonomy.

In the second paper, "Online Brands and Trademark Conflicts: A Hegelian Perspective," Richard A. Spinello (2006) draws on the philosophy of George Hegel, particularly his conception of property rights, to clarify and somewhat limit the legal claims of corporations to Internet domain names that incorporate their trademarks. As Internet commerce has mushroomed, various external parties have tried to incorporate famous names into their own domain addresses in order to create confusion, divert traffic to their own sites or extract ransom from the trademarked name owners. A widely reported incident of such usurpation in a non-commercial setting was whitehouse.com (a porn site) as contrasted with whitehouse.gov, the email contact address for staff serving the U.S. President. Spinello argues that Hegel's view of property appears to usefully balance the marketer's rights to trademark protection with competing consumer claims more fairly than other philosophies. For example, a reasonable person attempting to shop Wal-Mart online might well confuse Wal-Mart.org (a potentially bogus address) with Wal-Mart.com. And so, if there is a dispute about domain address rights, the trademark claims of Wal-Mart should prevail. However, using Hegelian reasoning, Spinello contends that Wal-Martsucks.com (a website likely critical of the firm) would *not* be confused by a reasonable person as the home page of the real Wal-Mart. So, in this latter case, private property rights to the disputed ether space—a legitimate forum for social criticism—ought not to be available to the corporation.

To be sure, these *BEQ* papers are just the opening round in what should be an on-going dialog about ethical issues emanating from the marketing and technology interface. We encourage interested scholars to further address the ethical implications of questions such as:

- Is it fair for marketers to use electronic customer profiles to actively *discourage* transactions from customers that are projected to be unprofitable to serve?

- Is it proper for online marketers to utilize targeted *price discrimination* based on the past online behaviors of individual consumers without acknowledging the protocol behind the practice?

- What can be done about *consumer abuses* caused by international emarketers not subject to local or national marketing regulations?

This last question raises one of the more poignant issues about the borderless world of Internet marketing. Since cyberspace is global, how can it ever be effectively regulated by governmental authorities that are geographically bound? It would seem that the universality of the web marketing world makes it critically imperative that prevailing ethical norms and values be established among citizens in order to reduce buyer exploitation and enhance transactional trust. In other words, the future fairness and justice of Internet marketing will depend far more on ethics than law. Finally, the discussion contained in this special issue of *BEQ* does not specifically address the ethical implications involved in the use of new marketing technologies not directly connected to a web selling environment. For example, the increased sophistication, miniaturization, and lower cost of surveillance capability has added to the arsenal of marketing researchers interested in doing covert observational consumer studies (Hagerty and Berman 2003). Who will watch these consumer watchers? Ethical evaluations of these offline applications of marketing technology are needed.

In the end, marketing practitioners adopt new technology because it promises to increase the efficiency or effectiveness of exchange. Such applications imply lower costs or greater convenience for consumers. In this manner, the use of new technology has always been a driver of the material abundance available in the marketplace. But typically, new technologies bring with them some questionable and often unintended side effects. One critical role for those in the Academy interested in ethics is to identify and evaluate those side effects in terms of how they must be balanced to promote greater economic fairness and justice.

A continuation of discussions contained in this issue of *BEQ* is welcomed, encouraged and anticipated.

References

Appleby, J. 2004. "FDA Guidelines Call for Radio Technology to Control Counterfeit Drugs." *USA Today* (November 16): 7B.

Berson, A., S. Smith, and K. Thurling. 2000. *Building Data Mining Applications for CRM* (Columbus: McGraw-Hill).

Borzo, J. 2004. "Something's Phishy." *The Wall Street Journal* (November 15): R8, R11.

Bowie, N., and K. Jamal. 2006. "Privacy Rights on the Internet: Self Regulation or Government Regulation?" *Business Ethics Quarterly* 16:3 (July): 323–42.

Caudill, E. M., and P. E. Murphy. 2000. "Consumer Online Privacy: Legal and Ethical Issues." *Journal of Public Policy & Marketing* 19(1): 7–19.

Chang, J. 2004. "Private Property." *Sale and Marketing Management* (December): 22–26.

Covert, J. 2004. "Down, but Far from Out." *The Wall Street Journal* (January 12): R5, R8.

Davidson, P. 2003. "FTC Told to Enforce Do-Not-Call List." *USA Today* (October 8): 1B.

_____. 2004. "Do-Not-Spam Registry Could Result in More Spam, FTC Says." *USA Today* (June 16): Bl.

De George, R. T. 1999. "Business Ethics and the Information Age." *Bentley College Center for Business Ethics/Bell Atlantic Lecture Series* (March 22): 1–20.

Donaldson, T. 2001. "Ethics in Cyberspace: Have We Seen this Movie Before?" *Business and Society Review* 106(4): 273.

Feder, B. J. 2003. "Wal-Mart Plan Could Cost Suppliers Millions." *The New York Times* (November 10): 1–2, http://www.nytimes.com.

Friel, A. L. 2005. "The Spam Spat: How Will Marketers Be Affected by the Fight Against Spam?" *Marketing Management* (May/June): 48–50.

Goldman, E. 2003. "Opinion: Hate Spam? Just Hit Delete." http://www.TwinCities.com (August 11): 1–2.

Gordon, J. R. 2002. "Legal Services and the Digital Divide." *Albany Law Journal of Science and Technology* 12: 809–19.

Grabner-Kraeuter, S. 2002. "The Role of Consumers' Trust in Online-Shopping."*Journal of Business Ethics* 39(1/2): 43–50.

Hagerty, J. R., and D. K. Berman. 2003. "New Battleground Over Web Privacy: Ads That Snoop." *The Wall Street Journal* (August 27): Al, A8.

Hajewski, D. 2003. "High-Tech ID System Would Revolutionize Retail Industry." *Milwaukee Journal Sentinel* (February 9): 1D, 3D.

Hays, C. L. 2004. "What They Know About You." *The New York Times* (November 14): section 3.

Hemphill, T. A. 2002. "Electronic Commerce and Consumer Privacy: Establishing Online Trust in the U.S. Digital Economy." *Business and Society Review* 107(2): 221–9.

Jamal, K., M. Maier, and S. Sunder. 2003. "Privacy in E-Commerce: Development of Reporting Standards, Disclosure and Assurance Services in an Unregulated Market." *Journal of Accounting Research* 41(2): 285–310.

Kelly, E. P., and H. C. Rowland. 2000. "Ethical and Online Privacy Issues in Electronic Commerce." *Business Horizons* (May–June): 3–12.

Kesmodel, D. 2005. "When the Cookies Crumble." *The Wall Street Journal* (September 12): R6.

Koehn, D. 2003. "The Nature of and Conditions for Online Trust." *Journal of Business Ethics* 43(1/2): 3–19.

Kracher, B., and C. L. Corritore. 2004. "Is There a Special E-Commerce Ethics?" *Business Ethics Quarterly* 14(1): 71–94.

Lager, M. 2005. "CRM in an Age of Legislation," *Customer Relationship Management* (August): 30–35.

Lans-Retsky, M. 2004. "COPPA Sets Tone for Privacy Policies." *Marketing News* (March 15): 8.

Linn, A. 2004. "Bugged By Spies: Imports Clog Computers." *USA Today* (November 1): 4D.

Loveman, G. 2003. "Diamonds in the Data Mine." *Harvard Business Review* (May): 109–13.

Loyle, D. 2003. "Privacy Under Scrutiny." *Catalog Success* (June 1); www.catalogsuccess.com, 1–7.

Mangalindan, M. 2003. "Putting a Lid on Spam." *The Wall Street Journal* (June 6): B1, B4.

Marshall, K. P. 1999. "Has Technology Introduced New Ethical Problems?" *Journal of Business Ethics* 19(1): 81–90.

McWilliams, G. 2004. "Analyzing Customers, Best Buy Decides Not All Are Welcome." *The Wall Street Journal* (November 8): A1, A8.

Milne, G., and A. J. Rohm. 2000. "Consumer Privacy and Name Removal across Direct Marketing Channels: Exploring Opt-In and Opt-Out Alternatives." *Journal of Public Policy & Marketing* 19(2): 238–49.

Murphy, P. E., G. R. Laczniak, N. E. Bowie, and T. A. Klein. 2005. *Ethical Marketing* (Upper Saddle River, N.J.: Pearson Prentice Hall), 205.

Ody, Penelope. 2004. "RFID Not Ready yet for Baked Beans." *Financial Times* (June 23): 3.

Peace, G., J. Weber, K. S. Hartzel, and J. Nightingale. 2002. "Ethical Issues in eBusiness: A Proposal for Creating the eBusiness Principles." *Business Society Review* 107(1): 41–60.

Peslak, A. R. 2005. "An Ethical Exploration of Privacy and Radio Frequency Identification." *Journal of Business Ethics* 59: 327–45.

Richtel, M. 2004. "In Texas, 28,000 Students Test an Electronic Eye." *The New York Times* (November 17): 1–3, www.nytimes.com.

Scheibal, W. J., and J. A. Gladstone. 2000. "Privacy on the Net: Europe Changes the Rules." *Business Horizons* (May–June): 13–18.

Spinello, R. 2006. "Online Brands and Trademark Conflicts: A Hegelian Perspective." *Business Ethics Quarterly* 16:3 (July): 343–67.

Swartz, J. 2004. "Is the Future of E-Mail Under Cyberattack?" *USA Today* (June 15): 4B.

Tedeschi, B. 2000. "E-Commerce Report: Giving Consumers Access to the Data Collected About Them Online." *The New York Times* (July 3): C6.

Corporate Citizenship: It's the Brand

As brand architect and steward, marketing should be a key leader in corporate citizenship.

LAWRENCE A. CROSBY AND SHEREE L. JOHNSON

Most executives acknowledge the importance of social and environmental responsibility. According to recent surveys, they see the significance to the bottom line, their companies' reputations, and their customers. But when it comes to translating citizenship into meaningful programs and embedding it in the business, companies range from leaders to laggards—with the majority somewhere in between.

Some progress is being made, perhaps because of new global corporate-citizenship initiatives such as the United Nations Global Compact. It asks companies to "embrace, support, and enact, within their sphere of influence, a set of core values in the areas of human rights, labor standards, the environment, and anticorruption." However, executives increasingly see themselves in no-win situations, caught between critics demanding ever higher levels of "corporate social responsibility" and investors applying relentless pressure to maximize short-term profits.

"To be a great company, you have to be a good company first," said General Electric (GE) CEO Jeffrey Immelt in a November 2004 issue of *Fortune* magazine. "The world's changed. Businesses today aren't admired. Size is not respected. There's a bigger gulf today between haves and have-nots than ever before. It's up to us to use our platform to be a good citizen. Because not only is it a nice thing to do, it's a business imperative."

Affecting Business

More and more, corporate citizenship is influencing consumer behavior. Over a 10-year period, the number of consumers willing to switch from one brand to another—if the other brand is associated with a cause—has risen from 66% to 86%.

Studies are also beginning to demonstrate that corporate citizenship can bring value to a company, from enhancing reputation to increasing sales. Research for BT, the British telecommunications giant, found that its corporate social-responsibility activities comprise 25% of the effect its reputation has on customer satisfaction figures. Furthermore, the research found that if BT no longer acted with integrity, then it could expect to reduce customer satisfaction by 10%—which could decrease revenues by 20%–30%.

And consumers want to know what companies are doing. Nearly nine in 10 agree that companies should tell them the ways they're supporting social issues. Whirlpool Corp., through customer research and causal modeling and analysis, discovered overwhelming evidence that (1) customers wanted a stronger emotional connection to the brand and (2) this connection could be built through social responsibility. For many years, Whirlpool had been donating a refrigerator and range to every Habitat home built in the United States. The problem: This was Whirlpool's best-kept secret. It changed that through the Reba McEntire Habitat for Humanity Concert Tour.

This initiative leveraged a well-respected spokeswoman through a creative execution, tying in multifaceted communications to create the emotional bonding and awareness that customers obviously craved. Subsequent consumer behaviors proved its positive business impact: All customer loyalty index measures improved significantly, Sears dealers' store sales for the Whirlpool brand increased 47%, and hits on the Whirlpool Web site rose considerably.

A corporation that practices solid citizenship has a long-term perspective about what's necessary to meet the expectations of customers, employees, and communities in which it operates. There's a clear recognition that good corporate citizenship is fundamental to good business. It builds brand loyalty, attracts and then helps retain skilled employees, appeals to a growing number of socially responsible investors, and enhances the company's public image and reputation—thereby opening doors to new markets across the world.

The challenge is to create a corporate-citizenship proposition that (1) expresses the benefit of the corporate values and (2) becomes an integral part of how wealth is created for the corporation. The social and environmental activism of businesses such as Timberland, Ben & Jerry's, and Patagonia is central to their missions and appeal to customers. And a number of large, global, and mainstream companies—such as Johnson & Johnson, 3M, IBM, Hewlett-Packard, GE, BP, Novo Nordisk, and Novartis—are building on strong cultures and historical commitment, to reinvigorate the status and strength of corporate-citizenship values in shaping strategies and decision making.

Living the Brand

The director of Unilever's Marketing Academy, Thom Braun, has stated, "Values are at the heart of branding. . . . Brand values should not just be 'attachments' to a product or service, but rather the driving force for what the brand can dare to become."

These intangible assets have become important to companies in establishing a global presence. By some estimates, brands make up as much as 40% of companies' market values. Protecting images and brand names has quickly evolved as a major challenge for globalization strategies and chief marketing officers.

Branding programs should be about enhancing corporate brands in ways that are meaningful to key constituencies: customers, employees, communities, public officials, suppliers, and so on. Avon's customers (primarily women more than 30 years old) did not need to be convinced that breast cancer posed a threat to them or to women in general. But in 1993, the cosmetics company committed itself to raising breast-cancer awareness in the United States—particularly among medically underserved women—as an essential first step toward early detection. Avon's independent sales representatives now routinely distribute educational materials on their sales calls, and participate alongside customers in fund-raising walks. All told, it has raised and contributed $250 million for breast cancer.

Executives increasingly see themselves in no-win situations, caught between social responsibility and short-term profits.

The business objective of any citizenship-branding campaign can be anything from increasing sales and improving customer loyalty to enhancing overall reputation. The philanthropic objective can be increasing awareness of a critical need, inspiring consumers and partners to take action, or raising money. However, if the business objective isn't also a strategic goal of the company, then even the worthiest cause will fail to (1) engage the company's energies and (2) build sustainable credibility with consumers.

For Bernie Marcus, cofounder of Home Depot, citizenship-branding efforts have to work that way. As he has said: "Habitat International came to us in 1991 . . . . 'Write a check to us,' they said, 'and we will distribute it to our affiliates.' But we said no. If we really want to have an impact in these communities . . . , then we have to build relationships." Throughout the United States, Home Depot's employees labor to build and rehabilitate affordable housing for the elderly and the poor. Like Marcus, leaders such as Wal-Mart's Sam Walton, ConAgra Foods' Bruce Rohde, Avon's Jim Preston, and Starbucks' Howard Schultz have viewed their employees as brand ambassadors.

Making Progress

Every day, more companies come to value the opportunities that corporate citizenship presents to business and society. Becoming a leading citizen requires companies to institutionalize and integrate corporate citizenship into their strategies, operations, and policies in all areas and at all levels. Marketing—being responsible for developing brand promise and message strategies—must take up a key leadership role in this imperative.

Keep in mind that it takes years to influence a social problem, and just as long to build a brand. You have to make sure senior management understands that this is long-term; don't confuse a citizenship-branding program with the monthly promotion plan. In an era that holds escalating expectations of business' role in society, good corporate citizenship rests at the heart of competitive business strategy.

LAWRENCE A. CROSBY is the CEO of Synovate Loyalty and is based in Scottsdale, Ariz. He may be reached at larry.crosby@synovate.com. **SHEREE L. JOHNSON** is global director of strategic marketing for Synovate Loyalty and is based in Vancouver, British Columbia. She may be reached at sheree.johnson@t synovate.com.

Lies, Damn Lies, and Word of Mouth

The hottest marketers in the country face their biggest challenge yet: marketing themselves.

MIKE HOFMAN

When some 450 attendees gathered at the Word of Mouth Marketing Association's conference in Orlando recently, they had many reasons to celebrate and a few to be fearful. Word-of-mouth marketing—by which companies encourage consumers to recommend products to one another—is currently among the brightest stars in the advertising firmament. But some practitioners worry that too many of their peers run campaigns that dupe consumers. The fear is that such abuses could undermine the credibility of a field that many marketers consider invaluable.

People have always recommended stuff to friends, of course, but the notion that companies can manage such exchanges has gained currency in the past few years. Techniques are still evolving as different companies experiment with wildly different strategies. Typically, though, marketers try to get samples of new products into the hands of individual consumers—often the connectors and mavens Malcolm Gladwell wrote about in *The Tipping Point*. The marketer encourages those individuals to talk up its products to friends, acquaintances, and total strangers.

How common are word-of-mouth programs? Very. Most major brands have one in the works. Dell, Hershey, Intuit, and Kraft belong to WOMMA, the year-and-a-half-old trade group. Entrepreneurial companies are also embracing word of mouth because it can be done cheaply and has an outsider appeal. Numerous start-up marketing firms and ad agencies specialize in it. Some of those have already sold to major agencies; others have raised serious money. David Baiter, founder of Boston-based BzzAgent, one of the best known firms, arrived at the WOMMA conference triumphant, having just secured $13.75 million in venture capital.

In short, buzz has buzz. Word of mouth is among the very few techniques to infiltrate the no-marketing zones people have built around their lives. Many marketers believe that informal, unmediated communication through blogs, social networking sites, or chats in the girls' bathroom is hands down more effective than even the most polished ads. Of course, that informal, unmediated communication is effective only so long as people trust it. Unfortunately, conventional wisdom these days is that

---

If You Can't Say Something Nice

One issue not addressed by the Word of Mouth Marketing Association's rules is what to do when those asked to spread the good word decide there's no good word to spread. Recently, several members of BzzAgent's word-of-mouth network complained on the company's blog about a new product: the Home Café coffee machine. Though many reviewers liked the Home Café just fine, some said it was poorly designed and brewed coffee that was either way too hot or tepid. Others referred readers to negative reviews of the product on Amazon.com. One man said he had promised to bring the machine to his book group and was disappointed when he received a broken sample.

In and among complaints about the grade of plastic used to make the lid and the machine's propensity to emit steam or (some said) smoke, a few people raised a more fundamental question: Are we obliged to talk up a product we don't like? No, a BzzAgent manager replied on the blog. All that is required is honest feedback.

As one member of the BzzAgent network pointed out, it seemed like an awful lot of excitement over a few people sharing their opinions about the product. Then again, the power of people sharing their opinions is exactly the point.

---

everybody lies, from auditors to *Oprah* authors. Consumers are aware that advertisers buy words on search engines, and that even some bloggers are on the take. If word of mouth becomes suspect, what's left for marketers?

Evangelists or Shills?

Marketers engage people to join word-of-mouth campaigns in several different ways. BzzAgent, for example, distributes rewards points to consumers in its network for every interaction

Words of Mouth	Word-of-mouth marketing is any initiative that prompts customers to talk to other people about a product or service. There are several breeds.
Buzz Marketing	Winning attention for products by putting them in the hands of celebrities.
Stealth Marketing	Marketing disguised as something else. Word-of-mouthers consider this their evil twin. Anyone who thinks ill of word of mouth, they contend, is probably confusing it with this.
Viral Marketing	Promoting products or services through messages and video spread by consumers via e-mail.
Influencer Marketing	Targeting the connected or cool people that lemmings will most likely follow.

they have in which they mention a product. Those points can be redeemed for prizes supplied by BzzAgent's customers.

Compensation schemes are uncontroversial in the industry. Transparency is another story. Outsiders often assume people enlisted in these campaigns hide their involvement to appear more credible. It's sometimes true. Some companies have employees write slanted reviews of products online, while others hire actors to pretend to recommend products.

Industry insiders say they view these tactics with alarm. In their perfect world, all word-of-mouth marketers would tell people what they were up to, says David Binkowski, of Hass MS&L, an agency in Ann Arbor, Michigan, that runs campaigns for General Motors, Procter & Gamble, and others. When he sends a sample product to a blogger, for example, he always asks her to say in her post that she received the item as part of a marketing campaign. Most boutique firms know enough to disclose, Binkowski adds. He says it's the large ad agencies that are jumping into this hot field that make clumsy mistakes like posting fake reviews online. (Big agency folks dismiss the charge.)

Whatever the source of abuse, duping not only sows suspicion in consumers' minds, it also raises the specter of government scrutiny. In October, an industry watchdog group called Commercial Alert, based in Portland, Oregon, sent a letter to the Federal Trade Commission, arguing that anybody who promotes a product without mentioning that he or she has been compensated is basically committing fraud. "There is evidence that some of these companies are perpetrating large-scale deception upon consumers by deploying buzz marketers who fail to disclose that they have been enlisted to promote products," wrote Gary Ruskin, Commercial Alert's executive director. The FTC should investigate word-of-mouth marketers, Ruskin continued, and create rules governing their conduct.

Though Ruskin's group is tiny, marketers take it seriously. In 2001, Commercial Alert petitioned the FTC to require search engines to disclose whether Advertiser payments influenced their rankings. "The FCC came back a year later and did exactly what we wanted," Ruskin says.

Lessons from the Spam Wars

To convince the world that their industry is under control, WOMMA has spent the past year developing its own rules, which it says obviate the need for government intervention. Never far

from members' thoughts is the fate of e-mail marketers. It was lack of self-regulation among early practitioners that "led to the rise of spam and that gave e-mail marketing a bad name," says Jamie Tedford, who oversees the word-of-mouth practice at Arnold Worldwide, an ad agency based in Boston. E-mail marketers failed to draw distinctions between good marketing and spam, the story goes. The response was technology that blocked marketing messages indiscriminately, and federal anti-spam legislation.

The word-of-mouth crowd is determined not to make the same mistake. "Every industry has sleazy players, and that's why word-of-mouth marketers have banded together to set rules and set the example," says Andy Sernovitz, WOMMA's Chicago-based president and founder. "Everything they asked for," he says, referring to Commercial Alert, "is something [we] already support."

Among other things, the code requires marketers to persuade recommenders to disclose what they are doing. As further inducement for full disclosure, WOMMA is touting a study by a professor at Northeastern University suggesting that people aren't turned off when told they are the subjects of a word-of-mouth campaign. In fact, they are more likely to mention the experience to someone else, creating a pleasant multiplier effect.

WOMMA's code also grapples with the charge that word of mouth often targets kids. "We stand against the inclusion of children under the age of 13 in any word-of-mouth marketing program," the code states. Teenagers are also a matter of concern. Tremor, a division of Procter & Gamble that helps companies promote products online to 250,000 teens, has drawn fire from Ruskin and even some WOMMA members for enrolling teens in a marketing service in return for free products. Robyn Schroeder, a P&G spokesperson, says that Tremor was contacted by the FTC to discuss its practices and "provided them with the information they were looking for." Though not a member of WOMMA, she adds, P&G "understands what they are trying to achieve."

The problem with any industry's code of conduct, of course, is enforcement. In theory, WOMMA could expel members who habitually violate its rules. But how the group would uncover transgressions and adjudicate complaints is unclear. Also, the idea of regulating informal conversations seems absurd on its face.

The good news for marketers is that the FTC seems willing to let the industry deal with these questions on its own. Speaking in Orlando, FTC official Thomas B. Pahl would not comment on whether the commission would pursue Ruskin's investigation request. But Pahl said he was impressed by WOMMA's efforts, and noted that the FTC prefers industries such as advertising and marketing to police themselves. "Self-regulation can be especially effective in making sure that most companies in an industry stay on the straight and narrow," Pahl said. That "permits the government to focus our resources and attention on those companies that are causing the most problems to consumers and competition."

MIKE HOFMAN can be reached at MHofman@inc.com.

Financial Scams Expected to Boom as Boomers Age

Seniors often hardest hit by aggressive sales pitches, fraud

Kathy Chu

In Michigan, an advertisement offers this come-on to those 60 and older:

"Come learn from the IRA Technician" at a seminar that more than 10,000 seniors have attended. Top sirloin steak will be served—along with tips on "how to guarantee your IRA will never run out, regardless of market fluctuations."

Just don't bring your financial adviser. Agents and brokers are not invited, the ad says.

As the first of 79 million baby boomers turn 60 this year, free-this and free-that financial seminars are thriving. Community centers and hotels have become a backdrop for what regulators see as aggressive sales pitches geared to seniors.

While people 60 and older make up 15% of the U.S. population, they account for about 30% of fraud victims, estimates Consumer Action, a consumer-advocacy group.

As this gargantuan generation of boomers starts to retire, "You're going to see more of these seminars and more of these sales pitches," says James Nelson, assistant secretary of state in Mississippi. "Wherever retirees are congregated, you're going to have these people preying on them."

Older people have long been a lucrative market for the financial-services industry because of the assets they've accumulated. But the sheer number of baby boomers approaching retirement and seeking a place to park their assets is causing a frenzy of aggressive sales tactics.

Boomers have more than $8.5 trillion in investable assets. Over the next 40 years, they stand to inherit at least $7 trillion from their parents, research firm Cerulli Associates estimates.

As baby boomers swell the retiree population, regulators worry not just about estate-planning seminars for seniors but also about sales of promissory notes, unregistered securities and lottery scams.

"It's the topic of the next few decades: senior investments and senior fraud," says Patricia Struck, president of the North American Securities Administrators Association, or NASAA.

"There are marketing seminars that are being held nightly and in every city," says Bryan Lantagne of the Massachusetts Securities Division. "They get you to come in and do a financial plan. Their goal is to put you in one of these products."

Senior estate-planning seminars aren't new. But they're drawing more regulatory scrutiny because they're ramping up in areas with large elderly populations. Typically, the people who attend them need advice about leaving assets to their children, managing income or minimizing taxes in retirement.

Beverly Buhs, 81, of Millbrae, Calif., attended one of these financial seminars with her husband, Art, in 1997. They bought a living trust on the spot, she says. They were told it would let them avoid probate court, the sometimes expensive process by which your assets are allocated after you die.

They also bought an equity-index annuity. That's a high-cost insurance product with returns based partly on the stock market.

After her husband died, Buhs found the trust didn't fully protect their assets from probate. And she couldn't access the money in the annuity without paying big penalties. Her complaints are part of a class-action lawsuit against the financial agents and companies involved in the seminar.

A 'Major Problem'

These seminars are a "major problem" in Texas, where many boomers retire, says Denise Voigt Crawford, the state securities commissioner.

North Dakota Securities Commissioner Karen Tyler calls these seminars a bait-and-switch tactic. The free seminar is the bait; the switch comes when the agents urge investors to liquidate the portfolio and put the money into other products, Tyler says.

Dan Danbom of the Society of Certified Senior Advisors— which helps train insurance agents, brokers and others to conduct senior seminars—says there's nothing "inherently dishonest

10 Tips for Dodging Scams

- **Don't be a "courtesy" victim.** Walk away or hang up if something sounds questionable. Con artists will exploit your good manners.
- **Check out strangers touting strange deals.** Say "no" to any investment agent who wants an immediate decision. Check out the salespeople and their firms with your securities department and NASD, a self-regulatory body. Find tips on avoiding fraud at the North American Securities Administrators Association's site: www.nasaa.org.
- **Stay in charge of your money.** Beware of anyone who suggests you invest in something you don't understand or who urges you to leave everything in his or her hands.
- **Don't judge a book by its cover.** Successful con artists sound and look professional and can make the flimsiest investment deal sound as safe as putting money in the bank.
- **Watch out for salespeople who prey on fear.** Con artists know you worry about outliving your savings or seeing all of your money vanish as the result of a catastrophic event, such as a costly hospitalization. Fear can cloud your judgment.
- **Don't make a tragedy worse with rash financial decisions.** The death or hospitalization of a spouse has many sad consequences. Financial fraud shouldn't be one of them. If you find yourself suddenly in charge of your own finances, get the facts before making decisions.
- **Monitor your investments and ask tough questions.** Insist on regular written reports. Watch for signs of excessive or unauthorized trading of your money.
- **Look for trouble retrieving your principal or cashing out profits.** Beware of advisers who stall when you want to pull out your principal or profits. Some investments restrict withdrawals for a certain period. But you must be told of these restrictions before investing.
- **Don't let embarrassment or fear keep you from reporting fraud or abuse.** Every day you delay reporting fraud or abuse, the con artist could be spending your money and finding new victims. You can file a complaint with law enforcement, with your state securities commissions and with the Federal Trade Commission, at www.ftc.gov or 877-FTC-HELP (877-382-4357).
- **Beware of "reload" scams.** If you're already the victim of a scam, don't compound the damage by letting con artists "reload" and take more of your assets. Con artists will promise victims they can get back the original money lost.

Sources: North American Securities Administrators Association, USA TODAY research

about seminars, any more than there's anything inherently dishonest about advertising or direct mail."

And some agents argue that their financial seminars fill seniors' very real need for education. Theresa Bischoff, an insurance agent in Palatine, Ill., says she holds seminars because, "Baby boomers are starving for information on retirement and estate planning."

But regulators worry that seminars often serve as tools for unscrupulous salespeople. NASAA issued an alert in December cautioning investors that such seminars were sometimes being used by "bogus" senior specialists. The specialists may take only a few courses to earn their titles, then use these designations to create a "false level of comfort" about their expertise, according to NASAA.

In a typical scenario, financial agents will find out, at the seminar and in follow-up meetings, what assets seniors have, NASAA says. Then they'll recommend these assets be liquidated and put into equity-index or variable annuities. (State regulators say these recommendations could be considered investment advice, and anyone not registered as an investment adviser could face enforcement action.)

Variable and equity-index annuities are complex insurance products whose returns vary with market performance. Variable annuities' returns are tied to the stock market. Equity-index annuities' returns fluctuate with the market but also provide a minimum guarantee.

Both can be appropriate for people who want tax-advantaged savings or an income stream in retirement. But they're generally ill-suited for people in their 60s, 70s or 80s who'll need access to their money over the next decade. These costly products usually have stiff penalties for withdrawing money before the end of a surrender period that can last up to 15 years.

Louise Renne, a former San Francisco city attorney, says financial seminars often "are really fronts for (insurance) agents who want to sell annuities to seniors." Renne represents Buhs and others in three lawsuits against financial pros who conducted the seminars and companies that supplied the products.

Michael DeGeorge, general counsel for the National Association for Variable Annuities, says, "The vast majority of annuity recommendations are done appropriately."

Emotional Pain

Whether scams involve inappropriate product sales or telemarketing fraud, they can be emotionally and financially devastating for victims of all ages.

Seniors, though, are particularly hard hit. Scams can wipe out an entire lifetime of savings. Unlike younger investors, seniors have few or no working years to recapture their losses.

The emotional pain of being scammed can also be magnified for seniors who keep silent about losing money. Many of them don't report suspected fraud out of shame and "fear that if the family realizes they've been ripped off, they'll be placed in an institution," seen as unfit to manage their finances and lives, says Jenefer Duane, chief executive of the Elder Financial Protection Network.

Thus, complaints about senior financial fraud are probably lower than they should be, Duane says. In 2005, consumers 50 and older filed 151,000 fraud and identity-theft-related complaints with the Federal Trade Commission. That total represented nearly one-third of total fraud and one-fifth of all identity-theft complaints among those who reported their age.

Online and telemarketing scams rank among the top complaints filed by older consumers.

Seniors who've been scammed often have to work longer than they'd planned—and harder. Take Neal Dukes, 71, of Grand Ledge, Mich. Dukes lost $250,000 a few years ago after a financial adviser persuaded him and 17 other people, mostly seniors, to put money into what the adviser said were high-interest-earning annuities.

The adviser, Daniel Neuenschwander, pleaded guilty, admitting he didn't invest the money in annuities but instead lost much of it in the commodities market or used it to support his family.

A Michigan circuit judge sentenced Neuenschwander in 2002 to up to 10 years in prison and ordered him to pay $2.2 million back to the seniors.

"It's tragic. Mr. Neuenschwander is very remorseful," says John Maurer, Neuenschwander's attorney.

Dukes says he hasn't gotten a dime back and isn't hopeful he will. He's been working eight to 10 hours a few days a week at his insecticide-spraying business to earn money.

'No Golden Years Left'

"When you're 71 years old, you should be able to enjoy your life and your golden years," Dukes says. "But when you've been taken like this, there are no golden years left."

Financial recovery in senior scams is rare but not hopeless. Shlimoon Youkhana, 80, was one of the lucky ones. He got his money back after what had seemed to be a promising investment turned sour, draining his money with it.

A few years ago, he and his children invested $15,000 in the stock of a company that was supposed to file for an initial public offering. But the company never gave them their stock certificates. It eventually merged with another entity and changed its name.

Youkhana, of Rosemont, Ill., spent more than two years and hundreds of hours researching the company and documenting his experience, reporting his findings along the way to the Illinois Securities Department. The department did its own investigation and recovered investors' money.

Now, Youkhana offers to help other seniors in his community do research before they invest. "I'm not a Don Quixote or anything," he says. He just doesn't want others to be victims, he says.

The easiest way to avoid scams? Beware of any opportunity that sounds too good to be true. Seniors who are pressured to make a financial decision on the spot should run—not walk—away.

Robert Inman, 69, was wary about the living trust and annuity being pitched during a December free-lunch seminar he attended in Jackson, Mich.

He didn't feel the presenters adequately answered his questions—such as, what happens if the company that created the trust goes under? And he was bothered that they wanted people to sign up on the spot.

Also, a salesman called him multiple times after the seminar, stopping only after being invited to the house. "We thought that maybe this is the way to get rid of him," Inman says.

He consulted an attorney and decided to forgo the products. Inman's advice to seniors? "Don't jump into anything hastily. Take some time to do some checking."

Consumer Groups Act

Consumer groups are also stepping up efforts to alert seniors to potential scams. In Michigan, AARP, the advocacy group for those 50 and over, has found a way to counter "free lunch" seminars: It holds its own "free lunch" seminars.

No products are sold at the sessions. Still, "They're wildly popular," AARP's Sally Hurme says of the educational seminars, which feature such names as "What You Should Know About Living Trusts" and "How to Tell the Difference Between An Estate Plan and a Sales Pitch."

Says Anita Salustro, who leads the seminars for AARP in Michigan: "People want some consumer protection. They've been to these free lunches and want some balanced information from someone who's not selling a product."

Managing for Organizational Integrity

**By supporting ethically sound behavior, managers can strengthen
the relationships and reputations their companies depend on.**

LYNN SHARP PAINE

Many managers think of ethics as a question of personal scruples, a confidential matter between individuals and their consciences. These executives are quick to describe any wrongdoing as an isolated incident, the work of a rogue employee. The thought that the company could bear any responsibility for an individual's misdeeds never enters their minds. Ethics, after all, has nothing to do with management.

In fact, ethics has *everything* to do with management. Rarely do the character flaws of a lone actor fully explain corporate misconduct. More typically, unethical business practice involves the tacit, if not explicit, cooperation of others and reflects the values, attitudes, beliefs, language, and behavioral patterns that define an organization's operating culture. Ethics, then, is as much an organizational as a personal issue. Managers who fail to provide proper leadership and to institute systems that facilitate ethical conduct share responsibility with those who conceive, execute, and knowingly benefit from corporate misdeeds.

Managers must acknowledge their role in shaping organizational ethics and seize this opportunity to create a climate that can strengthen the relationships and reputations on which their companies' success depends. Executives who ignore ethics run the risk of personal and corporate liability in today's increasingly tough legal environment. In addition, they deprive their organizations of the benefits available under new federal guidelines for sentencing organizations convicted of wrongdoing. These sentencing guidelines recognize for the first time the organizational and managerial roots of unlawful conduct and base fines partly on the extent to which companies have taken steps to prevent that misconduct.

Prompted by the prospect of leniency, many companies are rushing to implement compliance-based ethics programs. Designed by corporate counsel, the goal of these programs is to prevent, detect, and punish legal violations. But organizational ethics means more than avoiding illegal practice; and providing employees with a rule book will do little to address the problems underlying unlawful conduct. To foster a climate that encourages exemplary behavior, corporations need a comprehensive approach that goes beyond the often punitive legal compliance stance.

An integrity-based approach to ethics management combines a concern for the law with an emphasis on managerial responsibility for ethical behavior. Though integrity strategies may vary in design and scope, all strive to define companies' guiding values, aspirations, and patterns of thought and conduct. When integrated into the day-to-day operations of an organization, such strategies can help prevent damaging ethical lapses while tapping into powerful human impulses for moral thought and action. Then an ethical framework becomes no longer a burdensome constraint within which companies must operate, but the governing ethos of an organization.

How Organizations Shape Individuals' Behavior

The once familiar picture of ethics as individualistic, unchanging, and impervious to organizational influences has not stood up to scrutiny in recent years. Sears Auto Centers' and Beech-Nut Nutrition Corporation's experiences illustrate the role organizations play in shaping individuals' behavior—and how even sound moral fiber can fray when stretched too thin.

In 1992, Sears, Roebuck & Company was inundated with complaints about its automotive service business. Consumers and attorneys general in more than 40 states had accused the company of misleading customers and selling them unnecessary parts and services, from brake jobs to front-end alignments. It would be a mistake, however, to see this situation exclusively in terms of any one individual's moral failings. Nor did management set out to defraud Sears customers. Instead, a number of organizational factors contributed to the problematic sales practices.

In the face of declining revenues, shrinking market share, and an increasingly competitive market for undercar services, Sears management attempted to spur the performance of its auto centers by introducing new goals and incentives for employees. The company increased minimum work quotas and introduced productivity incentives for mechanics. The automotive service advisers were given product-specific sales quotas—sell so many springs, shock absorbers, alignments, or brake jobs per shift—and paid a commission based on sales. According to advisers, failure to meet quotas could lead to a transfer or a reduction in work hours. Some employees spoke of the "pressure, pressure, pressure" to bring in sales.

Under this new set of organizational pressures and incentives, with few options for meeting their sales goals legitimately, some employees' judgment understandably suffered. Management's failure to clarify the line between unnecessary service and legitimate preventive maintenance, coupled with consumer ignorance, left employees to chart their own courses through a vast gray area, subject to a wide range of interpretations. Without active management support for ethical practice and mechanisms to detect and check questionable sales methods and poor work, it is not surprising that some employees may have reacted to contextual forces by resorting to exaggeration, carelessness, or even misrepresentation.

Shortly after the allegations against Sears became public, CEO Edward Brennan acknowledged management's responsibility for putting in place compensation and goal-setting systems that "created an environment in which mistakes did occur." Although the company denied any intent to deceive consumers,

senior executives eliminated commissions for service advisers and discontinued sales quotas for specific parts. They also instituted a system of unannounced shopping audits and made plans to expand the internal monitoring of service. In settling the pending lawsuits, Sears offered coupons to customers who had bought certain auto services between 1990 and 1992. The total cost of the settlement, including potential customer refunds, was an estimated $60 million.

Contextual forces can also influence the behavior of top management, as a former CEO of Beech-Nut Nutrition Corporation discovered. In the early 1980s, only two years after joining the company, the CEO found evidence suggesting that the apple juice concentrate, supplied by the company's vendors for use in Beech-Nut's "100% pure" apple juice, contained nothing more than sugar water and chemicals. The CEO could have destroyed the bogus inventory and withdrawn the juice from grocers' shelves, but he was under extraordinary pressure to turn the ailing company around. Eliminating the inventory would have killed any hope of turning even the meager $700,000 profit promised to Beech-Nut's then parent, Nestlé.

A number of people in the corporation, it turned out, had doubted the purity of the juice for several years before the

Corporate Fines under the Federal Sentencing Guidelines

What size fine is a corporation likely to pay if convicted of a crime? It depends on a number of factors, some of which are beyond a CEO's control, such as the existence of a prior record of similar misconduct. But it also depends on more controllable factors. The most important of these are reporting and accepting responsibility for the crime, cooperating with authorities, and having an effective program in place to prevent and detect unlawful behavior.

The following example, based on a case studied by the United States Sentencing Commission, shows how the 1991 Federal Sentencing Guidelines have affected overall fine levels and how managers' actions influence organizational fines.

Acme Corporation was charged and convicted of mail fraud. The company systematically charged customers who damaged rented automobiles more than the actual cost of repairs. Acme also billed some customers for the cost of repairs to vehicles for which they were not responsible. Prior to the criminal adjudication, Acme paid $13.7 million in restitution to the customers who had been overcharged.

Deciding before the enactment of the sentencing guidelines, the judge in the criminal case imposed a fine of $6.85 million, roughly half the pecuniary loss suffered by Acme's customers. Under the sentencing guidelines, however, the results could have been dramatically different. Acme could have been fined anywhere from 5% to 200% the loss suffered by customers, depending on whether or not it had an effective program to prevent and detect violations of law and on whether or not it reported the crime, cooperated with authorities, and accepted responsibility for the unlawful conduct. If a high ranking official at Acme were found to have

been involved, the maximum fine could have been as large as $54,800,000 or four times the loss to Acme customers. The following chart shows a possible range of fines for each situation:

What Fine Can Acme Expect?

	Maximum	Minimum
Program, reporting, cooperation, responsibility	$2,740,000	$685,000
Program only	10,960,000	5,480,000
No program, no reporting, no cooperation, no responsibility	27,400,000	13,700,000
No program, no reporting, no cooperation, no responsibility, involvement of high-level personnel	54,800,000	27,400,000

Based on Case No.: 88-266, United States Sentencing Commission, *Supplementary Report on Sentencing Guidelines for Organizations.*

CEO arrived. But the 25% price advantage offered by the supplier of the bogus concentrate allowed the operations head to meet cost-control goals. Furthermore, the company lacked an effective quality control system, and a conclusive lab test for juice purity did not exist. When a member of the research department voiced concerns about the juice to operating management, he was accused of not being a team player and of acting like "Chicken Little." His judgment, his supervisor wrote in an annual performance review, was "colored by naïveté and impractical ideals." No one else seemed to have considered the company's obligations to its customers or to have thought about the potential harm of disclosure. No one considered the fact that the sale of adulterated or misbranded juice is a legal offense, putting the company and its top management at risk of criminal liability.

An FDA investigation taught Beech-Nut the hard way. In 1987, the company pleaded guilty to selling adulterated and misbranded juice. Two years and two criminal trials later, the CEO pleaded guilty to ten counts of mislabeling. The total cost to the company—including fines, legal expenses, and lost sales—was an estimated $25 million.

Acknowledging the importance of organizational context in ethics does not imply forgiving individual wrongdoers.

Such errors of judgment rarely reflect an organizational culture and management philosophy that sets out to harm or deceive. More often, they reveal a culture that is insensitive or indifferent to ethical considerations or one that lacks effective organizational systems. By the same token, exemplary conduct usually reflects an organizational culture and philosophy that is infused with a sense of responsibility.

For example, Johnson & Johnson's handling of the Tylenol crisis is sometimes attributed to the singular personality of then-CEO James Burke. However the decision to do a nationwide recall of Tylenol capsules in order to avoid further loss of life from product tampering was in reality not one decision but thousands of decisions made by individuals at all levels of the organization. The "Tylenol decision," then, is best understood not as an isolated incident, the achievement of a lone individual, but as the reflection of an organization's culture. Without a shared set of values and guiding principles deeply ingrained throughout the organization, it is doubtful that Johnson & Johnson's response would have been as rapid, cohesive and ethically sound.

Many people resist acknowledging the influence of organizational factors on individual behavior—especially on misconduct—for fear of diluting people's sense of personal moral responsibility. But this fear is based on a false dichotomy between holding individual transgressors accountable and holding "the system" accountable. Acknowledging the importance of organizational context need not imply exculpating individual wrongdoers. To understand all is not to forgive all.

The Limits of a Legal Compliance Program

The consequences of an ethical lapse can be serious and far-reaching. Organizations can quickly become entangled in an all-consuming web of legal proceedings. The risk of litigation and liability has increased in the past decade as lawmakers have legislated new civil and criminal offenses, stepped up penalties, and improved support for law enforcement. Equally—if not more—important is the damage an ethical lapse can do to an organization's reputation and relationships. Both Sears and Beech-Nut, for instance, struggled to regain consumer trust and market share long after legal proceedings had ended.

As more managers have become alerted to the importance of organizational ethics, many have asked their lawyers to develop corporate ethics programs to detect and prevent violations of the law. The 1991 Federal Sentencing Guidelines offer a compelling rationale. Sanctions such as fines and probation for organizations convicted of wrongdoing can vary dramatically depending both on the degree of management cooperation in reporting and investigating corporate misdeeds and on whether or not the company has implemented a legal compliance program. (See the insert on the previous page, "Corporate Fines under the Federal Sentencing Guidelines.")

Such programs tend to emphasize the prevention of unlawful conduct, primarily by increasing surveillance and control and by imposing penalties for wrongdoers. While plans vary, the basic framework is outlined in the sentencing guidelines. Managers must establish compliance standards and procedures; designate high-level personnel to oversee compliance; avoid delegating discretionary authority to those likely to act unlawfully; effectively communicate the company's standards and procedures through training or publications; take reasonable steps to achieve compliance through audits, monitoring processes, and a system for employees to report criminal misconduct without fear of retribution; consistently enforce standards through appropriate disciplinary measures; respond appropriately when offenses are detected; and, finally, take reasonable steps to prevent the occurrence of similar offenses in the future.

There is no question of the necessity of a sound, well-articulated strategy for legal compliance in an organization. After all, employees can be frustrated and frightened by the complexity of today's legal environment. And even managers who claim to use the law as a guide to ethical behavior often lack more than a rudimentary understanding of complex legal issues.

Managers would be mistaken, however, to regard legal compliance as an adequate means for addressing the full range of ethical issues that arise every day. "If it's legal, it's ethical," is a frequently heard slogan. But conduct that is lawful may be highly problematic from an ethical point of view. Consider the sale in some countries of hazardous products without appropriate warnings or the purchase of goods from suppliers who operate inhumane sweatshops in developing countries. Companies engaged in international business often discover that conduct that infringes on recognized standards of human rights and decency is legally permissible in some jurisdictions.

Legal clearance does not certify the absence of ethical problems in the United States either, as a 1991 case at Salomon Brothers illustrates. Four top-level executives failed to take appropriate action when learning of unlawful activities on the government trading desk. Company lawyers found no law obligating the executives to disclose the improprieties. Nevertheless, the executives' delay in disclosing and failure to reveal their prior knowledge prompted a serious crisis of confidence among employees, creditors, shareholders, and customers. The executives were forced to resign, having lost the moral authority to lead. Their ethical lapse compounded the trading desk's legal offenses, and the company ended up suffering losses—including legal costs, increased funding costs, and lost business—estimated at nearly $1 billion.

A compliance approach to ethics also overemphasizes the threat of detection and punishment in order to channel behavior in lawful directions. The underlying model for this approach is deterrence theory, which envisions people as rational maximizers of self-interest, responsive to the personal costs and benefits of their choices, yet indifferent to the moral legitimacy of those choices. But a recent study reported in *Why People Obey the Law* by Tom R. Tyler shows that obedience to the law is strongly influenced by a belief in its legitimacy and its moral correctness. People generally feel that they have a strong obligation to obey the law. Education about the legal standards and a supportive environment may be all that's required to insure compliance.

Discipline is, of course, a necessary part of any ethical system. Justified penalties for the infringement of legitimate norms are fair and appropriate. Some people do need the threat of sanctions. However, an overemphasis on potential sanctions can be superfluous and even counterproductive. Employees may rebel against programs that stress penalties, particularly if they are designed and imposed without employee involvement or if the standards are vague or unrealistic. Management may talk of mutual trust when unveiling a compliance plan, but employees often receive the message as a warning from on high. Indeed, the more skeptical among them may view compliance programs as nothing more than liability insurance for senior management. This is not an unreasonable conclusion, considering that compliance programs rarely address the root causes of misconduct.

Even in the best cases, legal compliance is unlikely to unleash much moral imagination or commitment. The law does not generally seek to inspire human excellence or distinction. It is no guide for exemplary behavior—or even good practice. Those managers who define ethics as legal compliance are implicitly endorsing a code of moral mediocrity for their organizations. As Richard Breeden, former chairman of the Securities and Exchange Commission, noted, "It is not an adequate

The Hallmarks of an Effective Integrity Strategy

There is no one right integrity strategy. Factors such as management personality, company history, culture, lines of business, and industry regulations must be taken into account when shaping an appropriate set of values and designing an implementation program. Still, several features are common to efforts that have achieved some success:

- *The guiding values and commitments make sense and are clearly communicated.* They reflect important organizational obligations and widely shared aspirations that appeal to the organization's members. Employees at all levels take them seriously, feel comfortable discussing them, and have a concrete understanding of their practical importance. This does not signal the absence of ambiguity and conflict but a willingness to seek solutions compatible with the framework of values.

- *Company leaders are personally committed, credible, and willing to take action on the values they espouse.* They are not mere mouthpieces. They are willing to scrutinize their own decisions. Consistency on the part of leadership is key. Waffling on values will lead to employee cynicism and a rejection of the program. At the same time, managers must assume responsibility for making tough calls when ethical obligations conflict.

- *The espoused values are integrated into the normal channels of management decision making and are reflected in the organization's critical activities*: the development of plans, the setting of goals, the search for opportunities, the allocation of resources, the gathering and communication of information, the measurement of performance, and the promotion and advancement of personnel.

- *The company's systems and structures support and reinforce its values.* Information systems, for example, are designed to provide timely and accurate information. Reporting relationships are structured to build in checks and balances to promote objective judgment. Performance appraisal is sensitive to means as well as ends.

- *Managers throughout the company have the decision-making skills, knowledge, and competencies needed to make ethically sound decisions on a day-to-day basis.* Ethical thinking and awareness must be part of every managers' mental equipment. Ethics education is usually part of the process.

Success in creating a climate for responsible and ethically sound behavior requires continuing effort and a considerable investment of time and resources. A glossy code of conduct, a high-ranking ethics officer, a training program, an annual ethics audit—these trappings of an ethics program do not necessarily add up to a responsible, law-abiding organization whose espoused values match its actions. A formal ethics program can serve as a catalyst and a support system, but organizational integrity depends on the integration of the company's values into its driving systems.

ethical standard to aspire to get through the day without being indicted."

Integrity as a Governing Ethic

A strategy based on integrity holds organizations to a more robust standard. While compliance is rooted in avoiding legal sanctions, organizational integrity is based on the concept of self-governance in accordance with a set of guiding principles. From the perspective of integrity, the task of ethics management is to define and give life to an organization's guiding values, to create an environment that supports ethically sound behavior, and to instill a sense of shared accountability among employees. The need to obey the law is viewed as a positive aspect of organizational life, rather than an unwelcome constraint imposed by external authorities.

Management may talk of mutual trust when unveiling a compliance plan, but employees often see a warning from on high.

An integrity strategy is characterized by a conception of ethics as a driving force of an enterprise. Ethical values shape the search for opportunities, the design of organizational systems, and the decision-making process used by individuals and groups. They provide a common frame of reference and serve as a unifying force across different functions, lines of business, and employee groups. Organizational ethics helps define what a company is and what it stands for.

Many integrity initiatives have structural features common to compliance-based initiatives: a code of conduct, training in relevant areas of law, mechanisms for reporting and investigating potential misconduct, and audits and controls to insure that laws and company standards are being met. In addition, if suitably designed, an integrity-based initiative can establish a foundation for seeking the legal benefits that are available under the sentencing guidelines should criminal wrongdoing occur. (See the insert on the previous page, "The Hallmarks of an Effective Integrity Strategy.")

But an integrity strategy is broader, deeper, and more demanding than a legal compliance initiative. Broader in that it seeks to enable responsible conduct. Deeper in that it cuts to the ethos and operating systems of the organization and its members, their guiding values and patterns of thought and action. And more demanding in that it requires an active effort to define the responsibilities and aspirations that constitute an organization's ethical compass. Above all, organizational ethics is seen as the work of management. Corporate counsel may play a role in the design and implementation of integrity strategies, but managers at all levels and across all functions are involved in the process. (See the chart, "Strategies for Ethics Management.")

During the past decade, a number of companies have undertaken integrity initiatives. They vary according to the ethical values focused on and the implementation approaches used. Some companies focus on the core values of integrity that reflect basic social obligations, such as respect for the rights of others, honesty, fair dealing, and obedience to the law. Other companies emphasize aspirations—values that are ethically desirable but not necessarily morally obligatory—such as good service to customers, a commitment to diversity, and involvement in the community.

When it comes to implementation, some companies begin with behavior. Following Aristotle's view that one becomes courageous by acting as a courageous person, such companies develop codes of conduct specifying appropriate behavior, along with a system of incentives, audits, and controls. Other companies focus less on specific actions and more on developing attitudes, decision-making processes, and ways of thinking that reflect their values. The assumption is that personal commitment and appropriate decision processes will lead to right action.

Martin Marietta, NovaCare, and Wetherill Associates have implemented and lived with quite different integrity strategies. In each case, management has found that the initiative has made important and often unexpected contributions to competitiveness, work environment, and key relationships on which the company depends.

Martin Marietta: Emphasizing Core Values

Martin Marietta Corporation, the U.S. aerospace and defense contractor, opted for an integrity-based ethics program in 1985. At the time, the defense industry was under attack for fraud and mismanagement, and Martin Marietta was under investigation for improper travel billings. Managers knew they needed a better form of self-governance but were skeptical that an ethics program could influence behavior. "Back then people asked, 'Do you really need an ethics program to be ethical?'" recalls current President Thomas Young. "Ethics was something personal. Either you had it, or you didn't."

The corporate general counsel played a pivotal role in promoting the program, and legal compliance was a critical objective. But it was conceived of and implemented from the start as a companywide management initiative aimed at creating and maintaining a "do-it-right" climate. In its original conception, the program emphasized core values, such as honesty and fair play. Over time, it expanded to encompass quality and environmental responsibility as well.

Today the initiative consists of a code of conduct, an ethics training program, and procedures for reporting and investigating ethical concerns within the company. It also includes a system for disclosing violations of federal procurement law to the government. A corporate ethics office manages the program, and ethics representatives are stationed at major facilities. An ethics steering committee, made up of Martin Marietta's president, senior executives, and two rotating members selected from field operations, oversees the ethics office. The audit and ethics committee of the board of directors oversees the steering committee.

Strategies for Ethics Management

Characteristics of Compliance Strategy

Ethos	conformity with externally imposed standards
Objective	prevent criminal misconduct
Leadership	lawyer driven
Methods	education, reduced discretion, auditing and controls, penalties
Behavioral Assumptions	autonomous beings guided by material self-interest

Characteristics of Integrity Strategy

Ethos	self-governance according to chosen standards
Objective	enable responsible conduct
Leadership	management driven with aid of lawyers, HR, others
Methods	education, leadership, accountability, organizational systems and decision processes, auditing and controls, penalties
Behavioral Assumptions	social beings guided by material self-interest, values, ideals, peers

Implementation of Compliance Strategy

Standards	criminal and regulatory law
Staffing	lawyers
Activities	develop compliance standards train and communicate handle reports of misconduct conduct investigations oversee compliance audits enforce standards
Education	compliance standards and system

Implementation of Integrity Strategy

Standards	company values and aspirations social obligations, including law
Staffing	executives and managers with lawyers, others
Activities	lead development of company values and standards train and communicate integrate into company systems provide guidance and consultation assess values performance identify and resolve problems oversee compliance activities
Education	decision making and values compliance standards and system

The ethics office is responsible for responding to questions and concerns from the company's employees. Its network of representatives serves as a sounding board, a source of guidance, and a channel for raising a range of issues, from allegations of wrongdoing to complaints about poor management, unfair supervision, and company policies and practices. Martin Marietta's ethics network, which accepts anonymous complaints, logged over 9,000 calls in 1991, when the company had about 60,000 employees. In 1992, it investigated 684 cases. The ethics office also works closely with the human resources, legal, audit, communications, and security functions to respond to employee concerns.

Shortly after establishing the program, the company began its first round of ethics training for the entire workforce, starting with the CEO and senior executives. Now in its third round, training for senior executives focuses on decision making, the challenges of balancing multiple responsibilities, and compliance with laws and regulations critical to the company. The incentive compensation plan for executives makes responsibility for promoting ethical conduct an explicit requirement for reward eligibility and requires that business and personal goals be achieved in accordance with the company's policy on ethics. Ethical conduct and support for the ethics program are also criteria in regular performance reviews.

Today top-level managers say the ethics program has helped the company avoid serious problems and become more responsive to its more than 90,000 employees. The ethics network, which tracks the number and types of cases and complaints, has served as an early warning system for poor management, quality and safety defects, racial and gender discrimination, environmental concerns, inaccurate and false records, and personnel grievances regarding salaries, promotions, and layoffs. By providing an alternative channel for raising such concerns, Martin Marietta is able to take corrective action more quickly and with a lot less pain. In many cases, potentially embarrassing problems have been identified and dealt with before becoming a management crisis, a lawsuit, or a criminal investigation. Among employees who brought complaints in 1993, 75% were satisfied with the results.

Company executives are also convinced that the program has helped reduce the incidence of misconduct. When allegations of misconduct do surface, the company says it deals with them more openly. On several occasions, for instance, Martin Marietta has voluntarily disclosed and made restitution to the government for misconduct involving potential violations of federal procurement laws. In addition, when an employee alleged that the company had retaliated against him for voicing safety concerns about his plant on CBS news, top management commissioned an investigation by an outside law firm. Although failing to support the allegations, the investigation found that employees at the plant feared retaliation when raising health, safety, or environmental complaints. The company redoubled its efforts to identify and discipline those employees taking retaliatory action and stressed the desirability of an open work environment in its ethics training and company communications.

Although the ethics program helps Martin Marietta avoid certain types of litigation, it has occasionally led to other kinds of legal action. In a few cases, employees dismissed for violating the code of ethics sued Martin Marietta, arguing that the company had violated its own code by imposing unfair and excessive discipline.

Still, the company believes that its attention to ethics has been worth it. The ethics program has led to better relationships with the government, as well as to new business opportunities. Along with prices and technology, Martin Marietta's record of integrity, quality, and reliability of estimates plays a role in the awarding of defense contracts, which account for some 75% of the company's revenues. Executives believe that the reputation they've earned through their ethics program has helped them build trust with government auditors, as well. By opening up communications, the company has reduced the time spent on redundant audits.

The program has also helped change employees' perceptions and priorities. Some managers compare their new ways of thinking about ethics to the way they understand quality. They consider more carefully how situations will be perceived by others, the possible long-term consequences of short-term thinking, and the need for continuous improvement. CEO Norman Augustine notes, "Ten years ago, people would have said that there were no ethical issues in business. Today employees think their number-one objective is to be thought of as decent people doing quality work."

NovaCare: Building Shared Aspirations

NovaCare Inc., one of the largest providers of rehabilitation services to nursing homes and hospitals in the United States, has oriented its ethics effort toward building a common core of shared aspirations. But in 1988, when the company was called InSpeech, the only sentiment shared was mutual mistrust.

Senior executives built the company from a series of aggressive acquisitions over a brief period of time to take advantage of the expanding market for therapeutic services. However, in 1988, the viability of the company was in question. Turnover among its frontline employees—the clinicians and therapists who care for patients in nursing homes and hospitals—escalated to 57% per year. The company's inability to retain therapists caused customers to defect and the stock price to languish in an extended slump.

> **At NovaCare, executives defined organizational values and introduced structural changes to support those values.**

After months of soul-searching, InSpeech executives realized that the turnover rate was a symptom of a more basic problem: the lack of a common set of values and aspirations. There was, as one executive put it, a "huge disconnect" between the values of the therapists and clinicians and those of the managers who ran the company. The therapists and clinicians evaluated the company's success in terms of its delivery of high-quality health care. InSpeech management, led by executives with financial services and venture capital backgrounds, measured the company's worth exclusively in terms of financial success. Management's single-minded emphasis on increasing hours of reimbursable care turned clinicians off. They took management's performance orientation for indifference to patient care and left the company in droves.

CEO John Foster recognized the need for a common frame of reference and a common language to unify the diverse groups. So he brought in consultants to conduct interviews and focus groups with the company's health care professionals, managers, and customers. Based on the results, an employee task force drafted a proposed vision statement for the company, and another 250 employees suggested revisions. Then Foster and several senior managers developed a succinct statement of the company's guiding purpose and fundamental beliefs that could be used as a framework for making decisions and setting goals, policies, and practices.

Unlike a code of conduct, which articulates specific behavioral standards, the statement of vision, purposes, and beliefs lays out in very simple terms the company's central purpose and core values. The purpose—meeting the rehabilitation needs of patients through clinical leadership—is supported by four key beliefs: respect for the individual, service to the customer, pursuit of excellence, and commitment to personal integrity. Each value is discussed with examples of how it is manifested in the day-to-day activities and policies of the company, such as how to measure the quality of care.

To support the newly defined values, the company changed its name to NovaCare and introduced a number of structural and operational changes. Field managers and clinicians were given greater decision-making authority; clinicians were provided with additional resources to assist in the delivery of effective therapy; and a new management structure integrated the various therapies offered by the company. The hiring of new corporate personnel with health care backgrounds reinforced the company's new clinical focus.

The introduction of the vision, purpose, and beliefs met with varied reactions from employees, ranging from cool skepticism to open enthusiasm. One employee remembered thinking the talk about values "much ado about nothing." Another recalled, "It was really wonderful. It gave us a goal that everyone aspired to, no matter what their place in the company." At first, some were baffled about how the vision, purpose, and beliefs were to be used. But, over time, managers became more adept at explaining and using them as a guide. When a customer tried to hire away a valued employee, for example, managers considered raiding the customer's company for employees. After reviewing the beliefs, the managers abandoned the idea.

NovaCare managers acknowledge and company surveys indicate that there is plenty of room for improvement. While the values are used as a firm reference point for decision making and evaluation in some areas of the company, they are still viewed with reservation in others. Some managers do not "walk the talk," employees complain. And recently acquired companies have yet to be fully integrated into the program. Nevertheless, many NovaCare employees say the values initiative played a critical role in the company's 1990 turnaround.

The values reorientation also helped the company deal with its most serious problem: turnover among health care providers. In 1990, the turnover rate stood at 32%, still above target but a significant improvement over the 1988 rate of 57%. By 1993, turnover had dropped to 27%. Moreover, recruiting new clinicians became easier. Barely able to hire 25 new clinicians each month in 1988, the company added 776 in 1990 and 2,546 in 1993. Indeed, one employee who left during the 1988 turmoil said that her decision to return in 1990 hinged on the company's adoption of the vision, purpose, and beliefs.

Wetherill Associates: Defining Right Action

Wetherill Associates, Inc.—a small, privately held supplier of electrical parts to the automotive market—has neither a conventional code of conduct nor a statement of values. Instead, WAI has a *Quality Assurance Manual*—a combination of philosophy text, conduct guide, technical manual, and company profile—that describes the company's commitment to honesty and its guiding principle of right action.

Creating an organization that encourages exemplary conduct may be the best way to prevent damaging misconduct.

WAI doesn't have a corporate ethics officer who reports to top management, because at WAI, the company's corporate ethics officer *is* top management. Marie Bothe, WAI's chief executive officer, sees her main function as keeping the 350-employee company on the path of right action and looking for opportunities to help the community. She delegates the "technical" aspects of the business—marketing, finance, personnel, operations—to other members of the organization.

Right action, the basis for all of WAI's decisions, is a well-developed approach that challenges most conventional management thinking. The company explicitly rejects the usual conceptual boundaries that separate morality and self-interest. Instead, they define right behavior as logically, expediently, and morally right. Managers teach employees to look at the needs of the customers, suppliers, and the community—in addition to those of the company and its employees—when making decisions.

WAI also has a unique approach to competition. One employee explains, "We are not 'in competition' with anybody. We just do what we have to do to serve the customer." Indeed, when occasionally unable to fill orders, WAI salespeople refer customers to competitors. Artificial incentives, such as sales contests, are never used to spur individual performance. Nor are sales results used in determining compensation. Instead, the focus is on teamwork and customer service. Managers tell all new recruits that absolute honesty, mutual courtesy, and respect are standard operating procedure.

Newcomers generally react positively to company philosophy, but not all are prepared for such a radical departure from the practices they have known elsewhere. Recalling her initial interview, one recruit described her response to being told that lying was not allowed, "What do you mean? No lying? I'm a buyer. I lie for a living!" Today she is persuaded that the policy makes sound business sense. WAI is known for informing suppliers of overshipments as well as undershipments and for scrupulous honesty in the sale of parts, even when deception cannot be readily detected.

Since its entry into the distribution business 13 years ago, WAI has seen its revenues climb steadily from just under $1 million to nearly $98 million in 1993, and this is an industry with little growth. Once seen as an upstart beset by naysayers and industry skeptics, WAI is now credited with entering and professionalizing an industry in which kickbacks, bribes, and "gratuities" were commonplace. Employees—equal numbers of men and women ranging in age from 17 to 92—praise the work environment as both productive and supportive.

WAI's approach could be difficult to introduce in a larger, more traditional organization. WAI is a small company founded by 34 people who shared a belief in right action; its ethical values were naturally built into the organization from the start. Those values are so deeply ingrained in the company's culture and operating systems that they have been largely self-sustaining. Still, the company has developed its own training program and takes special care to hire people willing to support right action. Ethics and job skills are considered equally important in determining an individual's competence and suitability for employment. For WAI, the challenge will be to sustain its vision as the company grows and taps into markets overseas.

At WAI, as at Martin Marietta and NovaCare, a management-led commitment to ethical values has contributed to competitiveness, positive workforce morale, as well as solid sustainable relationships with the company's key constituencies. In the end, creating a climate that encourages exemplary conduct may be the best way to discourage damaging misconduct. Only in such an environment do rogues really act alone.

LYNN SHARP PAINE is associate professor at the Harvard Business School, specializing in management ethics. Her current research focuses on leadership and organizational integrity in a global environment.

Psssssst! Have You Tasted This?

Mothers sound off in word-of-mouth advertising campaigns.

BARBARA CORREA

Just hours after Emily Grant plunked down a box of Hershey's Take 5 candy bars at a PTA meeting, a teacher who sampled the chocolate treat raced out to buy a king-size bar.

On the surface, the candy bar purchase was a simple act of impulse buying.

But in reality, it was the successful application of a clever marketing tool that uses everyday people to entice friends and family to buy products.

Word-of-mouth advertising has mushroomed in recent years as companies try to reach an increasingly inaccessible consumer base—one hiding in a multimedia fog of iPods, video games and infinite Web sites and cable channels. Advertisers simply can't reach consumers with traditional television, magazine and newspaper ads in such a stratified marketing environment.

So they're turning to women such as Grant—a well-connected mom whose opinion is valued within her peer group.

Secret-Agent Moms

Within the word-of-mouth advertising community, people such as Grant are known as "agents."

But these agents don't carry eavesdropping devices and disguises—they push household products in exchange for coupons and the very products they're promoting.

Throughout her agent career, Grant has soaked herself in a Ralph Lauren fragrance called Hot, taken Nutella samples to her sons' play dates and painted her hallway with a light-blue shade of Benjamin Moore paint.

The supplier of the products sent to her, Boston-based marketing company BzzAgent, instructs all its agents to tell people that they are getting freebies to promote them.

Grant says she doesn't see any conflict in marketing products to friends simply by sharing samples with them.

Social Networking

Bzzagent membership
www.bzzagent.com/

Procter & Gamble's program for teens
www.tremor.com/

Procter & Gamble's program for moms
www.vocalpoint.com/

Word of Mouth Marketing Association
www.womma.org/

"I'm not a big sales person with my friends," she said. "There's no need to push because it's just regular stuff."

Some Worry about Ethics

Some agencies and companies do not require their agents to announce that they are in fact pushing products, preferring to leave that decision up to the individual agent. While that has some worried about the ethical implications of the practice, advocates say tell-a-friend campaigns are more honest than traditional advertising.

"Word-of-mouth is actually the most honest form of marketing because you can't con someone about the experience of a product," said George Silverman, president of Market Navigation Inc., a company that, among other things, organizes conference calls for physicians to share opinions about pharmaceuticals. "You don't expect a salesperson to be objective, but I've always found that people don't lie to their friends, and they generally won't tell a friend about something unless they genuinely like it."

Silverman says traditional advertising has been losing consumers in recent years because people feel bombarded by information and are tuning out marketing messages. "People are overloaded. I've done focus groups with everyone from Hispanic gardeners to Fortune-500 executives. They're all overloaded. Word-of-mouth is the only thing that cuts through the overload. If you want to buy something, you can spend two months researching it or you can ask a friend. Which is more fun?"

For that reason, he said, more manufacturers are turning to word-of-mouth to sell everything from coffee makers to mobile phones.

Recruiting Teens, Doctors

Most programs target big-spending groups such as moms and teenagers, and efforts vary in how aggressive they get.

Mothers, especially working mothers, are especially prized by word-of-mouth marketers because they have a large sphere of contacts: through school, their kids' activities and co-workers.

"[Women] are the ones who are controlling all the consumer spending in this country," said Kevin Burke, president of Lucid Marketing, a word-of-mouth company in Burbank specifically focused on selling to moms. "Their roles have evolved in the last 20 years. The stereotype of the male controlling certain purchases is eroding."

The certainty of that buying power prompted consumer products giant Procter & Gamble to launch a program about a year ago called Vocalpoint. To date, the program has recruited well more than half a million moms, while another unit, Tremor, has enlisted several hundred thousand teenagers to talk to their friends about new music and video games.

'Straddles a Thin Line'

However, P&G is one of the word-of-mouth marketers that doesn't require its program members to disclose their involvement. The potential for infiltration of product placement in everyday life—such as name-dropping a particular dishwashing liquid to another mom watching football practice—has sparked a storm of controversy.

"It straddles a thin line," said George Silverman, the marketing strategist. "The bad side of it is using people as shills."

P&G does not require Vocalpoint and Tremor members to disclose that they are taking products because it does not want to tell members what to say, P&G spokeswoman Robin Schroeder said.

"They want it to be very natural," she said.

But the Word of Mouth Marketing Association, a fast-growing group founded in 2004, defines that approach as deceptive. "We were formed to take on that particular issue," CEO Andy Sernovitz said.

"Our code of ethics is, marketers have to disclose. . . . Tremor and Vocalpoint have not signed on to our code of ethics. They are conspicuously missing from the list."

Other marketing experts say companies that explicitly hide their marketing tactics are eventually found out, and the ethics surrounding word-of-mouth marketing are self-correcting.

"P&G is just hoping folks will talk about them," said Kevin Dugan, director of marketing communications at a design firm and author of a blog about public relations strategy. His wife became a Vocalpoint member when she found out about the program from him.

"There's no specific direction to go out and talk to people or to disclose. There are no talking points. The risk they have is, say my wife had Oil of Olay beauty mask. If she doesn't like it, she's going to tell someone about it. She doesn't feel compelled to talk about it because they sent it to her. With the Oil of Olay, she'll bring it up if it comes up, but it's not, 'I know we're talking about your kid's soccer game and I hate to interrupt, but I need to talk about this facial mask.'"

"It needs to be organic to be effective."

Like the recent outing of lonelygirl15, the homeschooled girl whose fictitious YouTube identity was revealed a few weeks ago by curious fans, some companies have posed as Regular Joes online and been punished by consumers who have unearthed their true identity. Carmaker Mazda turned off some loyalists when it launched a blog hosted by someone posing as a Mazda enthusiast.

All the Talk Can Backfire

Word-of-mouth also has plenty of examples of campaigns that backfired because products were not very good. Irina Slutsky, a video blogger and host of Geek Entertainment TV, received a mobile phone from Sprint six months ago apparently in the hope that she would write about it in her blog.

"The display screen broke two months after I got it, so if I had written about it, it would be all bad stuff," Slutsky said. "I thought, 'That's a silly marketing plan.'"

Folgers hired BzzAgent to create hype about its home brewing machines. The problem was the machines didn't work well, reportedly leaking water and emitting smoke.

Such backfire worries have kept some big companies form engaging in word-of-mouth marketing.

"Companies are very scared of it," Silverman said. "Nuclear power is very efficient and clean if it handles right, but you'd better know what you're doing, or you're going to blow up the place. Marketers are control freaks, and you can't control a lot of aspects of word-of-mouth marketing."

BARBARA CORREA—barbara.correa@dailynews.com (818)713-3662

Swagland

Where the writers are gluttons, the editors practice ethical relativism and the flacks just want to get their clients some ink.

DAVID WEDDLE

Swagland. It's not a mythical over-the-rainbow realm, an Eastern European country, a theme park. You might call it a state of mind, a wondrous alternate universe concocted by publicists, funded by corporations eager for media coverage of their wares and frequented by journalists who have cast off concerns about conflicts of interest and embraced a new creed of conspicuous consumption.

In Swagland, the streets are paved with freebies, from promotional T-shirts, CDs and DVDs, to designer clothing, jewelry and perfume, to spa treatments, Broadway show tickets and suites in five-star hotels, to cellphones, laptops and luxury sports cars on loan. Travel writers accept tree trips to exotic foreign lands. Automotive reviewers take junkets to Switzerland or the sun-dappled hills of Italy to drive the latest high-end roadsters. Entertainment hacks hobnob with stars and directors at the Four Seasons in Los Angeles. High-tech audio and video reviewers max out their home-entertainment centers with LCD HDTV screens, surround-sound systems and five-digit turntables, which they keep for months at a time—for research purposes. Surfing journalists travel to remote South Pacific atolls and stay with supermodels on "floating Four Seasons" luxury cruisers where the champagne never stops flowing.

Fashionistas have long been infamous for raking in the loot—the currency of Swagland. Designers lavish magazine editors with the latest styles because they're "celebrities in their own right," explains an editor at a major fashion daily. "They're gifted quite a bit because they are friends with these designers and they have a lot of access. They may get photographed with those items, and that influences what people buy. All the top editors take free clothes."

In recent years, Los Angeles has become the R&D capital of swag culture. The now-ubiquitous promotional gift bag grew out of Hollywood's plethora of award ceremonies and premiere parties. A gift bag may contain a T-shirt or coffee mug, or it might be crammed with thousands of dollars worth of goods. Whatever it may hold, the gift bag has an uncanny power to bring out the greedy 2-year-old in some members of the media. Many have come to view it not as a perk but a birthright. "When

I'm holding an event," says Susie Dobson of the Los Angeles firm Susie Dobson Global PR, "the magazine editors call and ask if there's going to be a gift bag. 'Will there be gift bags?' Yes. 'Will they be good?' Yes. 'Oh, great! I'll be there.'

At some events, journalists are allowed to pack their own gift bags. If the "merch" runs low, things can get ugly. "At the 2003 Environmental Media Awards," says freelance journalist Kyle Roderick, "there was a frenzy at the booth for Under the Canopy, which is this organic fiber fashion line. There was a jostling fight. . . . People were yelling, 'I want my T-shirt!' There were some shoulder blows. The sign was up that said 'Please take one.' People were grabbing three or four or five."

The abundance of swag fuels a thriving underground economy. Writers fence their T-shirts, designer duds and movie and automotive promotional memorabilia to a loose network of used-clothing stores (such as Decades in L.A.), entrepreneurs and Internet vendors. "I have editors calling me all the time and bringing me bags of stuff—designer shoes, jewelry, dresses, everything from Chanel to Gucci," says Keni Valenti, owner of Keni Valenti Retro-Couture, a vintage designer clothing store in New York's Garment Center.

Some journalists steal swag outright from photo shoot sets or magazine fashion closets. "I've had editors call me up and say, 'I have two fur coats here in a bag. I'm at 38th and 7th Avenue, right on the corner. If you can bring me X amount of dollars in cash, they're yours,'" Valenti says. "I said to one editor, 'What exactly are you going to say to the company?' She said, 'I'll just send back the bag empty and blame it on the messenger.'"

Others shake down merchants. Mary Norton, designer of Moo Roo handbags, was flabbergasted when an anchor for a prominent Los Angeles newscast walked into her showroom during the 2003 Oscar season and pointed to three of her creations. He told her that Moo Roo would never be mentioned on his show—ever—if she didn't give them to him.

Anne Rainey Rokahr, director of Red PR in New York, had a similar experience. A magazine writer offered to promote her clients' products on a TV morning show if Rokahr would pay her. "I was shocked and insulted," Rokahr says.

She's not alone. The guardians of journalistic ethics are horrified and dismayed by this subversion of all the values they hold dear. "There are no ifs, ands or buts about it, you put yourself in a compromising position if you accept any gift or free trip or anything from somebody you're writing about," says Edwin Guthman, a Pulitzer Prize-winning journalist and former editor of the Philadelphia Inquirer and national editor of the Los Angeles Times, who is now a senior lecturer at USC's Annenberg School. "It's something that a self-respecting journalist shouldn't do. There isn't any question about it, it's wrong. I'm sorry to hear that it's fairly prevalent."

Ethicists argue that the proliferation of swag has undercut the integrity of the press, blurred the lines between advertising and editorial and encouraged some publications to mislead their readership. "Very few readers have any idea how editorial staffs decide what gets reported on," says Jeffrey Seglin, an associate professor at Emerson College in Boston who writes a weekly column on ethics for the New York Times. "They don't know what the policies are at the magazines about accepting freebies. Readers need to be aware of this issue, especially when they're reading travel pieces and product reviews. There should be a clear distinction between what's advertising and what's editorial. Because when you purchase a magazine, you presume you are buying objective editorial. But that's not always the reality."

The perception that journalists can be bought contributes to an overall distrust of the media. A recent Gallup poll found that only 21% of those surveyed rated newspaper reporters' ethical standards as high or very high. Journalists ranked lower than bankers, auto mechanics, elected officials and nursing home operators. Kelly McBride, the ethics group leader at the Poynter Institute, a training school for professional journalists in St. Petersburg, Fla., laments that the press is "losing ground" in the battle for the public's respect, and believes that swag is a factor. "For people who are concerned about media bias, it is one more straw on the camel's back."

For publicists who practice giveaway marketing, however, such hand-wringing is futile, even a little comical. As far as they're concerned, the battle's already been won. The glittering utopia of Swagland is governed by one supreme precept, and Kelly Cutrone, founder of the firm People's Revolution, sums it up: "Here's the deal: Everything's a commercial."

The Age of Ethical Relativism

The rise of swag culture is no accident, according to McBride. "Corporations are spending a higher percentage of their annual budgets on marketing, and larger portions of those budgets are directed specifically at journalists, because marketing executives realize that ink on any given product is better than advertising," she says. "We've always known that, but they realize now, particularly in this age of an inundation of advertising, that advertising is limited in its ability to reach an audience. It's much more effective to create the elusive buzz about a product that everyone's after."

And the schizophrenic ethics policies of American publications make them an easy target. Many magazines and tabloids either turn a blind eye or encourage their writers to score freebies as a method of cutting expenses. The Robb Report, Motor Trend and Powder routinely send their contributors on junkets. Many others have strict rules against it. Travel + Leisure posts its policy in each issue, stating that its writers do not accept free trips. Most major newspapers and news magazines forbid employees and freelancers to accept merchandise or services from potential subjects, and some high-end glossies—Playboy, Harper's Magazine, Forbes, Fortune—have similar policies.

But even publications that enforce strict ethics policies do not have entirely clean hands. Most, including the Los Angeles Times, commission stories from freelance writers who operate as independent contractors. Freelancers are the migrant farmworkers of journalism—cheap labor that fills the gaps left by editorial downsizing and dwindling advertising revenue. As they scramble from publication to publication to make a living, some practice ethical relativism. If they're writing a story for a newspaper where accepting giveaways is forbidden, they adhere to that policy. But when they're on assignment for a lifestyle magazine that encourages them to accept free hotel rooms and airfare to cut expenses, they shift into high freebie mode. Thus, even the most scrupulous publications end up employing freelancers who may have accepted copious swag on other assignments.

When fashion writers come to town, they don't stop at taking a free hotel room. 'You ask them to come to an event,' says Kelly Cutrone, founder of the firm People's Revolution, 'and they say, "Can you send me a car?" or, "I don't have anything to wear. I'd really like to wear your designer to the show." You can smell a fashion editor who's looking for a free ride. They'll come to your showroom and they light up, saying, "Ohhhh, loooovvvveee!!! Oh my God, I've got to get one of these. I just love it, love it! Do you think there's any way I can get a deal on one of these?" That's classic.'

"There is an entire set of problems that comes with freelancers that does not come with staff writers, because there's a limited amount of control you can have over them," observes Stephen Randall, deputy editor of Playboy and an adjunct faculty member at USC's Annenberg School. "You don't know what freelancers are doing on other assignments. You don't know what hidden agendas they might have."

Some editors worry about ethics creep. Rick Holter, arts editor for the Dallas Morning News, points out that if an automaker decides to debut a new model in Germany, "there's no way my paper is going to pay for me to go to Germany." But what happens if five freelancers take the junket and come back with terrific stories, which they then submit to the paper? "If you're the car reviewer at Dallas Morning News, you look bad. Here's a freelancer coming in with a great story that you didn't get. Editors get tempted not to ask the tough questions of the freelancers they're buying something from."

Even more problematic are the pseudo-ethics policies of some publications. "One of the worst things that happens is when there is a policy and the publications don't enforce it," says Seglin. "On paper it may say, 'We will not do this.' But the staff and the freelancers see that everybody takes freebies and no one enforces the ethics code. It sends a message that the code is worthless."

Last month the editorial staffs of Jane, Details, Women's Wear Daily and W were banned from receiving gifts "of value" from advertisers. The New York Daily News reported that rebellious employees of Fairchild Publications planned to circumvent the ban by having publicists mail swag to their home addresses. Fairchild spokeswoman Andrea Kaplan averred that this would be against company policy and was quoted as saying, "We are not aware that this is happening."

Truth in Labeling

Many lifestyle scribes shrug off traditional ethics with the rationalization that they aren't really journalists. Julie Logan, a former editor for Glamour who has written for Self and InStyle, refers to fashion and beauty magazines as "service books." "I don't consider service books to be journalism," Logan says. "I consider it copy writing with a narrative. The function of a service book is to deliver readers to the advertisers. If the advertisers could find a way to put the magazine out without writers, they would. We're there because of their largess, not the other way around."

Yet the mastheads of service books list editors and correspondents and look identical to those of hard news publications. "They have all the trappings of regular journalism," McBride says. "They're doing what passes for consumer journalism—writing about products, places and things that people spend money on." And when consumers purchase a magazine, Seglin argues, "they expect objectivity. They don't expect the magazine to show favoritism. As readers, we want consumer journalists to do the legwork and review all of the available products, not just the ones they got for free."

Logan thinks service book readers could care less about the intricacies of objectivity. "These are people who look at advertorial the same way as they would editorial. These are not rocket scientists."

McBride counters that readers would care if they knew that not all magazines adhere to the same ethical standards. "If you're about to spend a lot of money on a vacation in a foreign country and are trying to decide what hotels to stay at, you would certainly want to know if a reviewer is raving about a place because he got a free room, or because he really did his homework on all the hotels in that area."

Seglin believes the solution is truth in labeling. Magazines should disclose their policies on freebies on the table of contents or masthead. "If editors argue that it's not a big deal to accept gifts and it doesn't affect the integrity of their reporters,

then why not tell the reader exactly what your policy is? Then the readers can make an informed decision about how to interpret the magazine's content."

But publications that allow acceptance of gifts have little or no incentive to do any such thing. McBride thinks there will always be a spectrum of publications and writers who take swag, and she sees this as an inevitable byproduct of a free market society. "Part of the beauty of American journalism is it's not licensed. Standards are voluntarily applied. There is no regulation," she says. "So I think the only thing we can do is put as much peer pressure as we can on our brethren and, in the spirit of a free market, give the readers the information they need to make intelligent choices."

The History of Swag

One of the most brilliant tactical breakthroughs in swag culture was developed in Los Angeles. In the late 1990s, publicists realized that the Academy Awards—a fashion vortex that draws the world's finest designers and jewelers and the international press together for one dizzying media-saturated weekend—presented an unprecedented opportunity to raise awareness for their clients' products. Thus the "swag suite" was born. Consortiums of designers rented out entire floors of such chic hotels as the Chateau Marmont, Raffles L' Ermitage and Le Meridien, and filled the suites with samples of their wares. They enticed celebrities and their stylists—and the media—with free champagne, facials, massages, makeup and hair styling, yoga classes and, of course, gift bags. The concept proved fantastically successful.

"Have you ever gone to a 99-Cents store on a welfare payday?" asks Kelly Cutrone. "It's basically like that. [Writers] will try to get four extra gift bags—one for their nanny, one for their sister in Oklahoma and one just in case they need to give it away for a Christmas present."

Cutrone's company, People's Revolution, has organized swag suites during the Oscars and the Golden Globes, and she's seen media greed escalate with each passing year. "It's gotten to the point where the vendors have to nail the stuff down. We've had to create a color-coded gift band system. The different editors and writers won't really know they're a part of it until they arrive. There will be different color codes: a silver bracelet, a gold bracelet and a white bracelet. The gold bracelet would be the highest rank. That means: This person is very, very credible and has a lot of power and you should gift accordingly. The silver one might mean: Give them a T-shirt. The white one is: Don't give them anything. They just need to be in here to feel important and we need their body to fill the space."

The swag suites proved so successful that they soon popped up at the Grammys and New York and LA's fashion weeks. At the Sundance Film Festival the swag suites have exploded into swag lodges, lounges and houses sponsored by Michelob, Skyy Vodka, Mystic Tan, Gap, Chrysler, Diesel, Tommy Hilfiger, Reebok, Ray-Ban and Black & Decker. Last year Volkswagen offered morning yoga classes, treated celebs and select members of the press to, free rides around town in its luxury Phaeton sedan and handed out $1,000 gift bags. The once sleepy main street of Park City, Utah, which used to host a quiet counterculture film festival, has become a gaudy carnival midway where New York fashionistas such as publicist Lara Shrift man hawk their clients' wares and writers for Women's Wear Daily, Us Weekly and the New York Post's Page Six hammer out exultant prose about the swagathon.

Juicy Couture is a textbook example of how swag suite marketing can propel a fledgling company into the limelight almost overnight. Founded in L.A. in 1994 by Gela Nash-Taylor—wife of John Taylor, bass player for Duran Duran—and Pam Skaist-Levy, it started as a T-shirt line and soon became known for low-cut, hip-hugging sweatpants with the words "Juicy" emblazoned across the butt. The product was hip, if no hipper than dozens of other start-up clothing lines that debuted and quickly vanished at around the same time. But Juicy had the marketing savvy of Nash-Taylor and Skaist-Levy.

"They really know how to work it in terms of getting free product into the hands of people," says Rose Apodaca, West Coast bureau chief for Women's Wear Daily. "Early on [in 2001], Juicy did a suite at the Chateau Marmont. It lasted all day. It was crazy chaos. Celebrities, media editors and all kinds of It Girls were there. Most people were given one free outfit. Others got more than that, I'm sure. Their track suits retail for about $175. The cashmere ones go for $500. Advertising Age wrote about the event as a case study. It put their name out there in a big way. They also sent a lot of swag to editors and celebrities and got the Juicy name out there on the people who mattered."

It cost Juicy anywhere from $20,000 to $100,000 to stage swag fests from L.A. to New York, but they proved to be extremely cost-effective. "In the fashion world it is much more impactful to see editorial than to see an advertisement," Nash-Taylor explains. "If you see an advertisement in Vogue, our customer will riffle past that. If the editor says 'Editor's Pick,' you're going to pay attention to that." Juicy's giveaway events generated articles in People, Women's Wear Daily, Us Weekly, the New York Post's Page Six, New York Daily News, Angeleno, OK!, Brntwd, New York magazine, Allure, Elle, Glamour, Harper's Bazaar, InStyle, Marie Claire, Vogue, W, the Los Angeles Times, Los Angeles magazine and the Boston Globe. In 2002 the advertising value equivalency of these articles was estimated to be $41,966,494.

In 2003 Nash-Taylor and Skaist-Levy sold the company to Liz Claiborne for an initial cash payment of $39 million, which may climb to $98 million after a required earn-out payment. And late last year they launched their first Juicy boutique, at the Caesars Palace Forum Shops in Las Vegas—chartering three planes to fly celebs and press to the opening night party.

"I don't know if they gave outfits to people," says Los Angeles Times fashion critic Booth Moore, who covered the opening. "Obviously, I didn't take the plane." (Los Angeles Times staffers and freelancers are not allowed to accept gifts of any kind, including travel, so she drove.) "But a lot of people at the opening were dressed in Juicy, and I don't imagine that they paid for it."

The Prehistory of Swag

Before the swag suite and the gift bag, there was the travel junket. Like D.W. Griffith's perfection of the close-up, the junket was a revolutionary breakthrough in its field. Developed by resorts and travel bureaus after World War II, it has become a surefire way of generating reams of ink.

The junket gives travel bureaus, resorts and hotels the biggest bang for their buck, far more than they could get by taking out ads in major magazines or newspapers. Full-page ads in national magazines run into the hundreds of thousands of dollars. In contrast, it might cost a grand to fly a writer to a hotel or resort for a week-end junket, and the results are far more effective. Kim Marshall, a fanner freelance writer who now runs a PR firm, the Marshall Plan, that organizes "press trips" for luxury resorts such as the Bora Bora Nui and Triple Creek Ranch in Montana, explains that "objective" copy in the form of an article is "seven times more believable. Because an ad is what you say about yourself. A third-party endorsement is far more credible in the mind of the reader."

Publicists refuse to admit that junkets compromise the integrity of participating journalists. "I'm a professional and I work with professionals, and they can't be bought," Marshall says. She claims the correspondents on her junkets adhere to backbreaking schedules to take in all of the sights and activities of the locales she promotes. Nevertheless, she expects at least half of them to get stories into print—"a minimum 50% return rate." Those who don't won't be invited on her next trip.

The spectacular success of travel junkets has led to the "Junketization" of a wide spectrum of industries. Movie studios were the first to realize the potential, and they began flying journalists to exotic locations to schmooze with movie stars. In 1969, more than 500 members of the press congregated on Grand Bahama Island for Warner Bros.' International Film Festival, which was in reality a giant junket to promote the studio's most prestigious summer films, among them "The Wild Bunch" and "The Rain People." The same approach was later applied to the music business.

Today, when auto companies debut their latest models, they invariably fly journalists in for the event. When Acura showed off its 2004 Acura TL in Seattle, dozens attended the junket at the W Hotel, where they were put up for two nights, treated to two dinners and cocktails, attended technical briefings on the car and test drove it. According to Mike Spencer, Acura's public relations manager, only a handful paid their own way. "Hopefully, we'll get at least 100 stories out of it," he says.

Jaguar held a junket in Scottsdale, Ariz., where the freebies included rounds of golf. Rolls-Royce offered reporters a drive up the coast from Santa Barbara to a private winery, where the vino flowed freely. Land Rover has held junkets on a ranch in Colorado and other rural settings where writers could practice skeet shooting, fly-fishing and falconry. According to a PR rep for the automaker—who asked not to be identified for fear that this article would reflect negatively on the industry—this isn't bribery but merely a way of contextualizing the product: "It's not just about what the vehicle physically does, it's also about the culture of the vehicle. The optional activities . . . are everything that you picture someone who ultimately would purchase a Land Rover would do."

Many auto magazines allow or even encourage their writers to take free junkets because, they claim, they can't afford to pay the costs themselves. "An airline ticket or hotel room is not, in this parlance, in our space, in any way a gift," says Matt Stone, executive editor of Motor Trend magazine. "Business travel is a tool necessary for us to do our job."

A veteran freelancer now employed by a major daily newspaper agrees. "To take the high road and accept no freebies is very, very expensive," he says. But, he adds, "the argument that this doesn't affect journalists' judgment is crap. Of course it does. And I'm an old hand at this. I've been to Europe maybe 50 times on product launches. They'll fly us into Frankfurt or Rome, the south of France. It'll be spectacular, right? Then they'll say, 'OK, drive this car. What do you think?' 'Gee, I don't know. Here I am bathed in the warm light of the Riviera. The car looks pretty good to me.' It really takes some doing to resist that tendency to be favorable."

How to Talk Swag

The gift bag, swag suite and junket paradigms have been adopted by almost every conceivable industry. Cosmetic companies fly beauty editors to Paris to present their new product lines. At the 2004 Republican National Convention, journalists received booklets full of discount tickets for New York retailers and were treated to martinis by Time Warner. Chris Mauro, editor of Surfer magazine, and Tom Bie, editor of Powder, say that their contributors accept free travel and product from manufacturers and promoters in the surf and ski industries, but without any guarantee of giving them ink.

"Outdoor writers are the biggest whores in the business," says the veteran free lancer. "I've seen outdoor writers who've had boats delivered to their house from manufacturers. Theoretically they're testing them, but the boat sits in the guy's yard—they just keep it, a 25- to 30-foot boat. There are $50,000 bass boats."

The freebie culture has engendered a sense of entitlement. Publicists love to do imitations of journalists who have tried to scam them. "Our company represents the Tribeca and SoHo Grand hotels," Cutrone says. "I get 10 e-mails a day from journalists who are coming to New York from all over the world. I'm talking about everyone from the Daily Telegraph to the Shanghai Times. They call and say, 'Hi, we're going to do this big, huge blowout story. We can only pick one hotel in New York City. Can you offer a press rate?' As a publicist, this is how I would translate that: 'We're sending this e-mail to every cool hotel in New York. This is a huge [tourist] market for you. We're not going to come out and say that we want a free hotel room.' So what I'm going to say to my client is: 'Can we offer these people a comped room? I think it could turn out to be a great story for us.' "

When fashion writers come to town, they don't stop at the free hotel room. "You ask them to come to an event," Cutrone explains, "and they say, 'Can you send me a car?' Or, 'I don't have anything to wear. I'd really love to wear your designer to the show.' You can smell a fashion editor who's looking for a free ride. They'll come to your showroom and they light up, saying, 'Ohhhh, loooovvvveee!!! Oh my God, I've got to get one of these. I just love it, love it! You knooooow, we're actually working on this amazing issue, which I think that this would be perfect for. But you know what, I'm going away with my boyfriend for the weekend. We're going to St. Bart's. Do you think there's any way I can get a deal on one of these?' That's classic."

Of course, publicists have no one to blame for this but themselves. They're the ones who addicted journalists to freebies in the first place. Many fashion publicists offer a "media discount" on their clients' products, which can range from 20% to 70%, depending on the client and the writer's clout. (A writer for a national glossy might get a larger discount than a reporter for a regional publication.) And then there's the "gifting" of designer clothing, shoes, purses, jewelry, sunglasses, watches and so on. Again, the status of the byline and the circulation of the publication calibrate the value of the gift. A junior editor at a regional publication might receive a $500 starter purse, while an editorial superstar could receive a $5,000 status bag.

Product is sometimes dispersed as part of a wider campaign to raise public awareness. Cutrone explains: "We'll go to the designer and say, 'Listen, we think that the green leather bag is a very cute must-have item for this season. What I'd like to do is order an extra 35 bags and do a gifting program to the editors.' Then the costs are rolled into production. Then the editors show up at fashion shows wearing it." And a trend is born.

No wonder Juicy Couture's Nash-Taylor proselytizes the virtues of swag. When I interviewed her for this story, I asked if she rewards journalists who write favorable articles with follow-up gifts. "You'd better believe it, David!" she exclaimed. "At the end of the conversation, we always say, 'Do you have Juicy? Do you want something for your wife?' We'll put you on with Kate and say, 'Kate, send David a great box.' Some journalists are not allowed to accept anything." And I was one of them, I informed her. "Oh, you are?" Nash-Taylor groaned. I admitted that my wife and daughter would be angry that I turned her down. She emitted a throaty laugh. "They're bumming. As a journalist, if you were allowed to do that, you'd understand our product better. So why not? That's how I look at it. Why not? I'm sorry I can't send you something for your wife and your daughter. They're going to be saying, 'You should have done it, Dad!' You too, David. We've got great men's stuff."

DAVID WEDDLE last wrote for the magazine about his daughter's college course work in film theory.

UNIT 5

Developing the Future Ethos and Social Responsibility of Business

Unit Selections

Key Points to Consider

- In what areas should organizations become more ethically sensitive and socially responsible in the next five years? Be specific, and explain your choices.

- Obtain codes of ethics or conduct from several different professional associations (eg, doctors, lawyers, CPAs). What are the similarities and differences between them?

- How useful do you feel codes of ethics are to organizations? Defend your answer.

Student Web Site

www.mhcls.com/online

Internet References

Further information regarding these Web sites may be found in this book's preface or online.

International Business Ethics Institute (IBEI)
http://www.business-ethics.org/index.asp
UNU/IAS Project on Global Ethos
http://www.ias.unu.edu/research/globalethos.cfm

We Want Your Advice

ANNUAL EDITIONS revisions depend on two major opinion sources: one is our Advisory Board, listed in the front of this volume, which works with us in scanning the thousands of articles published in the public press each year; the other is you—the person actually using the book. Please help us and the users of the next edition by completing the prepaid article rating form on this page and returning it to us. Thank you for your help!

ANNUAL EDITIONS: Business Ethics 08/09

ARTICLE RATING FORM

Here is an opportunity for you to have direct input into the next revision of this volume.
We would like you to rate each of the articles listed below, using the following scale:

1. **Excellent: should definitely be retained**
2. **Above average: should probably be retained**
3. **Below average: should probably be deleted**
4. **Poor: should definitely be deleted**

Your ratings will play a vital part in the next revision.
Please mail this prepaid form to us as soon as possible.
Thanks for your help!

RATING	ARTICLE	RATING	ARTICLE
	1. Thinking Ethically		26. The Parable of the Sadhu
	2. Ethical Leadership		27. Academic Values and the Lure of Profit
	3. Business Ethics		28. Does It Pay to Be Good?
	4. The Value of an Ethical Corporate Culture		29. Trust in the Marketplace
	5. Building an Ethical Framework		30. Businesses Grow More Socially Conscious
	6. Moral Leadership		31. Office Romance
	7. Ethics after Enron		32. Scams Unmasked
	8. Why Good Leaders Do Bad Things		33. Click Fraud
	9. Best Resources for Corporate Social Responsibility		34. Global Diversity: The Next Frontier
	10. Your Privacy for Sale		35. Trouble in Toyland
	11. Employers Look Closely at What Workers Do on Job		36. Japan's Diversity Problem
			37. How Barbie Is Making Business a Little Better
	12. Con Artists' Old Tricks		38. Is Marketing Ethics an Oxymoron?
	13. Corruption: Causes and Cures		39. Truth in Advertising
	14. Gender Issues		40. Marketing, Consumers and Technology
	15. Toyota's Sex-Harassment Lawsuit Could Set Standard		41. Corporate Citizenship: It's the Brand
			42. Lies, Damn Lies, and Word of Mouth
	16. Hiring Older Workers		43. Financial Scams Expected to Boom as Boomers Age
	17. Where Are the Women?		
	18. Crippled by Their Culture		44. Managing for Organizational Integrity
	19. Fear of Firing		45. Psssst! Have You Tasted This?
	20. Workplace Abuses That Guarantee Trouble		46. Swagland
	21. Birth of the Ethics Industry		47. Creating an Ethical Culture
	22. Learning to Love Whistleblowers		48. Hiring Character
	23. On Witnessing a Fraud		49. Go Green. Get Rich
	24. Erasing 'Un' from 'Unemployable'		50. The True Measure of a CEO
	25. The Ethics of Edits		

ANNUAL EDITIONS: BUSINESS ETHICS 08/09

BUSINESS REPLY MAIL
FIRST CLASS MAIL PERMIT NO. 551 DUBUQUE IA

POSTAGE WILL BE PAID BY ADDRESSEE

McGraw-Hill Contemporary Learning Series
501 BELL STREET
DUBUQUE, IA 52001

ABOUT YOU

Name   Date

Are you a teacher? ❏ A student? ❏
Your school's name

Department

Address   City   State   Zip

School telephone #

YOUR COMMENTS ARE IMPORTANT TO US!

Please fill in the following information:
For which course did you use this book?

Did you use a text with this ANNUAL EDITION? ❏ yes ❏ no
What was the title of the text?

What are your general reactions to the Annual Editions concept?

Have you read any pertinent articles recently that you think should be included in the next edition? Explain.

Are there any articles that you feel should be replaced in the next edition? Why?

Are there any World Wide Web sites that you feel should be included in the next edition? Please annotate.

May we contact you for editorial input? ❏ yes ❏ no
May we quote your comments? ❏ yes ❏ no